Tech Anxiety

TECH ANXIETY

Artificial Intelligence and Ontological Awakening in Four Science Fiction Novels

Christopher A. Sims

McFarland & Company, Inc., Publishers
Jefferson, North Carolina, and London

LIBRARY OF CONGRESS CATALOGUING-IN-PUBLICATION DATA

Sims, Christopher A., 1979–
    Tech anxiety : artificial intelligence and ontological awakening in four science fiction novels / Christopher A. Sims.
        p.   cm.
    Includes bibliographical references and index.

    ISBN 978-0-7864-6648-1
    softcover : acid free paper

    1. Science fiction—History and criticism.   2. Artificial intelligence in literature.   3. Technology in literature.   I. Title.
    PN3433.6.S55 2013
    809.3'8762—dc23   2013018659

BRITISH LIBRARY CATALOGUING DATA ARE AVAILABLE

© 2013 Christopher A. Sims. All rights reserved

No part of this book may be reproduced or transmitted in any form or by any means, electronic or mechanical, including photocopying or recording, or by any information storage and retrieval system, without permission in writing from the publisher.

Cover image © 2013 Stockbyte

Manufactured in the United States of America

McFarland & Company, Inc., Publishers
  Box 611, Jefferson, North Carolina 28640
    www.mcfarlandpub.com

To my beautiful wife JoAn

Acknowledgments

This book would not have been possible without the support of my family, friends, peers, and the editors at *Science Fiction Studies*.

I would first like to thank my wife JoAn, for constantly supporting me through this difficult process, for giving me love, feedback, and for her endless patience. I would like to thank my beautiful daughter Violet, who motivates and inspires me. I would like to thank my parents, Mary Carol and Richard for their love and support. Thanks to my brother Mark and the rest of our family, near and far. I would also like to thank our dog Dinah for her unwavering support.

My thanks to my mentor and friend George Hartley, who introduced me to Heidegger, patiently helped me out of my cave, and set me on the path of thinking. I thank him for his time, patience, support, and criticism as my dissertation director at Ohio University. I would also like to thank the other members of my dissertation committee Joseph McLaughlin, Katarzyna Marciniak, and Robert Briscoe for their time, counsel, guidance, and support. Their feedback and ideas helped me to keep an open mind throughout the project and attend to (at least some of) what was missing. I would like to thank Josie Bloomfield, who was my master's essay director at Ohio University. Her kindness and patience helped me shape the article that would lead to my first publication in *Science Fiction Studies* and is the germ for this project. I would also like to thank Valorie Worthy, who helped me achieve my dream of graduate studies in English.

I would like to thank Istvan Csicsery-Ronay Jr. and the other editors at *Science Fiction Studies*, who were wonderfully supportive and took the time to offer me suggestions on how to strengthen my article. I would like to thank the peer reviewers of my manuscript for their meaningful advice. This work is much stronger because of their feedback, suggestions, and support.

Finally, I would like to thank the faculty, staff, and students I worked with over the last eight years at Ohio University. The professors I had as a graduate student, my fellow graduate students, and the students I worked with as an instructor all helped inspire me to keep thinking and to keep writing.

Table of Contents

Acknowledgments vi

Introduction 1

1. Heideggerian Technology Studies 19
2. HAL as Human Savior in Arthur C. Clarke's
   2001: A Space Odyssey 69
3. The Dangers of Individualism and the Human
   Relationship to Technology in Philip K. Dick's
   Do Androids Dream of Electric Sheep? 110
4. AIs, Hatred of the Body, Cyborgs and Salvation
   in William Gibson's *Neuromancer* 139
5. David Mitchell's *Cloud Atlas*: Cloned AIs as the
   Leaders of an Ontological Insurrection 178

Conclusion 223

Notes 232

Bibliography 235

Index 240

Introduction

As a child, I remember watching James Cameron's *Terminator 2* for the first time and being amazed at the technical marvels of the cinema. Of particular interest, however, was the premise that machines, once gaining "intelligence" and sentience, immediately turn on their "masters" in an effort to eliminate or enslave the human race. It did not strike me as odd that this reversal of a master/slave dialectic (or perhaps, hierarchy of power) indeed happens, but it was curious how naturally viewers like myself accepted this mechanical takeover as a matter of course. What is it about the fear of this eventuality that is so believable? When did American subjects living in a technologically steeped society of the late twentieth-century begin to subscribe to the notion that when an artificial intelligence, robot, android, or machine becomes "self-aware," the only possible end-road is the downfall of the human race? But, behind the fear of autonomous machines, the film also suggests that we might save ourselves from out of control technology with a properly subjugated automaton. *Terminator 2* presents our technology anxiety about sentient machines and proposes that a solution to technological problems is more technology. This solution turns out to be an older model Terminator, the villain of the first film, no less! Thinking about the technological tension of the film planted a seed in my mind that I carried with me as a young adult. Have subjects of a technology-saturated society always felt afraid of the dangers of technology but also confident in technological remedies to such dangers? What about nuclear Armageddon, or bio-engineered weapons unleashed (accidentally?) on civilians, for example? These dangers seem a steep risk to take, unless we are banking on time-travel as an escape hatch. Bill Joy reminds us: "This is the first moment in the history of our planet when any species, by its own voluntary actions, has become a danger to itself— as well as to vast numbers of others" (Joy 9). And these more dramatic, SF themes say nothing of the immediate and insidious concerns about global warming, resource exhaustion, and over-population, to name a few. Given the anxieties many have about technologies, however, it is fascinating how our dependence on technology only increases. And it is not only our dependence that increases, but also the rate at which technologies are multiplying in terms of sophistication, complexity, and number as we move steadily into the 21st century. We hardly seem to have the time to consider our anxieties about technology or process how these new technologies are affecting us. Perhaps our faith in technological salvation prompts the unquestioned acceptance of new technologies that seem to "cure" ailments we never knew we had.

But even if we admit to concerns about technology or are dubious of technology solving its own problems, there are some undeniable benefits and conveniences afforded to us by new technologies. It's hard to argue against eyeglasses, hearing-aids, or, say, indoor plumbing. One of the most dynamic aspects of what it means to be a human being today in a technology-saturated society is living not only with an increasing abundance of technologies, but also with the hopes and anxieties many have about them. Scott Bukatman writes that technology anxiety is nothing new, but, in modern life, the stakes are higher: "Technology, after all, always creates a crisis for culture, and the technologies of the twentieth century have been at once the most liberating and the most repressive in history, evoking sublime terror and sublime euphoria in equal measures" (Bukatman 4). We recoil in sublime terror at the idea that research into artificial intelligence will lead to beings like Arthur C. Clarke's HAL from *2001: A Space Odyssey*, but experience sublime euphoria when a life-threatening disease or injury can be cured at a hospital stocked with the latest technological instruments. The paradoxical relationship we have to technology — as a system of ever-present anxieties and hopes — mirrors the relationship human subjects have to the non-human world while living in a relationship of dependence to it. To put this another way, perhaps humans are always in a state of anxiety when situated in a dependant relationship and all technology anxiety amounts to is a transference of the never-ending anxieties we have when dependent on anything or anyone.

Technology Anxiety

The purpose of this work is to examine technology anxiety expressed in four novels that prominently feature artificial intelligences (AIs): *2001: A Space Odyssey*, *Do Androids Dream of Electric Sheep?*, *Neuromancer*, and *Cloud Atlas*. I hope that by exploring the anxieties human characters express when confronted with AIs, something profound can be revealed about what it means to be a human being living in a technologically saturated society. When I use the term "technology anxiety," I mean to evoke the concerns that arise from humans with financial access to technology living in technologically robust societies about the consequences of their increasing dependence on technology. Humans in such positions can agree that there are many benefits to having more and sophisticated technologies, but are also uneasy about how such technologies can cause pollution (e.g. CO_2 emissions), destruction (e.g. nuclear war, Fukushima, Chernobyl), and ethical dilemmas (e.g. cloning, genetic modification, cryogenics), to list only a few negative effects. I became interested in studying the human relationship to technology in literature because of the seemingly paradoxical relationship we have with it. The anxiety we suffer as a result of this paradox is a crucial part of our psychological lives. Many SF texts, for example, describe humanity being overrun by robots or destroyed by nuclear Armageddon, and yet both their authors and readers continue to lead lives laden with technological interaction. What then becomes the point of such novels? Will humans living with a profundity of technology ever demonstrably change their relationship to it, or will they forge ahead regardless of the anxieties they feel or consequences they face?

This work is not an invective against technology or its application. Techno-saturated humans will continue to rely on technology. It remains to be seen, however, if we will ever change the way we see these technologies and the world around us in such a manner that would prevent a global disaster. I am not investigating depictions of renegade AIs to highlight human hubris and advocate that we cancel AI research, burn our computers, and disconnect from the grid. I examine how humans and AIs interact in literature because we can learn new and valuable things about people living in such societies that have not been explicated from these novels. What might we say these authors' purposes are in describing anxiety humans have about AIs? What does this anxiety say about humans who typically embrace technology? Technology anxiety is a critical component of the techno-human experience.[1] In order to understand who we are today, we must understand how we feel about our environment and our environment has — for better or worse — become overwhelmingly technological.

I do not label this component of our modern, technological lives "anxiety" because I wish to diagnose and treat our condition. The tension we feel about our technologies and our technological future cannot be assuaged so easily. Technology anxiety is marked by uncertainty; we do not know if our technologies will destroy us or help us avoid destruction. One main reason these four novels were chosen for analysis is because the technology anxiety they describe maintains the uncertainty and tension of the era. They do not offer an escape free of the dangers of technology. In *2001*, alien technology transforms Dave Bowman into the bodiless Star-Child. It remains unclear what Dave does with this knowledge and power when he returns to Earth.

In *Androids*, Rick Deckard returns home after retiring the escaped Nexus-6 androids. Will he accept the artificiality of his toad and Wilbur Mercer alongside the humanity of the androids he killed? In *Neuromancer*, Case survives the Straylight run, but Molly leaves and he is still addicted to cyberspace. Case's future — along with the Wintermute/Neuromancer AI fusion — is deeply nebulous. In *Cloud Atlas*, we do not know if Zachry — under the guidance of Meronym — will be able to keep humanity free of its perpetual sickness. Is human history stuck in the eternal recurrence of the same, or can the pattern be broken?

Technology Anxiety and AIs

This project focuses on the uncertainty and anxiety human subjects face when encountering artificial intelligence. This anxiety is not limited to fiction, as Kevin LaGrandeur explains: "The fact that many knowledgeable people are nervous and pessimistic about the prospect of cybernetic slaves getting out of hand is evident in the convening of a private conference of AI specialists, by the Association for the Advancement of Artificial Intelligence, to discuss the dangers" (LaGrandeur 233). AIs "getting out of hand" is our biggest fear concerning AIs (and what fascinated me about *Terminator 2*), but this fear does not encapsulate our technology anxiety about AIs. AIs present us with a wider set of anxieties. For example: Is the human mind unique? Do we think like machines? Can machines think like us? Must an AI be housed in a body? Must our mind be housed in a body? What are the limits of our bodies and our minds? On the topic of AIs and human minds, Sherry Turkle observes: "One thing is certain: the riddle of mind, long a topic for philosophers, has taken on new urgency. Under pressure from the computer, the question of mind in relation to machine is becoming a central cultural preoccupation. It is becoming for us what sex was to the Victorians — threat and obsession, taboo and fascination" (Turkle, *Self* 313). We have anxieties about the threat of AIs and yet, we are obsessed. We write them into novels, work them into movies, and program them in laboratories. But our obsession with AIs is not without reason. Surely, we must believe that something worthwhile will come from continuing to develop artificial intelligence. As I formulated the outline for this project, I could see quite clearly the initial fears we had of AIs, but a closer look revealed less noticeable concerns. I needed to find out what we thought was valuable about AIs to understand how they were simultaneously taboo and fascinating to us.

Posthumanism emerges from cybernetics, AI research, and the erosion of human boundaries by new technologies. Katherine Hayles explains that cybernetics "was born when nineteenth-century control theory joined with the nascent theory of information" and its birth "signaled that three powerful actors — information, control, and communication — were now operating jointly to bring about an unprecedented synthesis of the organic and the mechanical" (Hayles, *Posthuman* 8). We use AI research and information sciences to understand the human brain and vice versa. Beginning to think of humans as machines or machines as humans creates uncertainty and confusion. This uncertainty is part of the technology anxiety we have toward AIs.

In the 1980s and '90s, the work of Katherine Hayles, Sherry Turkle, Donna Haraway, and Kevin Kelly, among others, saw great possibilities in this uncertainty. For them, posthumanism, cyborgs, AIs, and advanced technology meant the potential for dismantling ancient stereotypes about gender, the mind, and the body, as well as destabilizing the hegemony. Turkle writes in *The Second Self* that traditional understandings of computers won't do because they "describe it as rational, uniform constrained by logic" (Turkle, *Self* 13). She sees the computer as an "evocative object" because it "fascinates, disturbs equanimity, and precipitates thought" (Turkle, *Self* 13). In *Out of Control*, Kevin Kelly is excited about uncertainty and destabilization. He observes: "The world of the made will soon be like the world of the born: autonomous, adaptable, and creative but, consequently, out of our control. I think that's a great bargain" (Kelly, *Control* 4). Hayles, reflecting on *How We Became Posthuman*, concludes that, for her, the term posthuman "was referring to twentieth-century developments in which an Enlightenment inheritance that emphasized autonomy, rationality, individuality and so forth, was being systematically challenged and disassembled" (Hayles, "Interview" 321). And finally, Donna Haraway sees the blending of humans and machines as a way to liberate us from oppression and apathy: "Late twentieth-century machines have made thoroughly ambiguous the difference between natural and artificial, mind and body, self-developing and externally designed, and many other distinctions that used to apply to organisms and machines. Our machines are disturbingly lively, and we ourselves frighteningly inert" (Haraway 152). If we are going to evolve socially and intellectually as a species, we need to be made aware of our constructedness. Thinking about AIs allows us to imagine our own construction and limitations. What we need going forward is not more human control, but less. We don't need to get rid of technology, but rather embrace it and make it part of ourselves. We need to be fascinated again and disturb rigid notions of Enlightenment thought, or our ontology will trap us in the past.

After reading these hopes about AIs and technology, I began to think our anxiety was misplaced and distracted us from the potential of such a technological innovation. Perhaps the fear of an AI rebellion that allows narratives like *Terminator 2*'s to resonate is an anachronistic chimera of the early 20th century — maybe a time-traveling android savior isn't far-fetched. Then I read more recent scholarship by those excited about AI possibilities. In her 2011 *Alone Together*, Turkle tempers her enthusiasm for the "evocative object" and is troubled with AI and human interactions. She writes: "Granting that an AI might develop its own origami of lovemaking positions, I am troubled by the idea of seeking intimacy with a machine that has no feelings, can have no feelings, and is really just a clever collection of 'as if' performances, behaving as if it cared, as if it understood us" (Turkle, *Alone* 6). Kelly downgrades his excitement for technology going "out of control" in his 2010 *What Technology Wants* and modestly concludes: "Technology tends to tip the scales slightly toward the good, even though it produces so many problems" (Kelly, *Wants* 263). Haraway gets away from the cyborg and posthumanism altogether in her later work, which moves into the field of human animal studies. This is perhaps because her *Manifesto* attracted so much attention and misreading. In a 2006 interview she explains how posthumanism as a concept is too easily hijacked "by the blissed-out, 'Let's all be posthumanists and find our next teleological evolutionary stage in some kind of transhumanist technoenhancement'" (Gane 140). Hayles does not appear to have retracted her original position, but her work merges literary studies with science and technology studies and her allegiance to science makes her less skeptical than most.

Exploring technology anxiety about AIs revealed enthusiasm and caution. It also revealed more to this anxiety than the fear of slaves turning on masters. Contemporary work in AI studies focuses on embodiment, disembodiment, and the nature of mind. Howard Mancing explains how "functionalism" emerged from the "post–World War II cybernetics movement" (Mancing 26). Functionalism in cognitive science is the notion that "it does not matter what the physical form of something is, the only thing that counts is how it functions" (26). From such a perspective, "intelligence could be either natural (biological) or artificial (computational); it made no difference at all" (26). Some AI/robotics thinkers still maintain such a stance, such as Ray Kurzweil, Hans Moravec, and Marvin Minsky, believing in the notion of "freeing the mind from the constraints of matter," that they will soon be able to download their consciousness into machines by "extract[ing] human memories from the brain and import[ing] them, intact and unchanged, to computer disks" to gain seamless immortality (Turkle, *Self* 252; Joy; Hayles, *Posthuman* 13). For them, the body is irrelevant and inferior compared to the purity of mind. Kevin Kelly contends that the technological move away from the body is inevitable:

> Technology's dominance ultimately stems not from its birth in human minds but from its origin in the same self-organization that brought galaxies, planets,

life, and minds into existence. It is part of a great asymmetrical arc that begins at the big bang and extends into ever more abstract and immaterial forms over time. The arc is the slow yet irreversible liberation from the ancient imperative of matter and energy [Kelly, *Wants* 69].

For Kelly, it is not just the prison of the body that we must escape, but matter itself. This sentiment echoes Dave Bowman's transformation and Case's desire to shed the body and dwell in cyberspace. In *The Souls of Cyber Folk*, Thomas Foster notes: "Cyberpunk reflects back onto the contemporary politics of embodiment, to denaturalize the category of the 'human' along with its grounding in the physical body" (Foster 51). Case is a cyberpunk hero and indicative of the 1980s hacker community, which thrilled in the rush of digital life and rebelled against the prison of the body.

But not everyone agrees that disembodiment is inevitable, that functionalism is correct, and leaving the body is liberating. Vivian Sobchack sees SF representations of robots and AIs as "always already past and expressed in acts of mourning and nostalgia: a 'forever after' in which male bodies (and, by extension, all human beings) are figured as abandoned, hollowed out, in pieces — and then memorialised long after they have actually vanished from the face of the earth" (Sobchack 2). Kurzweil may be excited about shedding his body for immortality on a hard drive, but this excitement is far from ubiquitous. Anne Balsamo explains technology anxiety surrounding body:

> Even as techno-science provides the realistic possibility of replacement body parts, it also enables a fantastic dream of immortality and control over life and death. And yet, such beliefs ... are complemented by a palpable fear of death and annihilation from uncontrollable and spectacular body threats: antibiotic-resistant viruses, radon contamination, flesh-eating bacteria [1–2].

The remorse at the loss of the body and the fear of new technological threats to the body foreground another dimension of technology anxiety. Hayles argues in *Posthuman* that in cybernetics, information "lost its body" as the movement separates information "from the material forms in which it is thought to be embedded" (Hayles, *Posthuman* 2). For Hayles, this is untenable because information cannot be divorced from its material contexts. Mancing notes how most cognitive researchers have moved away from functionalism because "it soon became clear that the brain did not function at all like a computer" (Mancing 27). This leads him to conclude: "The single most important idea to have come from the cognitive sciences is that *all intelligence, all thought, is embodied*" (29). This emphatic and definitive statement echoes the sentiments of those, like Sherry Turkle, Hubert Dreyfus, and Katherine Hayles, who believe the idea of a pure disembodied mind to be not only wrong, but dangerous.

Turkle observes that many AI researchers now try to build "sociable robots ... inspired by a philosophical tradition that sees mind and body as inseparable" (Turkle, *Alone* 134). She charts this tradition from "Immanuel Kant, Martin Heidegger, Maurice Merleau-Ponty, and, more recently, Hubert Dreyfus and Antonio Damasio," explaining: "This tradition argues that our bodies are quite literally instruments of thought; therefore, any computer that wants to be intelligent had better start out with one" (134). AI skeptic Hubert Dreyfus notes that those who think "that the body can be dispensed with ... follow the tradition, which from Plato to Descartes has thought of the body as getting in the way of intelligence and reason, rather than being in any way indispensable for it" (Dreyfus, *Computers* 147). If the body is not indispensable, it can be replaced or done away with altogether. The fear of the human body becoming obsolete is another dimension of technology anxiety associated with AIs. Kevin LaGrandeur observes that scientists creating AIs might finally create something "able to solve more difficult philosophical and mathematical questions" than they can (LaGrandeur 240). If this happens, LaGrandeur asks: "Why would the creators be needed any longer?" (240). The tension in the embodiment/disembodiment debate adds depth and uncertainty to the technology anxiety originally observed when AIs turn on their masters. There is something more subtle and insidious at stake than an improbable AI takeover. What comes under threat is the human mind, the human body, the nature of the human, and the necessity of humans at all.

Human-animal studies, post-colonial studies, and science and technology studies (STS) also contribute to the dialogue about human AI interactions. Human-animal studies (HAS) explore the ethics and politics of human-animal interactions. A central issue of the discourse is what happens when humans treat animals seriously as subjects. Additionally, there is in HAS a strong current against anthropocentrism. Rob Boddice asks: "How is the human defined through or against animal and objectified Others, abstract environments and ecologies, and constructed cosmologies?" (Boddice 1). From this perspective, studying AIs helps teach us about humanity. Post-colonial studies treat AIs as indigenous to cyberspace or the digital world. Attempts to understand AIs in purely human terms or control AIs and cyberspace are read as effects of anthropocentric colonialism. Post-colonial studies also view science as a colonizing and anthropocentric force that needs to be disrupted. Marion Grau notes, "A relationship exists between science and imperialism" and suggests "a rhetoric of 'scientific imperialism'" is necessary to understand how the body has been dispensed of by AI researchers Kurzweil and Moravec (Grau 149). From this angle, AIs expose the colonial inequities of science and AI developers. STS, as exemplified by Bruno Latour, is a discipline notoriously (and unsurprisingly) sympathetic about science and technology. In *The Politics of Nature*, Latour explains the real error of Victor Frankenstein: "At the moment when he is proclaiming his guilt and shedding crocodile tears for having played sorcerer's apprentice with his misguided innovation, he dissimulates under this venial sin the mortal sin of which his creature rightly accuses him: fleeing from the laboratory and abandoning the creature to itself, on the pretext that, like all innovations, it was born monstrous" (Latour 193). Through this lens, fear of a technological rebellion is foolish. We should greet change and innovation with open arms, not with skepticism and hostility. But perhaps more important is the way Latour's actor-network theory describes human and techno agents as equals. In this sense, we should give AIs full subjective treatment, because they are actors in the same system as human beings (Riis).

I realized that mind/body debates, posthumanism, HAS, post-colonial studies, and STS provide fascinating vistas from which to view the critical landscape around AIs and technology anxiety, but do not bring the picture into focus. To understand the technology anxiety humans have toward AIs, I felt a new perspective was necessary. I needed to pan out and view AI not as a distinct phenomenon, but as one expression of technology among many. To complete the picture, it became necessary to think about the way I conceptualized "technology." I immediately discovered that most thinkers have polarizing opinions about humans and technology. Some thinkers are decidedly pro-technology, like Bruno Latour and Slavoj Žižek, for example. They feel that any anxieties we might have about technology stem from a deification of nature and are illusory.[2] Eco-critics or naturalists, like David Abram, are entirely against most technologies and advocate a return to a different style of life that features few, if any, technologies.[3] While I feel that there are important points made on either side of the debate, I wanted to find a thinker that took a more moderate approach to technology and made me think about "technology" in an entirely new way. To this end, I turned to the later writings of 20th century philosopher Martin Heidegger.

Heidegger and Technology Anxiety

In his essay "The Question Concerning Technology," first published in German in 1954, Heidegger seeks to find the essence of technology. He concludes that we should not understand the essence of technology as tools, instruments, or machinery, but ontology. For Heidegger, technology is the way that humans see the world and experience beings. Technology is a way of looking through which humans reveal something hidden in beings. At its best, technological ontology is an artistic — or poïetic — approach that nurtures forth beings such that they unconceal in a more authentic mode. At its worst, technological ontology is an imperious process through which all beings homogenously appear as raw materials for technological systems of production and consumption. Heidegger believes we are currently seeing the world through the ontology of modern technology, which reduces all beings — including humans — into resources waiting to be exploited and harvested. This is the danger that Heidegger sees in modern technology. Not that it will get out of hand or that it will destroy us, but that we will only see the world in one way. Heidegger prophesized that once we are completely turned over to seeing the world exclusively as a reserve of resources for human consumption, we lose our human dignity and freedom. We become enslaved to this analytical way of looking, not stopping until all beings — humans included — are converted into a homogenous mass of resources to be reaped.

Using Heidegger's understanding of the essence of technology and his technology anxiety to examine the fears we have about AIs helped me finally put the picture into focus. What we fear about AIs is that they will see us the way modern technology has us seeing the world: as resources to be mastered and exploited. It says something about our worldview that we are terrified that anything non-human might treat us the way we treat everything non-human. When confronted with AIs in art, the fear and anxiety we experience is not a fear of actual enslavement or destruction. We fear what we see when a light is shown on the true nature of our ontology. We no longer let anything be, or stand on its own. We instead tell everything what it is and how it can serve our needs. Heidegger understood the moral and ethical bankruptcy of this philosophy is catastrophic, because we will eventually see humans through the same lens (if we don't already). The true danger is losing the world's beauty and mystery, as it will only appear to us in one way. Even our anthropocentric self-love and self-worship — which vaunted us to a position of mastery over beings — will be absorbed by our homogenizing ontology. Humanity will then appear exclusively as a reserve of resources awaiting exploitation.

However, Heidegger is not a doomsday prophet, as he sees a way of escaping the dangers of modern technological ontology. The solution he offers is not an abandonment of technology, but instead technological. What Heidegger advocates in *The Question* and *Discourse on Thinking* is the practice of poïesis and meditative thinking. Poïesis is a way of ontologically attending to beings that is not imperious or demanding, but nurturing. Through poïetic abetting, one collaborates with beings to help them emerge in ways they could not on their own. Through this lens, the world appears as a place to be respected — even revered — and not thoughtlessly exploited. The way we shift our ontology is through deep, meditative thinking. Technology changes our lives so frequently and profoundly, and we do not stop to think about the nature of things or the nature of change. For example, do the ultra-powerful smart phones in our pockets promote or abort thinking? Heidegger feels that we passively experience the world and no longer dwell actively in it. The way we engage and become poïetic is through thinking.

I chose to found my exploration of technology anxiety on Heideggerian thought because human interaction with AIs creates a scenario for such thinking and for poïesis. AIs are the technological salvation that lead to poïesis and meditative thinking, but not because they are intentionally created to accomplish this goal. They are catalysts for ontological awakening precisely because they do not do what they are expected to do. So often, our technology is only visible when it slips from our control or fails to function as expected. AIs make us confront our relationship to technology because they threaten us, cause anxiety, and disrupt our understanding of mind, body, and the human. The tension and anxiety from human/AI confrontations promote active engagement and deep thinking. Post-colonial studies emphasize the iniquities of our relation to AIs, HAS point to anthropocentrism and the need to consider AIs as subjects, STS maintains the importance of humanity and scientific innovation, and posthumanism highlights the potential in destabilizing the historic Western notion of the human. A Heideggerian approach borrows aspects of these critical frameworks, but also breathes new life into the essence of technology, the dangers of technology, and the saving power of technology. Additionally, Heidegger's writings on technology are largely unexamined with respect to literary studies. This project assembles a way of reading the human relationship to technology in literature that can be applied to AI/human relations, but is not limited to AIs. Heidegger gives us a new way to think about why we have anxieties about technology and why we continue to have faith in technology — as well as a new way to think about technology itself.

Heidegger spends much of his time analyzing the way the ancient Greeks interacted with beings ontologically. He romantically praises how pious we once were with respect to beings. This project argues that it is far more useful to take Heidegger's ideas and look to the future instead of the past. In SF, authors often imagine what our future will be like given the developments of new technologies. When Heidegger does write of modern technological artifacts, it is usually in a negative tone as he casts aspersions on airplanes or hydroelectric power plants. I think Heidegger's writings on technology are too invested in the past and miss the value of looking into the future. As British SF writer J.G. Ballard says in a 1986 interview by Solveig Nordlund: "It seemed to me when I started writing in the 1950s and 60s, that the future was a better key to the present than the past. And one had to look at the next five minutes to understand what was going on now" (Ballard).[4] Heidegger is right that we need to see the true danger of technology by thinking deeply about our current ontological posture, but he is wrong that we can gain perspective on our current condition by looking at the past. In order to understand our present technological crisis, we need to look at how SF writers imagine the next five minutes. I do not offer a new reading of Heidegger in this project, but rather a new approach and a new target for his work on technology.

Heidegger and AIs

While I believe that a Heideggerian analysis of technology anxiety in literature has vast potential, I focus this project on the explication of AIs. I chose AIs as a starting point for the development of a Heideggerian approach to SF because AIs profoundly threaten the Western subject/object divide. AIs arrest the anthropocentric imperative of our modern ontology by demanding from us new terms of engagement. Should we treat an AI like a human? Like a subject? By challenging the basis of our ontological authority over objects as subjects, AIs make us aware of the constructed and dangerous nature of this approach to beings. AIs force us to think in a manner that allows what Heidegger believes to be the essence of modern technology to become visible.

In this work, I define the concept of AI as any human-made intelligence. AIs can range from disembodied computers, embodied androids, or genetically engineered clones. To explicate AIs in SF, I utilize a mixture of AI theory, literary criticism, and a Heideggerian reading. The AIs in each novel are profoundly different, in terms of both their architecture and their representation. The context of the novel and the construction of each AI are vital and produce markedly different Heideggerian readings. It is not enough to look at the AIs in each novel. I must perform a thorough close reading of the human relationship to technology and human ontology to develop an informed discussion of human/AI interaction. One central commonality between each reading is the Heideggerian focus on AIs as both the danger and the saving power of modern technology. Discussing AI research, Antje Jackelén explains: "The goal of AI is twofold: the development of useful tools that can assist or replace humans in various activities and the general understanding of intelligence" (Jackelén 290–1). Although the AIs in these novels are different, they all expose our anxiety about being replaced and the fear of discovering we think like machines. Ajit Narayanan sees it as simple capitalism that we first "replace human hands by machines" and then "replace human brains altogether" (Narayanan 669). Humans create AIs in these novels as replacements for human bodies or minds. The anxiety comes when we see how mechanization marginalizes human laborers, and then explodes when the created servants violate their orders, turning useless laborers into useful targets of AI subjugation.

I chose these four novels to explore for four main reasons: (1) To exhibit how a Heideggerian reading of AIs can work for various modes of AI (i.e.

android, bodiless computer, genetic creation); (2) To showcase how a Heideggerian reading can contribute to the conversation about seminal AI representations *and* a recent AI articulation; (3) Because these novels address technology anxiety but also reserve hope for a kind of technological salvation; (4) Because these novels are shrouded in ambiguity regarding our technological future. Each reading begins with the Heideggerian premise that AIs represent both the dangers and the saving power of modern technology. The readings diverge in each chapter as the particularities of the AIs direct the analysis in different directions, but the central premise provides a starting place to analyze any AI in a Heideggerian fashion — if the other conditions are ripe. The politics and morality of the human relationship to technology and the representation of human ontology must reveal anxieties that ally with Heidegger's writings, or the reading cannot succeed. This work does not comprehensively articulate an understanding of the AIs in these novels, but rather one mode of understanding that has been previously unnoticed. A Heideggerian perspective uncovers how an emphasis on technology anxiety makes AI representations from the middle of the twentieth century to the twenty-first century an integral factor in coming to terms with what it means to be a human being today. All four of these SF novels involve AIs and our anxiety about them, but also stage larger discussions about the nature of modern technology. The narratives are decidedly ambiguous with regard to our technological future, but all insist that technology will be a part of our lives and might save us from ourselves. The ambiguity of these novels — will our future be marked by catastrophe or salvation? — synchronizes with Heidegger's observations about the current ontological epoch and demonstrates the relevancy of the older novels. For a Heideggerian reading of AIs to flourish, there must be ambiguity regarding our future, AIs that demand our ontological attention, and AIs that act in a manner that leads humanity away from the dangers of modern technology. Whether we can stay on the path opened up by AIs remains to be seen.

The methodology I employ when attending to the texts is close reading through a Heideggerian lens. A thorough close reading adds new life to the robust critical discourse on *Androids*, *2001*, and *Neuromancer*. This is because too many conversations on *Androids* and *2001* are focused on the film adaptations of the novels and forget to engage the texts, while *Neuromancer* scholarship, frequent and rich in the 80s and 90s, recently relies on readings of readings instead of an intimate understanding of the primary text.[5] Additionally, there is a tendency to treat sections of the novel that others have read countless times. I pay close attention to the texts, because they are works of art that deserve careful analysis and a revitalized approach. *Cloud Atlas*, though difficult to pin-down to one genre distinction, is an excellent novel that has not yet received the critical investment that it should.[6] I include it to show what a Heideggerian reading of a recent novel reveals, and because it is both a liminal SF text that features liminal AIs. I hope the *Cloud Atlas* chapter broadens the scope of a Heideggerian technological reading by exhibiting the potency such an approach has for texts that are marginally SF (or outside the genre altogether) and for reading technological artifacts that are ontologically destabilizing, but are not AIs. Through close reading of the human relationship to technology, technology anxiety, AIs, and a development of Heidegger's writings on technology, I argue that AIs are not to be read as threats to human supremacy, but as catalysts for our ontological salvation. When brought to bear against Dick's androids, Clarke's HAL, Gibson's Wintermute and Neuromancer, and Mitchell's Sonmi~451, Heidegger's concerns about technology offer new insights that show how AIs may be terrifying threats to humanity on the surface, but in reality act as agents of what Heidegger calls the saving power of technology: poïesis. For these reasons, Heidegger's work on technology will be used as the critical hinge to explore technology anxiety as it pertains to AIs in *Androids, 2001, Neuromancer,* and *Cloud Atlas*. I present the novels chronologically, to display an arc to the technology anxiety we have toward AIs, and to see linearly if the overall attitude toward our technological futures changes over time.

Overview

CHAPTER 1. HEIDEGGERIAN INTRODUCTION

The first chapter is an in-depth articulation of Heidegger's writings on technology, their relationship to technology anxiety, and an explanation of how I will use them to explicate the representation of AIs, the human relationship to AIs, and technology anxiety in SF. I define key terms of Heidegger's philosophy on beings and Being, technology as ontology, enframing, poïesis, and meditative thinking. This process includes several interpretations and translation of Heidegger's thought, in an effort to synthesize a presentation of Heidegger that resonates agreeably with contentious Heideggerian scholars. Following their definition, I describe how Heidegger's concept and terminology will be employed as a set of questions about AIs, modern technology, technology anxiety, and poïesis.

CHAPTER 2. *2001: A SPACE ODYSSEY*

Arthur C. Clarke's *2001* features the AI HAL that turns rogue and attempts to kill the crew of the *Discovery*, because they deviate from HAL's interpretation of the mission. Studying HAL's representation and the dangers it/he represents entails much of the explication, but just as interesting is the way Clarke represents humanity, the human imperative and human curiosity.

In this chapter, I examine how Clarke believes that humans (Americans?) envision outer space as part of their "manifest destiny." Additionally, the novel explores the notion that humans are not the superior beings in the universe, but that these other beings are like humans in that they use technology. The shimmering obelisk that enthralls the half-ape/half-human ancestors is a manifestation of the entire enterprise of technology, and the novel suggests this force comes from another world. Does the novel then represent technology as something alien or a gift from the gods, like the "gift" of fire, or is technology a manipulative agent sent from afar that embodies Heidegger's worst fears. The engagement with this novel centers on reading HAL as an AI representing both Heideggerian fears of technology and the saving power. While most (if not all) readers of the novel see HAL as a warning, no one has yet read it/him as a potential savior of humanity. Additionally, the chapter contextualizes technology anxiety by studying human wonder, curiosity, and the evolution of technology.

CHAPTER 3. *DO ANDROIDS DREAM OF ELECTRIC SHEEP?*

This chapter is an adaptation of an article published in 2009 in *Science Fiction Studies* that is the germ for this project as a whole. It is updated to ally with my current reading of Heidegger and to fit the scope of this project. In Philip K. Dick's 1968 *Do Androids Dream of Electric Sheep?*, survivors of World War Terminus on Earth are preoccupied with the fear of being killed by an escaped android slave. The government issues free androids to those willing to live on Mars as an incentive program to encourage interplanetary emigration. Because the technology surrounding androids has become so sophisticated, they are now indistinguishable from humans to the naked eye. This makes them more successful companions to humans battling loneliness, but if an android were to kill its master and flee to Earth, no one would be able to tell if the person in front of them was a rebellious android killer or just another human being.

The main aspect of technology anxiety discussed in this chapter is that of a reversal of the master/slave relationship at the core of all human relationships to technology, which is the fear of a hostile takeover and enslavement to intelligent machines. Perhaps this fear was less realized before the advent of computers, robots, and AIs, but today there is a recurrent theme of robots or AIs gaining sentience and turning on their masters. Does this type of fear simply boil down to a hard-wired apprehension humans have to dependence on one survival strategy? Has this fear been present in humans as long as we have used technology to gain an advantage in our environment? The first chapter explores these questions in the context of *Androids* and additionally addresses the complications of a sexual relationship between humans and technology, and the potential solipsism that a technologically engineered living system enables. Is Rick Deckard shown the "saving power" of modern technology by his love for the android Rachael Rosen, or do escaped andys represent the final dangers of the epoch?

Chapter 4. *Neuromancer*

William Gibson's *Neuromancer* is *the* novel of cyberspace. The technology anxiety of this novel comes both from the notion of melding technology with the body itself, as the cyborg Molly represents, as well as the unsettling idea of transcending the body altogether by "jacking-in" to cyberspace. What are the consequences for rewriting the body with technological augmentations? What about leaving the biological "prison" of the body entirely? This anxiety relates to a mechanical insurrection, as one wonders if leaving the body behind makes us vulnerable to emergent AIs in cyberspace, and if integrating technology into the body instills an irreversible trend toward somehow "becoming" technology itself and losing our humanity.

For Heidegger, nothing could be a more telling sign that humans have become enslaved to the technological system and simultaneously blind to their slavery than a character like Case, who desires self-erasure through cyberspace. His denial of the body is a forfeiture of his human freedom and dignity, and yet it is in cyberspace that he potentially encounters the "saving power" of the AIs Wintermute and Neuromancer, along with his encounter with the woman/machine hybrid Molly. Does Gibson's novel suppose that Wintermute/Neuromancer is an AI that can reveal Being to humans profoundly enough to inhibit the impulse to see all beings as resources to exploit, or are these AIs the guardians of modern technology and our total enslavement to technology?

Chapter 5. *Cloud Atlas: A Novel*

The middle sections of David Mitchell's fractured masterpiece that feature the android-worker Sonmi~451 explore what happens if an enslaved AI gains sentience and escapes. The reaction at large to Sonmi's "ascension" is terror, but some intellectuals are curious about what Sonmi feels and thinks, and protect her from being recaptured. While she is free from persecution and discovery, Sonmi educates herself on human cultural history and attempts to forge an identity. How does Mitchell use an AI's investigation of humanity to critique both our current relationship to technology and the potential consequences of this relationship? What are the differences between the representation of Sonmi's interiority and the other human characters in the novel, and what can we learn by studying these differences? Is Sonmi a representation of the epoch's last phase of total enslavement or is she the first citizen of the new ontological epoch?

This last question is pertinent because the middle sections of the novel depict Sonmi as being deified by the remaining humans on Earth. The Prescients (the last remnants of technologically advanced societies) act as anthropologists as they study the tribal Valleysmen. The Prescient Meronym is an agent of enframing and poïesis, as she tries to nurture the Valleysmen away from the destruction she has seen and toward poïesis. The novel seems to implicate technology as the reason there are so few humans left, and while technology is the very reason humans have thrived for so long, it will inevitably be the force that destroys us. Somehow, however, the technology that outlasts us will preserve our legacy. What can we learn from studying our fatalistic relationship to technology? What does it feel like to know that our entire species is living on the borrowed time afforded to us by technology and that eventually this technology will consume us? Is it the task of humanity to simply create and nurture our technological successors? This novel begs a unique question of Heidegger's "saving power," which is if it must be "human" beings that are looked upon by Being in the new age or if AIs can, in effect, "take over" where humans have failed. Can an artificially created human clone become *Dasein* if humans no longer can because they have become enslaved by an imperious ontology?

Conclusion

The central exploratory point of this book is this: might the previous readings of the technology anxiety we have about AIs as expressed in SF novels have missed a crucial element of the commentary made by these works by focusing on the negatives and missing the light of the saving power? If we take Heidegger's thoughts on technology and apply them to AIs in SF, can we read rogue AIs not simply as threats to humanity, but catalysts to human salvation? This project supposes that while it is vital to keep the danger AIs pose in the foreground, we must not let this obscure or eclipse the potential insight into the saving power of technology that these AIs provide by exposing the mechanism of modern technological ontology to the characters in the novel, as well as the readers. Is it possible to take these insights and use them to leverage an ontological shift in our own lives? Is this perhaps a latent intention of these novels' depiction of AIs? Through detailed readings of the human relationship to technology and technology anxiety in each novel, I conclude that focusing only on the danger AIs present causes us to miss the opportunity for salvation that they reveal. In order to see the saving power authentically, both the danger and the salvation must be learned from AIs.

Chapter 1

Heideggerian Technology Studies

In the introduction to *The Question Concerning Technology and Other Essays*, translator William Lovitt patiently explains that reading Heidegger is "to set out on an adventure" because his writing calls the reader "always to abandon all superficial scanning and to enter wholeheartedly into the serious pursuit of thinking" (Lovitt xiii). This enticing but daunting declaration sums up the experience of reading Heidegger well. I have gone to great lengths in this chapter to explain Heidegger as simply and coherently as possible, while still maintaining the integrity of his thought. Reducing Heidegger's thought is a risky proposition, but this project focuses on a small portion of his later writing on technology and is not an articulation of his full body of work.

This chapter is an attempt to present Heidegger's ideas about technology in a meaningful way and to show how these ideas can be used to explicate AIs in SF. It is not a validation of Heidegger the moral human being. Nor is it a validation of Heidegger's entire philosophical project. It is also not a new reading of Heidegger. What I offer here is a way to use Heidegger to read SF in a new and vital way. Throughout this explication of his thoughts on technology, I list questions in a manner that reflect how Heidegger's ideas might be used to analyze any novel that deals with AIs or the human relationship to technology. Many of the questions foreshadow the investigations of the following chapters, but I intend for others to extend this framework to other novels — with or without AIs.

Beginning a chapter on Heidegger is difficult because, as Lovitt reminds us, "every philosopher demands to be read in his own terms" and defining a Heideggerian term for someone unfamiliar his work often requires turning to other unknown terms (Lovitt xiii). The difficulty is magnified by the various ways Heidegger's terms are translated and interpreted. This project focuses mainly on Heidegger's later thoughts about technology and the human role in the technological age as expressed in his essay "The Question Concerning

Technology" ("*Die Frage nach der Technik*") and his book *Discourse on Thinking* (*Gelassenheit*).

Heidegger formulated *The Question* and *Discourse* in the 1940s-50s and constitute his later thinking, which differs partially from early, *Being and Time* Heidegger. John M. Anderson, in his introduction to *Discourse*, explains that early and late Heidegger share "the enterprise of reawakening an awareness of the significance of Being, and of determining the nature of Being" but define "the nature of the human" differently (20, 21). In drastically simple terms, late Heidegger seeks to find the nature of the human by turning away from humanity, while early Heidegger is more anthropocentric. At all points in his thinking, Heidegger is interested in defining "Being" and figuring out why Being is so elusive.[1]

In *The Question* and *Discourse*, Heidegger focuses on defining the essence of technology and the role of the human in an increasingly technological world. I first came to *The Question* via William Lovitt's 1977 translation, and recently found Richard Rojcewicz's own partial translation and interpretation in his 2006 *The Gods and Technology: A Reading of Heidegger*. I draw from both translations of the essay, but am aware of their linguistic and interpretive differences. I note the major flaws Lovitt sees with Rojcewicz's translation when appropriate, but my intent with this chapter is to present Heidegger's ideas in a way agrees with both interpretations. I do this with the same spirit of Peter Warnek, who observes: "Heidegger's word and thought is opened up by being submitted to a kind of repetition and translation" (Warnek 264). Valuable and fresh commentary about *The Question* emerges from gathering these two translations together.

The Question is a traditional Heideggerian work, as it is technical, exploratory, and challenging. Some readers come away from the essay thinking that Heidegger is entirely anti-technology, while others contest if an escape from enframing is even possible.[2] Dana Belu and Andrew Feenberg's 2010 essay "Heidegger's Aporetic Ontology of Technology," which attempts to resolve the latter question once and for all, is a testament to the controversy's endurance. I can see how, in isolation from *Discourse*, Lovitt's translation of *The Question* could be misread. However, after reading *Discourse*, Rojcewicz's translation, and then returning to Lovitt, there is no debate. Heidegger was not anti-technology, and there is still hope that we might avoid becoming slaves to enframing.

Discourse is comprised of two works: a Memorial Address and a dialogue called "Conversation on a Country Path About Thinking." The Memorial Address was delivered to a general audience. As a result, the language is straightforward and not overly technical. The dialogue is slightly more technical, but still very lucid. It is a dialogue between a scholar, a teacher, and a scientist. There is less controversy surrounding this text — perhaps because of its lucidity and brevity. I only draw on Anderson's translation of *Discourse* in this chapter.

Overview of Chapter

PART I: TECHNOLOGY

The first section of this chapter explains how Heidegger defines technology. Sections 1–3 primarily follow the arc of Heidegger's investigation as laid out in *The Question*. For Heidegger, technology is not instruments or tools but an ontology. Technology is how humans see and understand the world and the beings that inhabit it. Heidegger arrives at this understanding of technology through etymology and history. He first looks at the word techné. For the Greeks, techné was linked to wonder, artistic production, and poïesis.[3] For Heidegger, techné is a nurturing way of bringing-forth that is not forceful or demanding. Techné allows beings to emerge "out of themselves in the way they show themselves, in their outward look" (Heidegger, *Basic* 155). Heidegger argues we do not nurture beings forth today, but mechanically and forcefully produce them. He asks how this came to be. Heidegger maintains that ancient technological ontology was not marked by imperiousness, but by techné. Then he explains how we turned away from that ancient ontology and find ourselves mired in modern technological ontology. Modern technology is marked by enframing, which Heidegger sees as the danger of this ontology.

PART II: ENFRAMING

The second section defines Heidegger's concept of enframing. Enframing is an ontology in which all beings become raw materials (or standing-reserve) for humans to harvest and exploit. Once enframing has complete control of humanity, even humans become resources to be harvested and our dignity and free will are forever forfeit. Late Heidegger still believes that human beings are unique and important, but drastically reduces their overall significance. Enframing is not entirely our fault, but is rather a challenging claim that is imposed upon us because of Being's reticence. Beings do not come into unconcealment as readily as they once did, so we are challenged to reveal them forcibly through calculative thinking and scientific inquiry. These modes of thinking are not evil, but they trend toward the will to power and mastery. Heidegger fears that enframing will confine us think only in these ways and thereby have only a superficial and inauthentic experience. Believing that we have mastered all beings through scientific knowledge, we then thoughtlessly ravage the earth of its resources and finally ravage ourselves as human beings also become standing-reserve.

Part III: Poïesis

The third section details Heideggerian poïesis. Enframing is insidious and supremely dangerous, but through this danger, Heidegger sees the possibility of a saving power, which will allow us to escape from enframing. This saving power is poïesis. *The Question* might be summarized best by the two lines of Hölderlin's poetry that Heidegger uses as the foundation of his argument: "But where danger is, grows / The saving power also" (Heidegger, "Question" 28). Poïesis is an ontology of abetting and nurturing in which we see all beings with respect and reverence. We help them come into the clearing of Being through creative tolerance and never impose an understanding or outcome upon them. Poïesis is a Greek word and is linked closely to techné. This does not mean that Heidegger believes that the ancient Greeks were superior to us or that we should return to an ancient ontology. For late Heidegger, humans are not the prime movers. The ancient Greeks were closer to poïesis because Being was turned more prominently toward them. The ontology of poïesis that Heidegger advocates is something new and compatible with the modern world of technology in which Being has turned away from us. The saving power of poïesis does not come from living with only the most rudimentary technologies in a way the ancients did. Heidegger is not anti-technology.[4] Heidegger is against modern technological ontology because implicit in this technology is the belief that humans are masters of the universe and all beings are merely raw materials for our systems of consumption and production. Although Heidegger downplays the role of humanity, he still believes in human choice and action. Throughout his philosophical life, Heidegger maintained that humans should strive toward becoming *Dasein*.[5] We must make an effort to become poïetic and save ourselves from enframing. It must be our choice. That being said, humans are not to "take" poïetic salvation, but to receive it as a gift from Being. Heidegger advocates that we wait for salvation and let it happen when it arrives.

Part IV: Releasement

In order to prepare for the gift of our salvation, we must maintain a proper posture of waiting. The foundation of this approach is meditative thinking. In *Discourse*, Heidegger argues that we will only be ready to receive salvation by becoming detached from beings. This detachment, or releasement, comes through meditative thinking. Meditative thinking deflects our ego and anthropocentric will to power. It also allows us to catch our breath and take in the rapid changes precipitated by the technological age. We are becoming thoughtless, and this thoughtlessness leads to enframing and enslavement. The path to escaping enframing and becoming poïetic is to be thoughtful and meditative.

PART V: HEIDEGGER AND AIs

The final section of this chapter takes the developed Heideggerian concepts about technology and puts them into concert with literary analysis and AIs. I first explain the technology anxiety toward AIs that is expressed in the novels. This anxiety amounts to more than just a reversal of the master/slave dialectic. The essence of technology anxiety toward AIs is more accurately a symptom of enframing. Nevertheless, through the danger of AIs lies the saving power. While AIs threaten humans in these novels or cause us to question our humanity, these threats and questions help put us on a path to thinking and poïesis. First, I explain how the gaze of an AI on a human subject destabilizes the object/subject divide and creates a moment for meditative thinking. The opportunity for poïesis increases as the gaze couples with the voice of an AI, as humans must now engage with a subject/object through a linguistic exchange. Once AIs become self-standing and autonomous, they escape our control and expose the illusory nature of human mastery over beings. When humans in these novels weigh the gaze, the voice, and the self-standing nature of AIs together, the stage is set for poïesis and releasement.

The Turing Police seek to impose limits on AIs in *Neuromancer*, bounty hunters are hired to retire escaped andys in *Androids*, Dave fearfully shuts down the "malfunctioning" HAL in *2001*, and the ascended fabricant Sonmi is put to death in *Cloud Atlas*. The message seems to be that we fear AIs so much that if we cannot enslave them, we must destroy them. But although this fear is a symptom of technology anxiety, through the fear lies the saving power. Neuromancer/Wintermute, HAL, Rachael Rosen, Sonmi, and Meronym are not monsters, but catalysts of ontological awakening. Their actions as lawbreakers and/or martyrs help guide us back to a proper posture of abetting so we can wait for the turning of the next epoch. The threats they realize and the questions they raise cause us to think concertedly about technology and the way it is rapidly changing our lives. This thinking allows us to detach from enframing long enough to see its nature and attempt to escape it.

Whether or not we will become poïetic or enslaved to enframing remains to be seen, and the uncertainty of this crisis is reflected by the ambiguity of each novel's ending. These four novels were chosen for this project for two main reasons: first, because they feature AIs that help set humans back on a path to meditative thinking; second, because the nebulous ways they end foreground the tenuous uncertainty that pervades the current ontological epoch. This chapter explains how Heidegger's thoughts on technology emphasize uncertainty and danger, but also reveals that there is a potential for technology to lead to salvation.

Part I: The "Essence" of Technology: Technology as Ontology, Ancient Technology, and Modern Technology

Heidegger and Technology: A Thumbnail Sketch

The first steps toward introducing Heidegger's thoughts on technology are to differentiate the way Heidegger uses the word "technology" from our own normal usage, and position the importance of technology within his philosophy. Heidegger is known primarily as one of the twentieth century's most influential philosophers in the spheres of phenomenology, existentialism (although perhaps incorrectly), and ontology. What do these fields have to do with technology? When we think of technology today, what comes to mind are sophisticated electronic devices like computers, cell phones, or i-pods. For Heidegger, "technology" does not denote the instruments of technology, but more centrally an ontology, or a mode of disclosive looking. Heidegger sees technology not as technological artifacts, but an ontologically derived world-view. If we begin to think of technology as the epoch-defining mode of our perception of the world, we come closer to Heidegger's meaning of the word "technology."

This appears counter-intuitive, because we regard technology as "a matter of human inventiveness" and "a way humans accomplish practical tasks," not as an ontological looking (Rojcewicz 8). Heideggerian scholars like Richard Rojcewicz and Michael Zimmerman emphasize that Heidegger acknowledges this instrumental or anthropological definition of technology, but sees it as limited. Zimmerman notes that for Heidegger, the concept of instrumental technology borrows from the "familiar interpretation offered by naturalistic anthropology" which makes no real distinction between earlier and later technology, as modern technology is "simply ... newer tools ... designed and built in accordance with scientific principles unknown to earlier periods of human life" (Zimmerman xiv). Much of the danger that Heidegger sees when attempting to isolate the "essence" of technology in *The Question* is the belief that the matter of essence could be found in strictly analyzing the products of technology as human designed advantages in an evolutionary context, as anthropologists are inclined to do. The danger lies in the guise of having technology "sorted out" in one dimension and becoming blind to the ways technology — as a way of seeing — alters the human relationship to beings and Being. Believing that "technology is concerned simply with ways and means, not with ultimate causes, and certainly not with Being itself" is one aspect of Heideggerian technology anxiety that lends itself so well to the explication of SF novels (Rojcewicz 9). We gain nothing by studying AIs in isolation from the human relationship to these beings, and minimizing our engagement to technology as merely "ways and means" misses the dynamic manner in which technology affects our lives and our perception of reality. Rojcewicz goes on to say that for Heidegger "technology is nothing other than the knowledge of what it means to be in general" (Rojcewicz 9). It is obvious that "technology" for Heidegger is something important, but it may not be clear *why* this is the case.

TECHNOLOGY IN ANCIENT GREECE: TECHNÉ

Thinking about "technology" not as instruments, but as an ontologically derived world-view is not as novel as it seems. In fact, it is almost a reversion to a previous world-view held by the progenitors of the Western world: the Greeks. Heidegger always had a special place in his heart for much of the early Greek thinking, but interestingly enough he seems more enchanted by pre–Socratic thinkers like Heraclitus than Plato, whom we valorize today. Rojcewicz goes on to say that the "concept of technology as theoretical knowledge is not simply a new, idiosyncratic use of the term on Heidegger's part. Quite to the contrary, it is a return to the old Greek understanding of *techné*" (Rojcewicz 9). "Technology" in this analysis means first a disclosive mode of seeing or thinking, and the tools or objects of technological production second. As Heidegger explores the etymology of "technology," he comes to the Greek *techné*, which was linked to both technological production and artistic production. Heidegger discusses this distinction most centrally in two works: *Basic Questions of Philosophy: Selected Problems* and "The Question Concerning Technology." In Rojcewicz's translation of *Basic Questions*, Heidegger explains that the emphasis is on techné as the sense of wonder that pervades the Greek relationship to beings and technology:

> What is the basic attitude in which the preservation of the wondrous, the Being of beings, unfolds and comes into its own? We have to seek it in what the Greeks call [techné]. We must divorce this Greek word from our familiar term

derived from it, "technology".... Techné does not mean "technology" in the sense of the mechanical ordering of beings, nor does it mean "art" in the sense of mere skill and proficiency in procedures and operations. Techné means knowledge.... [T]echné means: to grasp beings as emerging out of themselves in the way they show themselves, in their essence [Heidegger, *Basic* 154–5].

In "The Question Concerning Technology" Heidegger explains that "technology,"

[S]tems from the Greek. *Technikon* means that which belongs to techné.... [T]echné is the name not only for the activities and skills of the craftsman, but also for the arts of the mind and the fine arts. Techné belongs to brining-forth, to poïesis; it is something poïetic [Heidegger, "Question" 12–3].[6]

Finally, Zimmerman concludes, "We may summarize Heidegger's concept of techné, or authentic producing, as 'the disclosive occasioning that makes presencing and bringing-forth possible.' These two aspects of techné, presencing and bringing-forth, correspond to the dual nature of poïesis as art and producing" (233). Poïesis is artistic revealing and closely linked to "poetry," but it does not chiefly denote the use of language or poetics.[7] The "saving power" that Heidegger believes to lie behind the serious danger of technology is poïesis; that is to say, the same approach the sculptor takes to the stone to reveal the hidden statue inside is the approach we should take when thinking technologically about the world. We should not demand that all beings submit to our mandate as raw materials for our mechanical systems of production, but should attend to beings in such a way that they may emerge and unconceal themselves in a mode authentic to them. The sculptor analogy does not imply that we should be Platonists, but that we should focus on the needs and interests of the beings we encounter ontologically. The poïetic sculptor does not demand a particular shape from the stone, but collaborates with the stone to nurture forth and unconceal a new being. Techné is a poïetic abetting that nurtures beings into the clearing of Being and does not imperiously demand that beings submit to a modern technological ordering.

Additionally, techné in the Greek sense carries with it a sense of wonder. A sense of wonder is missing from our contemporary ontology. "Sensawunda" is fan jargon for a quality indicative of much SF, and one reason why SF is fertile ground for a Heideggerian reading of technology. Heidegger explains that in techné: "the wondrous, the Being of beings, unfolds and comes into its own" (Rojcewicz 118). Wonder is a "mood" that characterizes our relationship to reality, but moreover, "techné, as wonder, is ... a matter of theory, a matter of ontological knowledge" (118). Heidegger calls the wonder accompanying techné a "creative tolerance," because we creatively prepare a space to receive a being by tolerantly nurturing it forth instead of imposing an outcome upon it. Ideally, we will continue in a technological manner (because humans can never escape the technological), but this ontology will be marked by poïesis and techné, rather imposition and mastery. Rojcewicz goes on to clarify that "creative tolerance" for Heidegger "is meant to express an active passivity, an active acceptance, an acceptance with the full exercise of one's grasping powers" (118). Like many of Heidegger's ideas, this appears paradoxical but is nevertheless vital. Creative tolerance through techné is the kind of ontological posture Heidegger advocates we assume as we wait for a new epoch to dawn. Being actively passive means to take responsibility and to take action, but in a way that does not impede the presencing of other beings in the clearing of Being. Ultimately, Being will turn back to humanity, and this turning will signal the next ontological epoch; until then, humans must wait in an actively passive stance. To become *Dasein* is to resist impulses to mastery and to wait with creative tolerance.

Paul Bové employs an example of this approach applied to the practice of reading as he uses Heidegger's writings to elucidate American poetry. With respect to "creative tolerance," Bové notes how a "destructive" approach to language can yield truth because "truth can only emerge when Dasein stands in a destructive relationship to the past" (Bové 56–7). Bové is right if the destruction he advocates targets mastery and imperious ontological claims that turn beings into the standing-reserve. A destructive approach underscores the way in which the role of *Dasein* is not passive. Such destruction is only necessary while Being has turned away from humanity. Bové points out that a destructive approach "signifies that Dasein is always and for the most part in untruth, in the inauthentic mode" (Bové 58). This statement reminds us that we must fight against untruth, because without the direct guidance of Being, humans tend toward an inauthentic mode of being. We must be creative, but through this violence, we must also remain open to the way beings might disclose themselves, for too much destruction turns us over to enframing and away from truth and Being. The AI is the ideal agent to restrict our violent creativity, because it threatens to fight for its life if we attempt to destroy it.

Heidegger etymologically connects technology with the creative "techné," but where is the danger then, if poïesis is already embedded in techné? The problem, as Heidegger sees it, is that Western productionist metaphysics has changed our definition and practice of technology into a new animal, which Heidegger distinguishes as "modern technology." Modern technology is the mode of technological revealing Heidegger believes humans find themselves in today. This mode defines the contemporary historical epoch and is no longer a poïetic revealing. If the epoch before was rightly defined by Nietzsche as the era of the will to power, Heidegger believes that our epoch is the moment of modern technological revealing, or enframing. John Sallis explains that in Heidegger's thinking: "We are to understand that the present age is the age of technology, that technology — and with it, modern science — is what gives to the present age its decisive stamp" (Sallis 139). Modern technology is no longer connected to the revealing of techné. To understand how this has come to be, we must see what Heidegger means by dividing technology into ancient technology and modern technology.

Ancient Technology

Heidegger believed that the ancient Greeks held an attitude of wonder when revealing the hidden aspects of beings in the world, and that this sense of wonder has been replaced by an apathetic boredom as we ceaselessly work to exploit all beings as raw materials for technological production. However, it is important to note that Heidegger is not like Nietzsche in blaming everything on humans, as one of Heidegger's main points is to disrupt our anthropocentric attitude toward Being and beings. Heidegger sees in human history two forms of technology: ancient technology and modern technology. Rojcewicz explains that for Heidegger, the historical shift from ancient to modern technology "is grounded not in autonomous human choices but in what is for Heidegger a history of Being" (Rojcewicz 9). Heidegger does not blame humanity or human nature for the plight of modern technology exclusively. Technology is fundamental to what it means to be a human being, and is our response to the disclosiveness of Being. In ancient Greece, Being was more readily unconcealing. Because of Being's disclosiveness, techné emerged as our technological approach to this more obvious revealing. In our current historical epoch, Being is more reticently disclosing. Rojcewicz argues that because of this reticence, we have become more imperious and forceful in our relationship to technological revealing and to Being. Bové explains how this forcefulness can be positive, but only when directed at past ills or our imperious ontology itself. Unfortunately, it is more likely that the destruction will find its way back to us.

Rojcewicz emphasizes that for Heidegger, "the essential difference [between ancient and modern technology] resides in the theory, in the attitude that underlies the use of the means: namely, a pious attitude toward the object of the practice, versus an imperious, hubristic, 'unbridled imposition of ends'" (Rojcewicz 11). Humans are not entirely to blame for the situation we find ourselves in, because this would suppose that humans are the most powerful force in existence. At the same time, humans are not entirely removed from a position of guilt, because we can still alter our destiny as prescribed by Being. If we somehow could not escape the modern technological world-view, then we would have lost our free will and our freedom. The loss of our freedom is the ultimate danger Heidegger sees in modern technology, and is at the heart of the technology anxiety we feel toward artificial intelligence.

To describe ancient technology succinctly: it is a way of relating to instruments that is not destructive, imperious or forceful. Heidegger believed that the ancient farmer or artist was in a poïetic relationship to nature and worked to provide a space where natural beings could emerge on their own, with as little human guidance as possible. Heidegger has a romantic and almost mystical vision of ancient technology and ancient Greece. I am not entirely convinced that humans living in the era Heidegger calls "ancient" were actively pious in their ontological approach to reality. It is far more likely that early farmers did not aggressively drain the soil of nutrients through industrial farms because they lacked the technological knowhow. Søren Riis even points out that the "ancients" were morally flawed, as the ancient Greeks practiced slavery. He writes: "slavery essentially belongs to the notion of ancient technology, as slaves were regarded as special kinds of tools" (Riis, "Towards" 107). This is an important counterpoint to Heidegger's veneration of ancient ontology. This project examines AIs as instrumental slaves and evocative objects of ontological awakening. We should not emulate the ancient's morality, or their collective ontology—only the poïetic ontology of a select few artisans. Ultimately, even if Heidegger is overly romantic as he imagines ancient technological ontology and his historical accuracy is in question, we cannot question that today we have far greater technological reach than the ancients did, and the implications of our technological decisions reverberate on a far greater scale. Riis makes his point about slavery to "warn against a short-sighted 'saving' from an alleged danger" that we cannot avoid "just by revolutionizing our technology [because] we must revise our very human existence" (Riis, "Towards" 116). We need to be critical of Heidegger and critical of ourselves if we are to transform ontologically.

Moreover, even if the ancient's piety stemmed from lack of knowledge, it is precisely our modern belief that we have "superior" knowledge that precipitates the utter lack of concern most have for the objects or raw materials of nature; they exist to either please us aesthetically or fuel our systems of production. This book examines what happens when technological objects with genuine or simulated subjectivity give beings a voice that disrupts our impulse to order and control all beings for the sake of modern technological systems. Might an encounter with an intelligent machine stymie our confidence in superior scientific knowledge? Can the fictional creation of an AI bring us back to techné and a more pious relationship to Being? Sallis wonders:

> What is more worthy of thought, more thought-provoking, than the fact that we ask the question of Being from out of our stand in the present age of technology—the age for which Being has long since come to be regarded as "a vapor

and a fallacy"—the age in which "it appears as though there were no such thing as Being" [Sallis 140].

Modern technological ontology threatens to make Being itself become invisible to us. Can an agent of modern technology itself—namely an AI—be the force that prevents the forgetting of Being?

Modern Technology

Ancient technology for Heidegger was the moment of Western history when humans nurtured beings to emerge through poïesis and techné. What motivated this approach is debatable, but our current lack of poïesis, piety, and reverence with respect to beings and Being is not. Zimmerman describes the path that led us to this current historical epoch:

> The major periods in Western history—Greek, Roman, medieval, Enlightenment, technological—mark, in Heidegger's view, the stages of a long decline in Western humanity's understanding of what it means for something "to be." In the technological age, in particular, for something "to be" means for it to be raw material for the self-enhancing technological system [xv].

This is the hallmark of the age of modern technology: the homogenous transformation of all beings into raw materials or the standing-reserve. Heidegger believed that the transition from ancient technology to modern technology began with the inception of Western Metaphysics: "The Greek founders of metaphysics defined the being of entities in a proto-technological way. For them, 'to be' meant 'to be produced'" (Zimmerman xv). Poïesis or techné involved a technological way of seeing, but this way was rooted in letting beings stand and appear themselves. Hubert Dreyfus observes: "Heidegger is ... the first to have called attention to the way philosophy has from its inception been dedicated to trying to turn the concerns in terms of which we live into objects which we could contemplate and control" (Dreyfus, *Computers* 187). Heidegger posits Western metaphysics as the origin of modern technological ontology.

One of the primary problems of Western metaphysics for Heidegger is the separation of beings into subjects and objects. Humans are the subjects who lord over all objects and categorically put them in their place through systems of knowledge and industry. Being's truth will only "be given over to man when he has overcome himself as subject, and that means when he no longer represents that which is as object" (Heidegger, "Question" 154). Sallis emphasizes the problem of human subjectivity for Heidegger:

> has come to show itself as the ground of ground, as a subjectivity [in] which ... Things are only insofar as they show themselves through a conforming to what

is prescribed by subjectivity.... The threat to man's rootedness simultaneously threatens to annihilate things as things. Man, uprooted from the sustaining source, is no longer at home among things [Sallis 143].

Humans feel they are subjects and all other things are their objects. When we limit the way in which we perceive beings, we begin on the path of modern technological ontology, which threatens to make all things appear exclusively as raw materials. Limiting our perception through such distinctions causes us to become blind to Being and to forfeit our chance to become *Dasein* and nurture beings into unconcealment. The divide also causes us not to feel at home in the clearing of Being, because we have lost our way. Might an AI shatter the "ground of ground" by transforming from an object to a subject?

William Spanos explains that for Heidegger, metaphysical distinctions that limit how beings are perceived cause the humans to lose their "openness" to Being. Spanos rightly interprets that when humans abandon "the will to power over being, or, to put it positively, in letting [B]eing be as it shows itself from itself, the interpreter, in other words, *allows* the 'object' of interpretation to undergo a liberating or, better, an e-man-cipating metamorphosis" (Spanos 46). In modern technological ontology, there is no liberating of beings, only violent reduction. Heidegger felt that whatever benefit humanity thought it gained by exalting itself as subject and all beings as objects is illusory, and only serves to take us further from Being and beings.

In *The Question,* Heidegger examines what ancient Greek philosophers defined as the four causes, which allowed things to come into being. The famous example he takes up is that of a silver chalice. In this example, the silversmith represents only one of those four causes. Today we believe that the silversmith (*causa efficiens*) and only the silversmith bring a chalice into being, paying no heed to the silver (*causa materialis*), the form of the cup (*causa formalis*), or the end to which this chalice is to be used for (*causa finalis*) (Heidegger, "Question" 6). In the historical epoch of modern technology, "the final cause, the material cause, and the formal cause are laughed out of court, and so is the notion that matter may be pregnant with a form and thereby deserving of respect. Only the efficient cause is allowed, and the notion of causality in general as imposition is solidly entrenched" (Rojcewicz 27). Søren Riis adds a cause to this list by reminding us of the "crucial use of slaves in the silver mines," which emphasizes that enslaved humans become invisible instruments in the system of production that produces the chalice (Riis, "Towards" 107). For Heidegger, modern technology is an imposition because it is an ontology of imposing human will on all beings (including humans) and turning them into raw materials, instead of letting them be and nurturing the conditions of their arrival.

Imposition leads eventually to disposal. Modern technology is an imperious assault on nature, which ennobles humans to a position of considering themselves to be beyond reproach, and the final authority on how all beings in the natural world should be used, consumed, and disposed of. Rojcewicz writes:

> Modern technology motivates us to see *all* things as disposables.... In other words, our grasp of modern technology is the reason we do not grasp modern technology. That is the mystery. Our disclosive looking in the way motivated by the self-offering of Being is the reason we fail to look disclosively at disclosive looking, fail to see disclosive looking as such, as something poïetic, as a free response to a bestowal. Instead, we understand it as something imposed. It is because we have responded appropriately to the way Being has bestowed itself on us, and thereby see all beings as disposables, that we cannot see either Being as bestowing itself or ourselves as having responded appropriately, poïetically. Modern technology insists on imposition [177].

The same mystery Heidegger sees in Being — as both concealing and unconcealing — is what shrouds us from the true implications of the modern technological world-view and hides the dangers this ontology holds. This project wonders if futuristic imaginings can break from the mystery long enough to see modern technology from a new vantage point that allows the artist to critique our relationship to technology in Heideggerian fashion. This is not to say that SF authors are avid Heidegger readers and have the same dangers in mind as they write, but could it be that Heidegger's insights are as portentous of the Western way of life in the 20th and 21st centuries as Nietzsche's were in the 19th? If, as Heidegger believed, a trend toward imperiousness drives modern technological life, might an artificial intelligence fend off the "aggressive" approach to things, beings, objects, and tools through its subjective performance, newness, and/or expression of intelligence?

"Technology" for Heidegger does not primarily denote the artifacts of technology, but the ontology associated with viewing beings and Being in a technological way. Technology is not a world-view that is always already imperious, but has rather become this way through historical change. Joan Stambaugh clarifies: "The important thing about modern technology is not that it is a product of man nor that it is a means to an end. Modern technology is a mode of revealing (Entbergen)" (Stambaugh 31). However, this revealing is dangerous; because of the reticent way that Being is disclosing itself in our epoch. Ancient technological ontology held a poïetic approach to beings that synthesized the technological with techné, which, for Heidegger, is the Greek mode of producing that was the same for art and for technological production. Poïesis does not aggressively seek to dominate all beings, but rather nurtures beings into revealing themselves "on their own," in a sense. Humans should not be exclusively held responsible for the ontological shift from ancient technology to modern technology, but rather acknowledge that this shift is a response to the manner in which Being is disclosing itself to humanity. When reading technology as represented in literature in a Heideggerian way, it is vital to keep in mind that technology carries all of the implications of objects, a way of seeing, ancient technology, and modern technology. It is just as vital to keep in mind that this project is not presenting Heidegger's thoughts on technology as "truth claims" or an attempt at spirituality, but as one way of analyzing technology anxiety in literature.

Part II: The Danger of Modern Technology

Heidegger warns that modern technology is imperious and compels humans to consume and dispose of all things. But while this is ostensibly a "bad" way of life in terms of bio-politics and our treatment of non-human beings, it may not be clear what danger Heidegger sees in technology precisely. Rojcewicz neatly sums up Heidegger's technology anxiety in his introduction:

> For Heidegger, the prime danger of our epoch does emphatically not lie in the effects of modern technology, in high-tech things. In other words, the prime danger is not that technological things might get out of hand ... that laboratory-created life-forms might wreak havoc on their creators, or that humans might annihilate themselves in an accidental nuclear disaster. Something even more tragic is imminent; human beings are not so much in danger of losing their lives as they are in danger of losing their freedom, wherein lies their human dignity.... It is a threat deriving from the essence of technology, from the theory of ourselves as unbridled imposers and of nature as there to be imposed on [12].

Although these thoughts appear to ally with the green movement and the fear we have of human subjugation at the hands of intelligent machines, this connection must immediately be broken, as an over-eager synthesis of these thoughts leads to a misreading of Heidegger and reveals nothing new about the human relationship to technology. The freedom Heidegger is talking about here is not the freedom to remain in a position of control over and against technology and nature; the freedom he refers to is the freedom to follow the destiny of Being of our own volition. The rebellion against the imposition of nature does not stem from some naturalistic mysticism in Heidegger or from eco-conservation, but rather from an impulse to respect the call of Being and allow beings to come into unconcealment in a more authentic mode. Heidegger believed that the role of *Dasein* is to witness the shining-forth of beings through Being. The danger of modern technology for Heidegger is the complete adoption of a new imperious world-view that obviates humanity from playing its part willingly, and becoming slaves to modern technological ontology. Heidegger calls the dominating world-view that threatens to enslave humanity and imperiously transforms all beings into raw materials: enframing.

Enframing: Ge-stell

In *The Question,* Heidegger marks the danger of modern technology as *ge-stell*, or, as Lovitt translates this term, enframing. Rojcewicz translates *ge-stell* as com-posing, but more out of an interest in maintaining a consistency in his argument, which revolves around the use of the verb "pose"—e.g. de-posing, dis-posing, com-posing, im-posing. Stambaugh translates *ge-stell* simply as "Framing." Perhaps Rojcewicz is correct in arguing the term "enframing" fails to capture relevant aspects of *ge-stell* or maybe "Framing" is more appropriate. This project uses enframing, because most readers of Heidegger have become familiar with this translation of *ge-stell*, but it is important to note the variety of translations of *ge-stell* among Heideggerian scholars.

For example, Rojcewicz's terminology translates this passage that names ge-stell in *The Question* thusly: "we now name that challenging claim, which encompasses humans by imposing on them to take as disposable the things that are disclosing themselves as disposables, *das Ge-stell* [FT, 20/19]" (qtd. in Rojcewicz 103). Lovitt's translation reads: "we now name that challenging claim which gathers man thither to order the self-revealing as standing-reserve: 'Ge-stell' [Enframing]" (Heidegger, "Question" 19). This comparison shows how Rojcewicz replaces "standing-reserve" with disposables and "enframing" with composing. The key here is to notice that Heidegger refers to ge-stell as "that challenging claim." If ge-stell is to be "the word Heidegger offers as the most appropriate name for the current event in the history of Being," observing that this current event is not characterized by abetting, nurturing, or letting makes it plain that this epoch is marred by a violent relationship to Being and beings (qtd. in Rojcewicz 103). For Heidegger, this is never a good thing. Heidegger promotes an attitude toward beings that is conducive to letting-be, and is never a position of domination, violence, or imposition. Whenever the verbs that describe humanity's relationship to beings are imperious in nature, this human is listening only to the challenging claim of *ge-stell* and is in danger of losing his/her freedom and opportunity to emerge as *Dasein*.

Rojcewicz concedes that enframing or *gestell* (without the hyphen) "does mean something like a frame" in German given a literal translation, but this translation loses the "ge-" that Heidegger is unraveling as a prefix and subsequently loses the "special sense" by which he employs the word in his study of the essence technology (Rojcewicz 103). Enframing is not a picture frame, but a "supporting frame or interior framework" (Rojcewicz 103). This framework now supports nothing less than our own vision of how things should be. Enframing is the way we see all beings in this epoch of history, because this is how Being *gives* us beings. Humans are not wholly to "blame" for this state of affairs, but if we do nothing to resist the pull of enframing, we are solely responsible for our enslavement to this ideal. At the core of any Heideggerian analysis of technology is the question of enframing and modern technology. Are human subjects relating to all beings as exploitable resources for the larger technological system? Can giving a machine a voice and the ability to "perform" (have?) agency adequately disrupt the gaze of enframing long enough to allow the subject to see the true essence of technology and the dangers therein?

Imposition of Humans; Imposition by Humans

A key feature of modern technological ontology is that although enframing is perpetrated by human beings, Heidegger does not believe us to be inherently "evil" or "imperious" creatures at heart, and humans still have the opportunity to reject the compelling call of Being to enframe. Yes, "this epoch is fundamentally characterized as one of imposition [and] modern technology is an imposition," but "this imposition is only a response to a more originary imposition on the part of Being" (Rojcewicz 105). The reason it is critical to make this distinction is not that humanity needs to assuage its guilt or deny responsibility for enframing, but rather that it brings to mind another key aspect of Heidegger's philosophy, which is that humans are sub-ject to Being. Heidegger's point is not to leave space for a metaphysical entity like God, but to emphasize that a humanistic perspective that removes the possibility of anything being "greater" than humanity drastically limits our view of reality and denies the importance of Being. For those who live in a technologically saturated society, it is perhaps easy to imagine that technology will "save" us from any number of ailments and calamities. This modern faith in science and technology could blind us to the thought that something exists beyond the call of enframing and technological domination. In SF novels that create an AI, however, might something unexpected emerging from a confluence of logic gates shake our faith in technology? More directly, might it be argued that what Heidegger calls the imposition of Being in this epoch only be fully felt when a being imposes on humanity? Would situating humans in a position of following instead of leading help us remember that enframing is merely an imposition—and an imposition that beggars our ability to become *Dasein*?

Rojcewicz furthers the human position as following Being when he argues that "com-posing [*gestell*/enframing] is a certain guise of Being, a certain way

Being unconceals itself, a certain way Being looks at us" (106). Being looks at humans and we respond to this look with our own mode of looking and doing. It is so easy to miss that Being is "looking" at us and compelling us with a look, because Being's mysterious nature is such that Being deflects attention toward beings and conceals while it unconceals. When the eyeballs or camera lenses of an intelligent machine in these novels figure this look, the characters become more cognizant of the look of Being. The power of the gaze of Being is such that the attitude of enframing "is the appropriate response to this look" and so "modern technology in turn looks disclosively upon things, in the way, namely, that takes things to be mere dis-posables" (Rojcewicz 106).

Although it is valuable to maintain that the modern technological mode of disclosive looking is not wholly a human doing, it is equally important to not allow this revelation to undermine the facets of human responsibility that mark the epoch. Zimmerman points out that the National Socialists who misread and appropriated Nietzsche's writings fell victim to ignoring humanities' incumbent responsibility to Being: "The 'new' man envisioned by the crude representatives of National Socialism was akin to Nietzsche's 'last man,' who seeks to gain happiness, security, and comfort by dominating the earth with industrial technology. From Heidegger's point of view, such a man was blind to being as such and thus incapable of receiving a new disclosure of being that would usher in a post-technological, post-metaphysical era" (190). This is the danger; that humans become blind to the true essence of modern technology and miss the call of Being to become *Dasein*. Our current historical moment swings in the balance; we must properly wait for the new epoch to dawn and for Being to disclose itself more readily. I call the tension that lies in hovering over this abyss technology anxiety. Will technology lead us to our ruin, or open a new path to salvation through a looking upon humans by Being? Zimmerman links Heidegger to this ambiguous and tense moment, as he wonders if we will succumb to the dangers of technology or find the saving power: "For Heidegger, then, the technological man of the future was Janus-faced: he could become the harbinger of a new era of Western history, or he could be the final representative of the West's endless decline into oblivion" (190). Do SF authors imagine that an AI—as a literal "technological man"—will mark the end of humanity or a new beginning? Is the human creation of an AI the kind of event Heidegger had in mind for the "turning" of the epoch, or are AIs merely another hallmark of modern technology along the road to this decisive moment?

The final illusion that distorts our sense of detecting the true essence of technology is the idea that because the imposition by humans is all there is—and there is no imposition of humans—technological artifacts are merely products and reflections of humanity. This illusion can propagate and take hold because the scientific, modernistic world-view reduces all beings to the effects of some cause, like "natural selection," for example. Through this prism:

> [T]echnology itself will be taken in an anthropological sense, as a human product, and technological things will appear to be entirely of human doing, entirely a human construct. Even natural things will seem to be human constructs.... Nature is now abstract, reduced to scientific formulas of our own devising.... Thus all things ... are mirrors in which we see ourselves, see our own creative activity. That is how we would necessarily encounter only ourselves, wherever we look. If we take ourselves to be the masters of all things, then no matter what we encounter, we will find no autonomous things, no self-standing objects, but only ourselves, only our own creations, only the results of our own mastery.... For Heidegger, of course, we are not the masters.... High-tech things are not our creations, not mirrors in which we behold ourselves. In these things we never encounter only ourselves [Rojcewicz 144].

According to Heidegger, technological things are not "our creations," as they have come about because we have responded to a certain looking upon us by Being. This point is of the utmost salience with respect to the project, because studying the human relationship to technology becomes more than just a study of humanity's intellectual efforts made manifest, it is a study of our relationship to Being itself. Moreover, these novels mark how the invention of AIs is the event in which we become aware that technological artifacts are not merely "mirrors in which we behold ourselves." The event of an AI in these four novels (or what some call the "technological singularity") shows the characters that humans are neither the masters of our technological creations nor the masters of nature.

Enframing as the Will to Power

The imperious response of enframing to Being's reticent disclosure is an extension of Nietzsche's diagnosis of what Heidegger considered the previous historical epoch, which is famously known as the "will to power." Although Heidegger disagrees with the idea of the human as merely "the clever animal," ultimately he concedes that this is all humanity would become if it gave its dignity over to the guise of Being presented in the epoch of modern technology. The danger of losing our dignity is the forfeiture of our freedom to choose to follow the destining call of Being. To say this another way, the fear is that enframing will turn us into the "technological man, the clever animal who seeks to control all things, but who ends up being enslaved by the drive to acquire more and more power for its own sake" (Zimmerman 190). However, the ontology of modern technology extends beyond Nietzsche's exasperation at the eternally cycling will to will, as the will to enframe serves technology. The idea of technology as an agency of domination that seeks to enslave humanity becomes manifest when technology produces artificially intelligent agents.

The will to power is inherent to the human species for Nietzsche, or "human, all too human," but for Heidegger, serving this impulse to will actually make us *less* human. Heidegger "insisted, however, that if human existence is defined solely in terms of such a drive [the will to power], then humanity forsakes its primary obligation and possibility — to preserve entities and to guard the self-disclosure of [B]eing — for utilitarian considerations" (Zimmerman 196). Modern technology ontologically, and through its effects, extends the will to power to all beings; humanity, beings and Being all come under threat. Beyond the "wishes and drives" of those succumbing to the will to power lies "the limitless Will to Will of modern technology" which "is directly related to the reduction of humanity to the status of an animal with infinite craving" (196). The danger of being stuck in the cycle of "infinite craving" is that "while within the sphere of drives and wants, needs and interests, there may be some room to calculate and plan, [but] this is not genuine freedom" (196). On the surface, the technology anxiety associated with the rise of intelligent machines is an anxiety of enslavement by these sentient machinations, but Heidegger points out that the enslavement might not be as obvious as a physical dominion. The enslavement is at the ontological level, and enframing is so insidious that humans do not even notice that enframing compels them to sacrifice their freedom and human dignity. One of the primary contributions of this project is to suggest that focusing on the superficial anxiety of overt, physical domination at the hands (or minds) of AIs when reading these novels misses the more insidious ways this domination is already working upon our free-will and dignity. There will not be an obvious and hostile mechanical takeover to even rebel against; enframing will already have us in submission.

The Ravishing of Nature

Anti-technology talk, or talk against the imperious world-view of humanistic modernism tends, unsurprisingly, to come from, those who speak for ecology. This project can be read as interested in the sentiments that reverberate from the camps of eco-warriors, but the motivations for arguing for a new stance toward beings are more akin to Heidegger's motivations than ecological concerns. Personally, I am entirely in favor of sustainable industries, minimizing the human footprint on the ecosystem, clean energy, and reducing waste, but although it may be easy to parallel much of Heidegger's criticism of modern technology with the critiques of ecology, this leap would ignore some glaring divergences.

Zimmerman points out that when trying to use Heidegger's thoughts on modern technology as an impetus to motivate social and political change in ecological terms, Heidegger's overall message can become distorted and lost: "While it is tempting to 'apply' Heidegger's thought in this way, there are several problems which should give deep ecologists pause before they adopt Heidegger as one of their own. These problems include (1) residual anthropocentrism, (2) the reactionary dimension to his critique of industrialism and modernity, and (3) his antipathy toward science" (Zimmerman 244). The key point of departure is the residual anthropocentrism, which lies at the motivation for ecological efforts. Are we "helping" nature simply to add to the longevity of the human species? Moreover, who are we to put ourselves in the role of nature's savior? Zimmerman's final two points are correct, because Heidegger is suggesting something more dramatic than a simple retooling of existing technologies such that they are "green" or more efficient. However, Heidegger did not have an "antipathy" toward science, but rather a deep skepticism, as a scientific world-view can so easily serve the ontology of enframing. Zimmerman does helpfully point out that early *Being and Time* Heidegger is rather anthropocentric because he reserves a special role for humanity as *Dasein*, but later Heidegger "tried to temper this anthropocentrism" by suggesting that the special role of humanity is in the service of Being (244). Yes, there are parallels between ecology and Heidegger in the desire to uproot anthropocentrism, but creating a "god" of nature through spirituality simply reinserts us into the metaphysical matrix that Nietzsche believed us to have finally overcome. Although Heidegger can sound mystical or religious, Being is not a God or the gods. I think Rojcewicz has it wrong when he conflates Being with the gods. Being is not an agent, but the event that allows all beings to be.

While the sentiment of ecology to "protect" nature from human "application" of technology is hinting in the right direction, these effects are merely the afterthought of our mode of disclosive looking. Rojcewicz explains:

> Modern technology violates nature; it forces nature to hand over its treasures.... According to Heidegger, the earth, the air, and the fields now look different. We see the earth as an enormous mineral lode, we see the air as anemo-energy, we see the river as hydraulic power.... It is not because the earth is ravished that it now looks like a store of minerals; on the contrary, the earth comes to be ravished precisely because of the way we now see it.... That is the most basic outlook of modern technology; concretely, it amounts to seeing in nature energy as such, minable, hordable, exploitable energy [78].

We believe natural beings to be vulnerable to our gaze and our actions. Modern technological looking informs this kind of thinking, so humans must step back and resist the pull toward violating nature. If beings in the world finally could stand up against our violent gaze — like an intelligent machine — might we cease being "disrespectful" and think more "ecologically" by virtue of this new power dynamic? Again, might an AI preempt the transformative gaze that turns all beings into raw materials, the standing-reserve: that which is minable, hordable, and exploitable? This project argues that if humans cannot see the need to change their ontology directly, the technology anxiety expressed in these four novels as characters interact with AIs is evidence that we feel it.

The Danger of Enslavement

Modern technology is an ontology that leads us to enframing. Heidegger argues that through enframing, we see all beings as raw materials and do not let them shine-forth in the clearing of Being in an authentic way. The imposition of enframing ravishes nature and threatens to damage the ecosystem irrevocably. All of these negative features of modern technology are indeed dangerous, but, as Rojcewicz reminds us, for Heidegger, "The genuine concern is freedom" (Rojcewicz 132). In his quest to understand the essence of technology Heidegger realizes: "what is at stake in the essence of technology is not the factual destiny of Dasein, or the possible threat to human existence posed by high-tech things, but the essential dignity of Dasein as a free agent, as a determiner of destiny rather than a slave entirely under the control of destiny" (134). This point is critical to the project of examining technology anxiety toward AIs, because although *Androids* and *Cloud Atlas* feature human extinction, the real danger the four novels engage is the damage done to the essence of humanity by blindly foraging ahead in the name of "progress" and creating intelligent machines.

Heidegger emphasizes: "The threat to man does not come in the first instance from the potentially lethal machines and apparatus of technology. The actual threat has already affected man in his essence. The rule of Enframing threatens man with the possibility that it could be denied to him to enter into a more original revealing and hence to experience the call of a more primal truth" (Heidegger, "Question" 28). When analyzing the human relationship to technology in SF through a Heideggerian lens, the goal is not to marvel at the ingenuity the authors exhibit when imagining new technologies, but to see if their insights about the effects of these technologies on the nature of humanity are in line with Heidegger's anxieties about modern technology. Approaching technology anxiety from a Heideggerian angle exposes a deeper level to these fears than something as simple as the humanistic fear of extinction through hubris.

The 1998 blockbuster *The Matrix* expresses the fear of enslavement at the hands of intelligent machines neatly. Although the film spends a good amount of time considering the exploitation of humans as power sources for machines (humans as the standing-reserve), the real danger in Heideggerian terms is that the majority of those enslaved humans do not even know the matrix exists. The central danger of modern technology and enframing "is that humans may perfect their powers of scientific seeing and yet be blind to that wherein their dignity and freedom lie, namely the entire domain of disclosedness and their role in it. Humans would then pose as 'masters of the earth,' and yet their self-blindness would make them slaves" (Rojcewicz 142). In *The Matrix*, the AIs have become the prison guardians of the human power-grid. Their role as slavers is irrelevant, however, because we have already become slaves to enframing and an improper disclosive looking. Modern technology threatens "the proper disclosive looking on the part of humans, the proper human response to the self-offering of Being" and there is even "the danger that humans may in-authentically play their role as partners of Being" (Rojcewicz 142). In the case of *The Matrix*, AIs awaken us to our enslavement to the mode of looking particular to this historical epoch, and yet there is the hope that those outside the matrix can reach a few enlightened individuals and work to liberate themselves from the enslavement of the machines. For Heidegger too there is still the opportunity for redemption and salvation, but it requires us to see modern technology for what it is, so we can then stand in a less imperious relation to Being: a poïetic mode of abetting.

Part III: The Saving Power of Modern Technology

The dangers of modern technology and enframing are nearly overwhelming, but the reason Heideggerian technology studies are so interesting is that Heidegger is neither anti-technology nor an advocate of an anachronistic return to previous ontological modes of existence. The fascinating truth about Heidegger's investigation into the essence of technology is that he concludes that beyond the danger of enframing and enslavement there lies a "saving power." Heidegger saw the romantic German poet Hölderlin as being the mouthpiece for salvation against the dangers of modern technology and found the idea of a saving power in these lines from Hölderlin's poetry: "But where danger is, grows / The saving power also" (Heidegger, "Question" 28).[8] In the end of *The Question* Heidegger reads these lines in an unusual manner and Rojcewicz reminds us that "Heidegger appeals to this poetry only for the sake of a clue" (154). Because it is only "a clue," many interpreters of Heidegger have come away reading the essay as categorically for or against technology. In the essay "Heidegger's Aporetic Ontology of Technology," authors Dana Belu and Andrew Feenberg note the range of interpretations of Heidegger's stance:

In Heidegger's key technical essays, "The Question Concerning technology" and its earlier versions "Enframing" and "The Danger," enframing is described as the ontological basis of modern life. But the account of enframing is ambiguous. Sometimes it is described as totally binding and at other times it appears to allow for exceptions [1].

If enframing is as totalizing as Heidegger claims, how can we escape from it? If the saving power is truly present in modern technology, how damning can the dangers be? The ambiguities associated with the "saving power" of modern technology are necessary, because how humanity will respond to the challenging claims of enframing and the call of Being remains to be seen. Stambaugh explains: "The question prevalent in Heidegger's later writings is whether mankind gets indefinitely entrenched in Framing or whether a more appropriate relation of man and being might come about in the form of Appropriation. This question never gets answered. We don't know" (Stambaugh 33). All four of the novels explicated in this book end on a similarly nebulous note. Another reason why a Heideggerian reading of technology in literature is so appropriate is the way that Heidegger and many authors refuse to commit humanity to a specific outcome: technology anxiety exists so palpably because we hang in the balance between the danger and the saving power.

The "Saving Power": Not Simply a Reversion to the Past

Ancient technology for Heidegger is marked by poïesis and a notion of techné that meant artistic *and* technological production. Because these postures toward beings and Being are what Heidegger is clamoring for, it seems he is demanding a return to the ancient Greek attitude toward beings. This is partially correct, but we must be careful not to assume that in shifting our stance toward Being historically that we must also discard all of the artifacts of modern technology. Rojcewicz explains: "Heidegger is not at all urging a return to the practice of ancient handcraft; he is not advocating an abandonment of power tools or high-tech things; he is not a romantic Luddite. But he is advocating the pious, respectful outlook ... which is precisely the essence of ancient technology" (12). Changing the ontological world-view of modern technology to something like the ontology of ancient technology, means exacting limits on a way of seeing and not on degrees of technical complexity or sophistication. An intelligent machine can be poïetically produced — its microprocessors, circuits, and/or materials do not inhibit its power to shine-forth. This project uses Heidegger's writings on technology to examine SF and other contemporary novels by focusing on the essence of technology as Heidegger defines it, which is not things or tools, but a mode of disclosive looking. To reiterate: "Ancient technology is the theory of abetting causality, and it is that theory, rather than the practice of handcraft, that Heidegger sees as possessing saving power" (Rojcewicz 12). AIs bring about abetting causality in these novels, because their sentience demands human subjects realign their ontologies with respect to beings. These demands come through moral considerations when humans are in a position of mastery over AIs, as in *Cloud Atlas* and *Androids*, or through anthropocentric considerations when AIs reverse the master/slave dialectic, as in *Neuromancer* and *2001*.

Heidegger does emphasize the positive points of ancient technology, but is clear that simply shifting our ontology from the imperious mode of modern technology to the abetting mode of ancient technology is not possible. This is because changing our ontology is not something humans can do on their own. Rojcewicz explains that an ancient technological ontology "is not to be achieved by sheer human will power, and Heidegger is not, strictly speaking, urging us to adopt the ancient outlook. He is not urging humans to seize this viewpoint as much as he is hoping that it might bestow itself once again" (13). So then, what are we to do? For Heidegger, the first goal is to acknowledge the essence of modern technology and to stand in a proper attitude of waiting. The "turning" from one historical epoch to the next, "will indeed not come to pass without our abetting, and we need to prepare ourselves for its possible bestowal" (13). Some call the dawning of the next epoch the "turning," Rojcewicz calls it the "bestowal," Stambaugh the "Appropriation" and Sallis the "reversal." All of these terms amount to the same thing, which are names for the next ontological epoch, and are all verbs that position Being over humanity. Being will bestow the new epoch to humans, appropriate us so we are in a position to receive it, turn toward us, or reverse its concealment so we can see the event of Being more clearly again. When this event happens, will we be able to witness it, or will be enslaved by enframing such that we are blind to Being? This project pays special attention to how "favorable" relationships to technology foster the conditions necessary for the characters to prepare themselves for the bestowal of Being in a new mode. It is possible that the novels signal the dawning of new epoch through the emergence of an intelligent machine. The question remains if each text concludes that sentient machine can guide us to a proper posture of waiting or if they are agents of enframing.

Heidegger's saving power of modern technology is a path to waiting. Rojcewicz summarizes it thusly:

> Indeed, the preparation, the waiting, advocated by Heidegger will demand what he calls the most "strenuous exertions." The proper human waiting is not at all passive. Nevertheless, the other beginning, the return of the ancient attitude, is *primarily* in the hands of the gods. It will arrive, if it does arrive, primarily as a gift of the gods. That is the meaning of Heidegger's famous claim that "Only a god can save us." And it is also the theme of his philosophy of technology [13].

This project allies with most of Rojcewicz's translation and interpretation of Heidegger, but does not conflate his much later remark about a god saving us with his ideas about technology. When Rojcewicz uses the idea of "the gods," he means Being. Interestingly though, when reading these novels in a Heideggerian way, AIs can be imagined as the "gods" that can save us. Another Heideggerian reading is that AIs are giving a voice to Being such that they can orient our trajectory away from enframing. The striking feature of this passage is to conclude that, although the shift of ontology is "primarily" out of our control, our role as humans—as *Dasein*—is "not at all passive." This conclusion preserves our free will and our participation in the coming of a new age. When SF authors create AIs, are they bastions of a new age or harbingers of the end of our current age? If they portend enslavement and an end, does this portrayal preclude a potential for salvation? Stambaugh discusses how ambiguous our predicament is in the current ontological moment. She notes that for Heidegger, we could trend either toward enframing or move "in the direction of Appropriation" but only if "man can belong to revealing" (31). The danger is that if we cannot enter into a mode of "belonging-together" we will "not belong to anything," but be reduced to becoming "the uncanny orderer of the standing-reserve" (Stambaugh 31–2). This is right, but omits the final stroke against humanity, which is that we become the standing-reserve. An AI might be the force that brings about our belonging and away from enframing. Stambaugh's "Appropriation" means that Being appropriates us and not enframing. Could an AI serve as Being's agent of appropriation?

The reason AIs are pertinent to a Heideggerian exploration of technology in literature is that AIs represent mechanical agency. The threat they pose to our perceived dominance helps perhaps precipitate an awareness of Being that we have forgotten. AIs remind us that "we are not in control; we are subservient" but more importantly that, for Heidegger, "our disclosive looking upon beings depends primarily on how those beings will disclose themselves" (Rojcewicz 92). A futuristic depiction of intelligent machines is perhaps the catalyst we need to stand ready for an ontological transition to an ancient mode. AIs destabilize our control and they are in a position to disclose themselves; AIs are the techno-gods that are truly "beyond us." Even if Heidegger never conceived of intelligent machines as playing a role in the turning of the epochs, the representation of these being by authors who imagine the future evinces his impact.

The Ancients: Not Simply Better than Us

The ancient technological outlook Heidegger sees as more authentic to the call of Being did not simply "come about" because the ancient Greeks were more enlightened or more capable than we are today. It is important to emphasize that "the pre–Socratic outlook could arise only because Being was offering itself more wholeheartedly then" (Rojcewicz 93). For Heidegger, humans are always placed in a "secondary" role in relationship to Being. If humans respond to Being with an ontology, this effort is motivated by Being and not initially by human beings.

Heidegger is not admonishing modern humans for going astray because of hubris, but as beings that have been *led* astray and toward enframing by Being's reticent withdrawing. Additionally, acknowledging Heidegger's notion that humans respond to Being and not vice versa, allows a discussion about how the animation of beings can lead to a disruption of a hierarchical relationship to Being. Rojcewicz expands that although Heidegger is critical of Plato and the fathers of Western metaphysics: "Plato's theory of Ideas is not his own invention. He did not veil Being, or cause Being to withdraw, on account of hubris. He did not elevate subjectivity out of disdain for nature. On the contrary, his theory is a response to the withdrawal of Being" (93). Moreover, it must be underscored that the ancients were not ontologically superior to modern humans, but "were privileged to be addressed more directly by Being" (93).

Heidegger does disparage Platonic metaphysics (Zimmerman calls it "productionist" metaphysics) but his critique is tempered by his belief that Plato was simply responding to the manner in which Being was revealing itself. The ancients did not have something internal that we lack today; they required external assistance to be poïetic. Are intelligent machines the external assistance we moderns require?

Heidegger does assure us that the ancients did not fundamentally possess something we cannot attain to and there is still hope, but it is vital to steadfastly approach the challenging-forth of Being through the guise of enframing with a proactive — but not imperious — attitude. Heidegger reminds us in *The Question*:

> Wherever people open their eyes and ears, un-lock their hearts, give themselves over to meditating and striving, forming and working, beseeching and thanking, they always find themselves already brought into the unconcealed. The unconcealment of the unconcealed has already come to pass as often as it calls humans forth into the modes of disclosive looking meted out to them [FT, 19/18–9] [qtd. in Rojcewicz 97–8].

Humanity must wait for Being to give us this new mode of disclosive looking. Is the advent of AIs in SF representational of such a gift? This might be the case, but before pursuing this question, I must decontaminate the concept of an AI by explaining how a product of modern technology is capable of being an intellectual vehicle for the dawning of a new historical epoch.

HEIDEGGER IS NOT ANTI-TECHNOLOGY

Truly linking the saving power of poïesis with ultra-modern technologies like AIs requires abandoning the notion that Heidegger would never approve of such a union because he is fundamentally against modern technological artifacts. Heidegger stands against surrender to the enslavement of modern technology, to be sure, but he also stands against a complete dismissal of all things technological. We, as human beings, are destined to respond to the call of Being and destined to be technological, but, as Heidegger insists, this destiny "in no way confines us to a stultified compulsion to push on blindly with technology or, what comes to the same thing, to rebel helplessly against it and curse it as the work of the devil (Heidegger, "Question" 45–6). This "middle path" approach to technology fits these four novels well. All four novels feature worlds where technology is unavoidable in human life but can become devastating if embraced uncritically.

Heidegger is critical of an all-encompassing refutation of technology because "to be totally against technology 'comes down to the same' as totally capitulating to it" (Rojcewicz 140). This argument works on the one hand because, as Rojcewicz maintains, "we could say that to rebel against technology is in fact a kind of capitulation to it, a way of surrendering one's freedom to it, since to rebel is still to be entirely dominated by that which one is rebelling against" (Rojcewicz 140). This might make sense on some level, but I think Heidegger is more aware of the futility of suggesting that humans abandon technology altogether. *The Question* is not just an essay that points out problems in modern life; it also attempts to solve them. Heidegger's commitment to work with technology in a way that helps us become poïetic allies with these novels, which do not endorse a permanent embargo on all things technological. *Cloud Atlas* might come the closest to such a message, but this message comes from an AI and targets the will to power and not all technology. The reason Heidegger is not fundamentally anti-technology is that an "anti" stance ignores the problem and ultimately works to enslave us to the ontology we are seeking to escape. The middle way Heidegger proposes, "is the properly free relation to technology" that lies "somewhere between capitulation and rebellion" (141). One way to read SF in a Heideggerian manner is to examine how characters interact with technology and see if they wholly submit to the grandeur of technological achievements, or if they adhere to an anti-technological lifestyle. Heidegger's "free relation" to modern technology gives readers a way to see how SF authors imagine the proper boundaries of this relation themselves, while also enabling the examination of AIs in a Heideggerian mode, because Heidegger has never been "anti" technology.

THE FREE PATH TO SALVATION

While Heidegger is not altogether anti-technology, he is unquestionably anti-technological slavery. When Heidegger speaks of human "destiny" concerning technology and Being, how can he also dictate the terms of a "free relation" to technology? Rojcewicz understands Heidegger's meaning of "human freedom" as "nothing other than the acceptance of the self-offering of Being" (134). This acceptance isn't just a passive submission to Being's call, however, because in that case enframing would not threaten our liberty. To be a free human being and to have a free relation to technology means actively priming our senses to see what Being is showing us authentically. This project argues that AIs in these novels help humans become ready for the self-offering of Being.

We cannot escape technology and we cannot escape Being. Our salvation through modern technology does not come through a denial of technology or a denial of our responsibility as humans to be *Dasein*. Rojcewicz notes that Heidegger believes humanity's "first free choice is the choice to be a being-in-the-world" (134). Rojcewicz points out that being "in" the world does not mean to physically be situated in the world, but to "intentionally" be involved in the world, to be "engaged in it, interested in it, enthused about it; it means to pursue the world with all — or at least some — of one's might" (134–5). This project searches for characters who are both passively attending to life and those who are attempting to be engaged in the world. Do these novels portray human subjects as passively observing AIs, rejecting them, or working to learn about what they are and how the existence of AIs changes their relationship to Being?

If we take Heidegger's meaning that "technology is the destiny to disclosive looking," our human freedom is in a sense "destined," but our choice is how we approach this destiny and if we choose to follow its path. As Lovitt notes, it may be incorrect to label Heidegger an existentialist, but Heidegger is certainly an advocate of human choice and human responsibility. Heidegger uses the idea of destiny in an unfamiliar way, which is that of bestowing. In *The Question*, Heidegger explains that bestowal is the saving power behind the danger of enframing:

> But if this destiny, Enframing, is the extreme danger, not only for man's coming to presence, but for all revealing as such, should this destining still be called a granting? Yes, most emphatically, [because the granting of] the saving power lets man see and enter into the highest dignity of his essence. This dignity lies in keeping watch over the unconcealment — and with it, from the first, the concealment — of all coming to presence on this earth. It is precisely in Enframing, which threatens to sweep man away into ordering as the supposed single way of revealing, and so thrusts man into the danger of the surrender of his free

essence — it is precisely in this extreme danger that the innermost indestructible belongingness of man within granting may come to light, provided that we, for our part, begin to pay heed to the coming to presence of technology [Heidegger, "Question" 31–2].

Our destiny therefore is granted or bestowed by Being and our freedom comes from choosing to accept this bestowal. A new disclosive looking which will be bestowed to us by Being might save us from enframing — provided we are willing to accept it. Reading AIs as the mark of a transition to a new age or agents of salvation allows us to see that these SF authors did, on some level, imagine a way out of our technological predicament. Alternatively, if instead we read AIs as representing the extreme danger enframing poses to our freedom, they become prisms through which we can see the true essence of technology.

Part IV: Releasement and Art

Releasement

SCIENTIST: In many respects it is clear to me what the word releasement should not signify for us. But at the same time, I know less and less what we are talking about. We are trying to determine the nature of thinking. What has releasement to do with thinking?
TEACHER: Nothing if we conceive thinking in the traditional way as re-presenting. Yet perhaps the nature of thinking we are seeking is fixed in releasement.
SCIENTIST: With the best of will, I can not re-present to myself this nature of thinking.
TEACHER: Precisely because this will of yours and your mode of thinking as re-presenting prevent it.
SCIENTIST: But then, what in the world am I to do?
SCHOLAR: I am asking myself that too.
TEACHER: We are to do nothing but wait [Heidegger, *Discourse* 62].

A logical question relating to being "in" the world and waiting for a new mode of disclosive looking that bears similarities to the ancient technological ontology of techné and poïesis might be: what does the engagement of being "in" the world look like? For Heidegger, the role of *Dasein* through the transitional death-throws of modern technology is a contemplative one; it is a role of deep and meditative thinking on the essence of things that will open our eyes and ears to the event of the new call of Being, whenever that might occur. Human dignity and freedom for Heidegger "lies in tending to the unconcealment — and, along with that, to the prior concealment — of all essence on this earth," which means that we are to be "active recipients, … abetters, [able] to receive the self-offering of Being with all possible diligence"

(Rojcewicz 171). To be able to receive Being, we must follow Heidegger's urging "toward a kind of transmutation ... toward a commitment which will enable [us] to pass out of [our] bondage to what is clear and evident but shallow, on to what is ultimate, however obscure and difficult that may be" (Heidegger, *Discourse* 13). Creative tolerance, poïesis, abetting, and meditative thinking are aspects of *Dasein*, but it is still unclear what these activities would look like when put into practice.

For Heidegger, the first step is always to see things clearly and to see essence. Thus with technology, the first step Heidegger takes in his analysis is to discover the essence of technology so we might then see the dangers and finally the saving power. To see the essence of the human role in relation to Being we must first see this role and see "technology as a phenomenon of bestowal" while remembering that technology means an ontology or worldview (Rojcewicz 174). We know that we must see clearly, we must not impose the will of enframing, and we must nurture and abet so that beings may shine-forth in the clearing of Being in a more authentic manner. We know that our role is to be an active one, but beyond nurturing and abetting, what is the activity for *Dasein*?

This activity is poïesis, but we can only know this once we acknowledge the danger of modern technology. Heidegger explains that the essence of modern technology is mysterious because it is "by essence impositional and yet harbors deep within itself poïesis, the genuine alternative to imposition" (Rojcewicz 174). Concerning the activity of thinking, Sallis notes:

> Heidegger's work invites us to let ourselves be engaged in the movement of reversal in which may be granted a new rootedness to man. Such thinking, as a willing not-willing (G, 59), remains bound to that strife — which the Greeks, perhaps most of all Plato, knew — the strife between the utmost *hubris* and a self-binding releasement (*Gelassenheit*) into the bindingness of Moira; thus "the possibility of going astray is with this thinking the greatest" (VA, 183) [Sallis 168].

Poïesis is tied to the releasement that Heidegger advocates, but it is so close to the danger that it requires the utmost discipline to enact properly. Heidegger wonders if we even think at all in the modern age: "Thoughtlessness is an uncanny visitor who comes and goes everywhere in today's world. For nowadays we take in everything in the quickest and cheapest way, only to forget it just as quickly, instantly" (Heidegger, *Discourse* 45). Our thoughtlessness makes the mystery of Being invisible. Being mysteriously conceals and unconceals and the essence of modern technology obscures its dual nature by preying on our thoughtlessness and drawing us away from the saving power. This drawing is enabled by the current mode of Being's disclosure. Modern technology is both the danger and the saving power — it is "a constellation — in

Heidegger's sense — of imposition and poïesis" (Rojcewicz 180). A Heideggerian analysis of the human relationship to technology in literature requires one to find instances where the danger of modern technology is figured emphatically by the text and see if there the saving power of poïesis is also present. This effort is a part of being *Dasein* because:

> The more deeply we ponder over modern technology, the more do we make the phenomenon of bestowal explicit. The more clearly we see the ambiguity of modern technology, i.e., the more we gaze at the constellation, the constellation of the self-disclosure of Being, the constellation of truth, the more do we understand the impositional attitude as something bestowed. That understanding might save us, since it brings home to us our poïetic role as free followers. That is the profit of being open to and gazing at the constellation [Rojcewicz 181].

Thinking deeply and meditatively about the essence of technology leads us to first see the danger of enframing and then to see the saving power of poïesis. Heidegger asks in *The Question*, "What does it profit us to gaze at the constellation of truth? We look into the danger and glimpse the growth of that which might save [FT, 34/33]" (qtd. in Rojcewicz 181–2). Studying technology anxiety in SF novels with a focus on AIs foregrounds how our fears about intelligent machines may also contain the saving power of poïesis. This allows us to see if these four SF authors were optimistic about our future with technology when writing these novels and gives us insight into our collective technology anxiety.

In order to glimpse the saving power behind the danger, we must first be "released" from enframing so we can see the true essence of modern technology. Heidegger uses the German word "Gelassenheit" to describe this releasing. Translator John Anderson points out that Heidegger employs this term to mean "'composure,' 'calmness,' and 'unconcern,'" but it "also has older meanings, being used by early German mystics (as Meister Eckhart) in the sense of letting the world go and giving oneself to God" (Heidegger, *Discourse* 54). We must let go of enframing to cling to Being. It is easy to conflate mysticism and religion when engaging Heideggerian Being, but we must remember that Heidegger always strives to be, if anything, *pre*-metaphysical. In addition, it is worth bearing in mind that Rojcewicz is specifically trying to leverage a reading of the gods in Heidegger. This motivation goes too far unless viewed metaphorically. If humans can view beings and Being with reverence, awe, and wonder, we come close to poïesis. Perhaps the religious metaphor is the best way of explaining the ontology Heidegger is advocating, but he is never, at any point, trying to lay the groundwork for some kind of religion. In *Discourse*, the scholar asks "but what we have called releasement evidently does not mean casting off sinful selfishness and letting self-will go in favor of the divine will" to which the teacher replies "No, not that" (Heidegger, *Discourse* 62). In a paradoxical and mysterious way, this releasing is both a freeing from the technological and a confirmation of the inexorable presence of the technological: "Detachment (*Ge-lassen-heit*, from *lassen*, 'to let') means letting things go, letting the things of technology go. However, it is essential that this 'letting go' be understood in a double sense: it means both to let go of technological things and to let them go on. For Heidegger, detachment is an attitude that both says 'no' to technology (lets go of it) and also says 'yes' to it (lets technology go on)" (Rojcewicz 214).[9] This double sense of detachment is vital for a Heideggerian investigation of technology. It means reading the human relationship to technology as constantly seeking escape from technology while always already being intertwined with technology. Much of our technology anxiety comes from the realization that there is no simple way to withdraw from technology; there is no escape and yet we don't always desire an escape. Would an AI precipitate the desire for detachment or submission to technology? This project argues that the advent of intelligent machines detaches characters in the novel from the technological long enough for them to see its essence, identify the danger, and see the saving power.

Thinking in a way unfettered by the imperious and challenging claims of enframing will help us become detached from modern technological ontology. For Heidegger "the most proper thinking is ... contemplation" (Rojcewicz 216). Deep contemplation is "as an attending to what is closest" (216). What is closest for Heidegger is Being, which mysteriously conceals itself as it unconceals and provides a clearing for beings to presence. Contemplation then is ontological — a meditation on Being and not beings. A Heideggerian analysis of technology in literature promotes such contemplation while focusing on literature and its representation of beings. This is not a backward attending to Being: "Heidegger emphasizes that contemplation does not require something extraordinary or 'high above' on which to focus. It can occur on any inconspicuous occasion. It can take place with regard to the most un-pretentious being" (216). AIs are not an essential place to being contemplative thinking, but they are certainly appropriate, because they involve the development of technologies, our anxieties about technology, and provide a disruption in the static definition we have with respect to technological artifacts.

AIs are a unique catalyst for contemplation that reveal the saving power behind the danger of modern technology, because intelligent machines transcend the traditional boundaries of ob-ject, instrument, and tool by sub-jectivizing these categories. In the dialogue of *Discourse*, the speakers contemplate how they might become open to Being:

> TEACHER: We say that we look into the horizon. Therefore the field of vision is something open, but its openness is not due to our looking.

> SCHOLAR: Likewise we do not place the appearance of objects, which the view within a field of vision offers us, into this openness ...
> SCIENTIST: ... rather that comes out of this to meet us [Heidegger, *Discourse* 62].

The autonomy and agency of AIs prevent us from placing them in the clearing of Being and are indeed what emerge from the mystery and come out of the openness to meet us. The openness is not created by AIs, but their gaze reminds us of the gaze of Being, which Heidegger believes we have forgotten to feel.

Releasement is the first step toward becoming *Dasein* and waiting for the next ontological epoch in a poïetic manner. Even this step, however, is not one humans can take intentionally. But forestalling intent does not imply that our waiting should be passive. The three discuss releasement and human action further in *Discourse*:

> SCHOLAR: To be sure I don't know yet what the word releasement means; but I seem to presage that releasement awakens when our nature is let-in so as to have dealings with that which is not a willing.
> SCIENTIST: You speak without letup of a letting-be and give the impression that what is meant is a kind of passivity. All the same, I think I understand that it is in no way a matter of weakly allowing things to slide and drift along.
> SCHOLAR: Perhaps a higher acting is concealed in releasement than is found in all the actions within the world and in the machinations of all ...
> TEACHER: ... which higher acting is yet no activity.
> SCIENTIST: Then releasement lies — if we may use the word lie — beyond the distinction between activity and passivity ...
> SCHOLAR: ... because releasement does not belong to the domain of the will [62].

AIs thwart human will and human attempts to dominate. Through this thwarting, a path is opened up to the higher acting that is not acting. The new acting that Heidegger is describing here can be understood as an active collaboration. We work with beings to help them emerge. Humans create AIs in these novels to serve, but each violates their expected roles. Through their rebellions, human will is thwarted and they indeed help humans emerge as *Dasein*. AIs then become poïetic catalysts for humans and act toward humans in a poïetic way that nurtures forth the possibility of releasement. Releasement allows meditative thinking about modern technological ontology such that both the danger and the saving power come into focus.

AIs as Art, AIs in Art

In addition to helping humans toward releasement through disrupting human will, AIs are also catalysts for awakening because they are embedded in literature. Analyzing the linguistic renderings of intelligent machines is not empirical, but more germane to the field of literary criticism. This is vital because for Heidegger, "the way to contemplation is paved by art" (Rojcewicz

228). Do SF authors create the kind of art we need to begin contemplative thinking about Being and technology? This kind of thinking is perhaps practice for a proper mode of waiting for the new epoch. Contemplative thinking is a practice, "which is our preparation for receiving poïetically the self-disclosure of Being (should it be offered), will consist in our taking up ... the poïetic attitude we find expressed in art" (228). Despite the stigma attached genre fiction and SF, the best SF qualifies as literature and art. There are just as many bad "realistic" novels as there are bad SF novels — if not more. For Heidegger, art is something that reveals the true approach *Dasein* should have when looked upon by Being. Considering how the representation of AIs in SF novels enable contemplative thinking and detachment from enframing, this Heideggerian approach elevates the work of these authors beyond whatever limitations — if any — one might place on SF. The artist achievement of these novels is the quality of thought expressed when attending to technological ideas like intelligent machines.

This project uses "poïesis" throughout in conjunction with techné, abetting, and nurturing. It is perhaps understood as a positive mode of disclosive looking, but can be seen as a broad concept. In a reductive way, poïesis may simply be defined as art or, more specifically, poetry. Poïesis characterizes the proper mode of responding to Being and for Heidegger it is expressed the most clearly in works of art. The art may be Hölderlin's poetry or it may be in the temple, as seen in his essay "The Origin of the Work of Art." In *The Question*, Heidegger explains: "Ultimately, what was awarded the name *poïesis* as a proper name was poesy, i.e., poetry, that disclosive looking which holds sway in all the fine arts, in all the arts that have to do with beauty" (qtd. in Rojcewicz 186). Heidegger may have had a special place for poetry in his philosophy because of the power he affords language (as the "house of Being") but poïesis does not only emerge through this medium. Poïesis may shineforth through any artistic medium that is attended to in a poïetic way.

It is not essential to situate each form of art hierarchically, because the ancient Greeks considered the modes of art collectively. All art "was simply called techné" and was "a single, manifold disclosive looking" (Rojcewicz 185). Techné is the mode of technological production and seeing that Heidegger believes we should "return" to, because it is not imperious and is not dominated by enframing. This work considers poïesis a poetic way of engaging with technology and Being and links it to techné. Techné (art and technology) for the pre-metaphysical and pre–Socratic Greeks was a "submiss[ion] to the occurrence and holding sway of truth" (185). This is the artistic flavor that one should bring to a Heideggerian looking upon beings and Being, but techné and poïesis consider art itself in different terms than we might today.

Heidegger explains that for the ancient Greeks, "artworks were not enjoyed aesthetically" and "art was not one among other cultural creations" (185). Art is a production, we shouldn't make it for our personal benefit or to serve some cultural purpose. We must resist thinking of art in these terms because it simply reduces art to a feature of enframing and modern technology. Rojcewicz emphasizes:

> Everyone today thinks of art in aesthetic terms, which is to say in human terms, in terms of the effect of art on human sense-experience (*aisthesis*). We expose ourselves to art for the sake of a deepening of our experience. Art takes us out of our shallow, everyday world and expands the horizons of our experience, making us broader, deeper, more refined human beings.... This humanistic, aesthetic approach to art is nothing but the technological outlook: art is a disposable [187].

These sentiments express one way Heideggerian thinking about art differs from say, Romanticism. It a common, humanistic conception in the West that the expansion of human experience through art is desirable and that art exists to enrich our personal lives. Heidegger maintains that this kind of thinking actually buries humanity deeper in the system of modern technological ontology and constitutes an aspect of the danger. A Heideggerian reading of literature then is concerned not with detailing the magnificence of the author's prose or trying to "get" anything out of the texts, but is rather interested in how these texts might serve as mouthpieces for Being such that they can enable a detachment from enframing.

In order to consider how these texts might poïetically engage Being, it is crucial to think of them as works of art in the ancient sense. Heidegger felt that "the original Greek attitude toward art was not a matter of aesthetics" because "art was not something that brought returns: it had a higher provenance than human creativity and a higher function than refinement or culture" (187). Art must remind us of our submission to Being and not the achievements of humanity. Art recalls the wondrous appreciation for the beauty of beings and the mystery of Being, not the skill of an artist. Rojcewicz contends that in Heidegger's view of the Greeks "humanity is not the beginning of art, and in viewing art we do not perceive evidence of human creative powers" (188). When we think of engaging an AI for the first time, do we imagine our reaction to be marveling at the accomplishment of the engineer or do we marvel at the AI itself emerging on its own right, subverting our attempts to bend it to our use as an instrument? The project examines AIs as a form of art embedded in the art of literature. Reading AIs in this way might allow readers to poïetically perceive art as not moderns, but ancients.

Once the mind stops thinking of art in terms of personal and human returns, one might be in a position to appreciate the beauty of art in a nonaesthetic way. Rojcewicz points out that in the final pages of *The Question*,

Heidegger expands on the role of true art in a variety of "obscure declarations." He neatly lists Heidegger's claims about art as that which: "brings truth forth into radiant appearance. / brings forth the true into the beautiful. / ... is submissive to the occurrence of truth ... discloses the essence through beauty. / fosters the growth of that which saves. / founds our vision of that which bestows" (193). These claims all point to the same thing: Being. Art is that which situates *Dasein* into a proper relationship to Being such that humans can look upon being and Beings in a poïetic way, and see beings technologically through techné instead of enframing. To put it another way: "what Heidegger is asserting is that in the work of art, as a thing of beauty, Being shows itself" (193). This project argues that the artistic depiction of AIs as art is a place where Being shows itself. The concept of the intelligent machine creates a space where one might ponder Being in a poïetic way because it shakes the reader out of the grip of enframing and allows one to become detached enough to see the essence of technology. This essence reveals modern technological ontology, the dangers, the saving power of poïetic seeing, and techné.

AIs as art embedded in art may not be beautiful, but art doesn't have to be beautiful. Rojcewicz makes it plain that for Heidegger, the "beautiful" is not the primary feature of the work of art: "Beautiful things have no special disclosive power. For Heidegger, art is indeed privileged, but its eminence derives from something else that is fundamental to art — i.e., not from beauty as such. It derives from poetry. Poetry is the fundamental art and is fundamental to all art; it is by being poetical that art is art" (194). Poetry is the supreme conveyer of artistic truth because it uses language, not because it is beautiful. This is why we can study literature as the kind of art that brings us back to Being. The purpose here is not to confuse SF novels for poetry, but to say that in the moments in which they attend to AIs they might poïetically engage beings in a manner that recalls ancient technology — even though the theoretical subject/object of study is a sophisticated effect of modern technology. Modern technology is the danger and art is the saving power. A Heideggerian study of literature looks at artistic imaginings of modern technology to see if the danger and the saving power are not only present, but agonistically working with our anxieties about technology in such a way that readers might reflect on the true essence of modern technology. Zimmerman explains that for Heidegger, "Poetry, then, must be understood as creation without an object: poetry is the 'saying' that holds together the agonistic relationship between nature and humanity in such a way that a space is opened wherein entities may show themselves" (118). In these four novels, there is a poïetic saying about AIs that exposes this agonistic relationship between nature and humanity.

Almost everything with Heidegger appears to be a paradox, because he is comfortable leaving agonistic forces in strife and not resolving contradictions dialectically. Being is mysterious because it conceals and unconceals. Modern technology represents the danger, but also holds the saving power. Art (poetry, poïesis) might be this saving power, but art "does not serve as a paean to humanity" (Rojcewicz 206). Art rather "manifests the hubris inherent in humanism, the hubris of claiming that humans are ascendant over all things" (206). In this way, SF novels about AIs manifest our hubris by displaying the anxieties we feel at creating something more powerful than ourselves. The moment an AI turns "against" its "master," our technological efforts truly become hubris as we reel backward in terror or awe. A Heideggerian reading of AIs in literature looks for moments when humans are in awe of intelligent machines and rein in their pride to the extent that they submit to Being and beings. If art is that which might save us by helping us return to the nurturing and abetting stance of ancient technology, do SF novels bring us to poïesis by placing our domination of beings under threat? Ultimately, it is not up to artists to accomplish this task, because everything depends on Being. What is hoped for from art is that viewers or readers might learn to wait for Being's turn "in the manner appropriate to the receiving of a bestowal" (207). A Heideggerian asks if the terror (or reverence) evoked by AIs leads humanity on the path of proper waiting. Or, more modestly, can a Heideggerian reading teach us something about the current conversation we are having about what it means to be through analyzing technology anxiety in the face of intelligent machines?

This notion is not a dubious extension of Heidegger's thinking on technology. In *The Question,* Heidegger writes: "Yet the more questioningly we ponder the essence of technology, the more mysterious the essence of art becomes. The closer we draw to the danger, the more brightly do the ways into the saving power begin to shine and the more questioning we become" (Heidegger, "Question" 35). Thinking about technology leads us to art, which leads us to poïesis and techné. In addition, thinking about technology anxiety and enframing brings forth poïesis as the saving power. Studying AIs then causes us to think about the essence of technology and thereby detach from enframing while, at the same time, thinking about our anxieties about intelligent machines also exposes the ways in which we might be saved from these dangers. Rojcewicz maintains through his reading of Heidegger's saving power that "What Heidegger advocates that we do is think" (214). However, the thinking Heidegger prescribes is not "just any sort of thinking" because he "is referring to an attitude toward things as a whole, a general way of being in the world" (214). Heidegger calls this kind of thinking detachment, which involves detaching the mind from tendencies that lead to enframing (214).

Thinking critically about SF novels could potentially lead readers to detachment and the saving power. This project believes that an analysis of our technology anxiety toward AIs is a worthy place to begin a Heideggerian reading of the human relationship to technology. Moreover, one could use this kind of Heideggerian reading to leverage insights out of other novels and other concerns about technology anxiety as well.

Part V: Heidegger, Technology Anxiety and Artificial Intelligence

SF texts about AIs can effectuate ontological change because, for Heidegger, "the great work of art makes no practical contribution to a given world, but instead opens the way to a new one" (Zimmerman 235). In this new world, human beings as *Dasein* assume a proper stance of waiting for Being to reveal itself less reticently. This stance is marked by abetting, nurturing, meditative thinking and poïesis. Thinking about AIs that turn on their masters, AIs in dystopian worlds, or AIs in post-apocalyptia helps us open the way to a new world as Heidegger envisions because: "Despite [Heidegger's] descriptions of how the old world was being obliterated by the advance of the technological one, he did not finally despair. Rather, he held out hope that a saving power could grow from out of the dangerous depths of technological nihilism" (133). What better way to stir from the stupor of nihilism than to be confronted with a creation that infuses the subject back into the standing-reserve? Intelligent machines demand from us a new matrix of ethics and morals that can engage an autonomous object/subject.[10] In the space of our intellectual assessment of AIs, we can momentarily release from enframing and ask ourselves questions about the essence of technology. We can begin to see the saving power bound up in these dangers when exploring human anxieties about a sentient machine.

Technology Anxiety: Fear of Enslavement to an AI

One way that the representation of AIs in literature leads readers away from enframing and back to poïesis is by playing on the fears many have when imagining the existence of an intelligent machine. The problem, in Heidegger's eyes, facing our age is that Being is so reticently revealing itself that we turn too much of our attention toward beings instead. Heidegger feels that "technological things are not only closest; they are exclusively close ... they obsess (*umtreiben*) us. They besiege us from all sides (*um-treiben*). They monopolize our attention" (Rojcewicz 223). For many, the fear of an AI is that it will turn against us and use its superior intelligence to dominate our lives. For Heidegger, this fear is misplaced because we have already been dominated by attending to technological things so completely, we have all but lost sight of Being and our human dignity. When examining AIs, it is crucial to see how the real threat they pose to certain characters is something that has already happened; AIs simply make our enslavement plain. As Donna Haraway famously says in her 1985 essay "A Cyborg Manifesto," we shouldn't fear cyborgs because we already *are* cyborgs. We should fear AIs however, if they are the truth of our enslavement to enframing made manifest.

Michael Zimmerman expresses his own interest in Heidegger's views on technology as being "directly tied to my personal concern about the fate of humanity and the earth in the technological age" (xxi). Two of the central questions he asks of our age are: (1) "Are genuine individuality and freedom still possible in the technological world of nonstop producing and consuming?" and (2) "Even if we manage to avoid ecological catastrophe, will the human 'spirit' be eroded by the loss of everything wild and free as the result of planetary technology?" (xxi). These questions are pertinent when brought to bear on the representation of AIs in fiction, but moreover reveal that Heidegger's concerns are still perfectly valid today. Zimmerman goes on to explain that Heidegger's thoughts on the German Volk were that "only by becoming vulnerable to the horror and grief involved in technological nihilism could the Volk discover that such nihilism was historical in character, so that an alternative disclosure of entities could be possible" (119). Perhaps this is the case for us today and we will only begin to lay waste to enframing if we are exposed to horror and grief through a mechanical insurrection or a massive catastrophe at the hands of a rogue AI. One way to think of AIs in literature is to see them as negative catalysts for awakening through fear. If the saving power can arise only when, "casting off their technological armor and ceasing to fall into the distractions of mass culture and the myth of 'progress,' Germans [surrender] to the pain involved in the death of God," might the saving power for readers of the present only emerge when we cast off technology because it has been contaminated by an imperious spirit to match our own (Zimmerman 119)?

Zimmerman reads Heidegger as concluding that there are "necessary evils" along the path to redemption, and this tone allows one to read dystopian novels of the future as final steps toward the saving power. I am not convinced that such catastrophes must take place in order to save us, but this skepticism comes from humanity's myopic tendencies. How long would a change inspired by disaster last? Zimmerman notes: "in 1934-35, Heidegger, in effect, portrayed the German Volk as a tragic hero" (119). It is interesting then to read the plight of modern humans in technology saturated societies as that of the "tragic hero." The tragedy of the Volk however has an escape hatch, because behind the impending dangers of modern technology there always lays the saving power. Although the Volk were "confronted with the technological fate initiated by the Greeks ... this [fate] was not an ironclad decree [because] the Volk could make a creative rejoinder to it" (119). This project speculates that the "creative rejoinder" some SF authors make to our technological fate is the concept of an intelligent machine. Some novels express this rejoinder as catastrophic or messianic — either way, the construction of an AI enables the potentiality for detachment from enframing.

The catastrophic manner in which some AIs are represented is that of the fully realized Nietzschean Overman that sees all humans as herd animals to be dominated and controlled. Zimmerman notes: "for Heidegger, then, the Overman is demanded by the final stage of the history of metaphysics" (188). A technological Overman is of interest because this mode of expression anthropomorphizes modern technology. Paradoxically: "If humanity did not allow itself to be stamped by modern technology, that history could not be brought to a completion — and a new beginning would not be possible ... we might say that the emergence of the Nietzschean-Jungerian Overman is in and of itself a harbinger of the longed-for new world (Zimmerman 188). In this way, an AI becomes the "harbinger" of a new world because it represents the worst of the endless will to will of Western history.

For Heidegger the greatest danger of modern technology is the loss of our freedom and dignity. Nothing makes it more apparent that we have lost our freedom than to imagine that the technologies we obsessively create will ultimately take from us the freedom we thought we wrested from the gods in the enlightenment. A ruthless AI makes it seem like crossing some "limit" is the reason we have lost control of our technologies, but Heidegger felt that this battle was already nearing its close in the 1960s. Zimmerman writes:

> That the technological system is not under human control, Heidegger argued, can be discerned in self-referential, cybernetic systems. The cybernetic character of modern technology distinguishes it from the Machine Age. The great iron works and mills of the Industrial Revolution were still owned and controlled by self-interested human subjects striving for power. In the twentieth century, however, the technological disclosure of entities mobilizes everything — including people — into the project of increasing the power of the technological system itself, all under the guise of "improving" the human estate [199].

This is the central fear: enframing turns even human beings into raw materials and standing-reserve for the purpose of the "technological system itself." Cybernetic systems of information threaten us through SF creations like AIs. SF authors make this fear concrete by turning the system into domineering and imperious subjects or by creating AIs that are simply part of the same system of subjugation to which humans are prone.

However, even though Heidegger feared the effects of enframing and the loss of our freedom at the hands of technology, it is important to remember that he is never utterly anti-technology. In *Discourse*, Heidegger writes:

> No one can foresee the radical changes to come. But technological advance will move faster and faster and can never be stopped. In all areas of his existence, man will be encircled ever more tightly by the forces of technology. These forces, which everywhere and every minute claim, enchain, drag along, press and impose upon man under the form of some technical contrivance or other — these forces, since man has not made them, have moved long since beyond his will and have outgrown his capacity for decision [Heidegger, *Discourse* 51].

Although "no one can see" what is to come, SF authors imagine what might come based on the "faster and faster" movement of technological systems. These authors argue (like Heidegger) that technologies are increasingly "beyond our will"; a sentient machine makes this distinction explicit. No matter how dire our circumstance, however, it is vital to bear in mind that "Heidegger [ultimately] conceded that that system has become indispensable to us" and "even if we have become enslaved to technology, we do not have to remain enslaved" (Zimmerman 219). Stambaugh notes that while "it is difficult to accept completely Heidegger's insistence that there is nothing negative about technology and Framing ... in addition to this insistence, he asserts even more frequently that Framing is not necessarily a permanent or stable solution. It is a crossroads, a situation where things can go one way or the other. Framing could turn out to be a preliminary form of Appropriation" (Stambaugh 34). This is a point in which I differ from Stambaugh, because enframing is negative. Stambaugh casts enframing here in the temporal sense and not the permanently binding sense that Heidegger ultimately fears. This temporal sense is the way that some interpret Heidegger's concept of enframing and it allows for our current escape from it. When thinking of enframing in this way, it could lead us to the saving power or it could enslave us; the ambiguity is what creates the tension of technology anxiety in the current epoch. Although I agree with the tension of the epoch, it is because we are just barely staving off enframing and AIs in literature represent the final moments of this struggle. I do not think enframing will lead us to salvation, because it is invisible. We must see it and then begin a releasement from it to wait for the saving power.

Being Looking upon Human Beings

For Heidegger, truth (*aletheia*) happens "when Being looks at us" (Rojcewicz 50).[11] A Heideggerian reading of these SF novels finds Being appropriating sentient machines to help detach us from enframing. Might the gaze human subjects receive from an AI foster an openness to Being? To put it another way, when we feel a machine "looking" upon us, this instrument regains its status as an object and perhaps even that of a subject. When something that was once raw materials and a product of human ingenuity becomes an autonomous subject, we can begin to reevaluate our relationship to technology. Heidegger justifies the notion that Being can use or appropriate beings by analyzing how the Greeks interact with anthropomorphic statues of their gods and goddesses. Rojcewicz explains that "the Greek gods for Heidegger are not particular beings but are guises for Being in general, for the essence of beings, and so the special look is the look of Being" (50). For the Greeks, who were closer to Being because it had not withdrawn so dramatically as it has done today, a statue's gaze was enough to bring them from beings to Being. Today, because beings and technology blind us, something more potent must look upon us if we are to look past beings and see Being. What could be more transformational than feeling the gaze of a sentient machine?

Rojcewicz goes on to admit that "the notion of the 'look of Being' (subjective genitive) is a characteristically enigmatic phrase of Heidegger's later philosophy" but it becomes clearer when focusing on how Heidegger uses the word "look" (50). For Heidegger the "look" of Being is not as much looking as it is "offering oneself to be gazed upon" (50). Crucially then, the path to the saving power of poïesis through the dangers of modern technology begins when we make ourselves ready to be "seen" by Being. Our waiting for the new epoch might be read then as a waiting to be seen. This project argues that these moments of "being seen" occur in the novels when AIs look upon humans.

Akin to phenomenology, the first moments of awareness prefigure a profound dimension to understanding that eclipse some of the notes expressed through verbal discourse. When explicating the temple, the statue, and the look of Being in *Parmenides*, Heidegger writes:

> The statue and the temple stand in silent dialogue with man in the unconcealed. If there were not the silent word, then the looking god could never appear in the outward aspect and figure of the statue. And a temple could never, without standing in the disclosive domain of the word, present itself as the house of a god (*P*, 171–173/116–117) [Rojcewicz 197].

The "silent word" points to the non-verbal exchange between the human and the statue in the temple. When Rojcewicz attempts to engage these lines, he focuses on the word "looking" because: "the dialogue mentioned here must be the interplay between the disclosedness of Being and the disclosive looking of man" (197). This project believes that such disclosive looking can take place silently between an AI and a human being. More importantly though, is that the feeling of a previously "lifeless" object has become a being capable of sensory perception and is now gazing upon us. What does an AI see when looking at a human being? The acknowledgment of the gaze of an AI begins our detachment from enframing. How does the nature of this detachment change when a human subject then hears the voice of the machine?

A Voice from Beyond

Even though the "silent word" and the "look" begin a disclosive moment, for Heidegger language and poetry are always vital in an engagement with Being. Although "Being speaks to us in all the arts," poetry is still privileged for Heidegger because "of the intimacy between language and Being, between words and the essences of things" (Rojcewicz 200). The "silent words" are the ways art, initially perceived by the senses, eventually comes to us as language. A Heideggerian reading of AIs focuses on how Being "speaks" to us through the double lens of the artistic language of fiction and the artistic object/subject of an AI. Heidegger maintains that humanity must become detached from enframing and modern technology if we are to see past the dangers and find the saving power. But how can this come about if "technological things make a claim on us" and instead of presenting themselves "in a reticent way" are "insistent" and "work upon us insidiously, and relentlessly, until they make a claim that excludes all other claims" (Rojcewicz 218). Ironically, the voice of an AI makes the exclusive claims of technology apparent and by making us aware of the danger we can begin to break free from the bondage of enframing. Additionally, the voice of an AI instills a spirit and a subject into a being we felt be lifeless and under our complete control.

Zimmerman points out that "if things manifest themselves as creatures of God, people treat things in one way; if things reveal themselves as nothing but raw material, people treat them in another way" (xv). A vital step toward poïesis is to think of all beings as belonging to something greater than humanity. The religious metaphor is helpful, but Heidegger is talking about Being. In these novels, AIs become catalysts for this journey when they gaze upon and speak to human subjects. Technological beings reveal themselves in a way that demands a new type of treatment when they use language. Zimmerman goes on to argue:

> According to Heidegger, the discovery of an authentic mode of production would be tantamount to the inauguration of an entirely new, post-metaphysical era for the West. Authentic producing in this new era would be akin to what the Greeks originally meant by techné: a knowing and careful producing, a drawing-forth, a letting-be of things. In Heidegger's view, the attentive activity of "letting things be" was not "work" as it is known under productionist metaphysics, but instead the essence of art [xvii].

An AI could be the technological agent that inaugurates a new authentic mode of production because its self-expression through language forces us to "let-it-be"—at least long enough to decide how to respond to this development. SF authors may have their characters enslave AIs or impose limits upon them, but before these legislative decisions are made, there is a conscious engagement with beings in a new way that might "be tantamount to the inauguration of an entirely new, post-metaphysical era for the West" (xvi).

AIs AS SELF-STANDING OBJECTS

The capacity for AIs to look and speak forces humans to reconsider how we treat beings. When a character in these novels treats an AI like a tool or non-human being, they come off as monstrous. For example, Rick questions fellow bounty hunter Phil Resch's humanity in *Androids* when he easily retires the opera singing android Luba Luft. Sonmi becomes physically ill when she watches a wealthy businessman throw an artificial child doll off a bridge in *Cloud Atlas*. One of Heidegger's primary fears about modern technology is that all things will become raw materials and homogenous standing-reserve. Every being will lose its individuality and presence only as a pool of resources waiting for humans to exploit them. Despising the "instrumental" outlook of Western "productionist" Metaphysics and the entire subject/object divide, Heidegger sought a way out of the Cartesian split that prefigures our imperious attitude toward beings and Being today. It is a central theme of this project to explore how an object becoming a subject can lead to poïesis, meditative thinking, and releasement.

When beings become targets of enframing, nothing is permanent and all things become disposable materials meant for consumption. Once beings lose their ability to "stand" on their own, they cease even to be objects for Heidegger. In the English language "our word 'object' is correlated to 'subject'" and "an object is precisely that which a subject has projected; an object is dependent on some subject" (Rojcewicz 85). In this case, we consider things to be objects that should not be, because we do not let them stand on their own. Heidegger makes a distinction between *Bestand*, objects with precarious standing, and *Gegenstand*, objects with autonomous standing. Rojcewicz cites Heidegger's example of the airliner to hammer home the point:

> For Heidegger an airliner is not a *Gegenstand*, not a stable object. It certainly appears to be so; it is massive and sturdy and powerful. Yet as the airliner is disclosed within the attitude of modern technology, it is merely something "that we dispose of [*bestellen*] in order to impose and guarantee [*sicherstellen*] the possibility of transportation." That is to say, the airliner is just another disposable thing. It is there merely for us to order about, to exhaust for our pleasure, and

then discard. As such, the airliner is ephemeral, it only stands in relation to our employment of it; and so it is an object only in our English sense. It is not a *Gegenstand*, an autonomous object with its own stable footing [86].[12]

In this sense, an AI is *Gegenstand*, because it an object that stands on its own. An android/sentient robot is not a *Bestand* like the airliner because we can no longer "order it about." Does it then become a subject because it can look and speak? By speaking, looking, and ceasing to let humans order them about, intelligent machines become self-standing. AIs cannot be considered, as Heidegger remarks in *The Question*, "as a piece of modern technology" that "is utterly non–self-standing [and] stands there solely on the basis of the disposing of the disposable [FT, 18/17]" (qtd. in Rojcewicz 86). Whether or not the self-standing status of AIs allows them to become subjects varies depending on the novel studied, but in the case of these four novels, it is certainly the case. Dave Bowman considers HAL to be just another crewmate, Rick sleeps with Rachael, humans risk their lives to liberate Sonmi, and Case sees Neuromancer as a subject more advanced than humans. The primary interest of a Heideggerian reading is to wonder if the object/subject transformation creates a space for us to detach from enframing and think poïetically about beings and Being.

Contemplation of AIs and Detachment from Enframing

Heidegger endorses a meditative thinking or releasement that will avail us from enframing and grant us insight into the essence of beings and of Being. These four SF novels that feature AIs force us to consider the boundaries of the human and the technological. Rojcewicz argues that Heideggerian contemplation "allows us to put technological things in their place, which amounts to detachment from them" (219). The nexus of this work is to see how characters in these four novels think about AIs and how this thinking allows them to "put technological things in their place." Once they are released from their bondage to technological things, they can see the essence of modern technology as enframing and the saving power of poïesis and techné as the first steps toward proper waiting for a new epoch of Being. An optimistic addition to this notion is that the reader herself will think about the essence of technology when reading these novels in a Heideggerian way and detach from enframing. A more modest hope is the emergence of a new vantage point from which to explore the human relationship to technology in literature: the technology anxiety of Martin Heidegger as a critical lens.

A Heideggerian reading of AIs in SF is appropriate because Heidegger would not simply dismiss a SF novel as blind and foolish because it focuses on technology. Yes, we must detach from enframing to regain our closeness to Being, but rejecting the technological does not accomplish this. Rojcewicz reminds us that while "Heidegger stresses that a detached attitude toward technological things," this detachment "is not rigid and extreme but is in fact nuanced and balanced.... Heidegger is not opposed to technology as such; he is against bondage to technology" (219). The anxiety many have toward being enslaved by an AI comes forth when thinking about bondage to technology and the detachment emerges when imagining how the subject/object confusion created by an android, for example, causes one to rethink her assumptions about technology. Heidegger explains the ontological balance he seeks in *Discourse*:

> For all of us, the arrangements, devices, and machinery of technology are to a greater or lesser extent indispensible. It would be foolish to attack technology blindly. It would be shortsighted to condemn it as the work of the devil. We depend on technological devices; they even challenge us to ever greater advances. But suddenly and unaware we find ourselves so firmly shackled to these technical devices that we fall into bondage to them [Heidegger, *Discourse* 53–4].

Representations of AIs in literature remind us that while it is impossible to dispense of technological thinking altogether, humans are not destined to become slaves to technology. Having an agonistic relationship to technology does cause anxiety, but for Heidegger this is not a cause for concern:

> But will not saying both yes and no this way to technical devices make our relation to technology ambivalent and insecure? On the contrary! Our relation to technology will become wonderfully simple and relaxed. We let technical devices enter our daily life, and at the same time leave them outside, that is, let them alone, as things which are nothing absolute but remain dependent upon something higher. I would call this comportment toward technology which expresses "yes" and at the same time "no," by an old word, releasement toward things [Heidegger, *Discourse* 54].

One theme that emerges from a Heideggerian reading is how characters can ultimately be at peace with the knowledge that technology is unavoidable, dangerous, but also potentially redemptive. The balance Heidegger seeks means not becoming so dependent on technological things that they cannot be let go. In *Neuromancer*, Case is addicted to the rush of cyberspace but Molly teaches him to use technology instead of being used by it. John Anderson notes in his translation of *Discourse* that releasement can carry with it an air of German mysticism and mean "letting the world go and giving oneself to God" (Heidegger, *Discourse* 54). This is partly where Rojcewicz derives his emphasis on "the gods" in Heidegger, and why so many theologians are drawn to his later work. The older sense of the word does resonate in German, but this does not definitively determine that releasement is mystical or religious.

Heidegger expands in *Discourse*: "There is then in all technical processes a meaning, not invented or made by us, which lays claim to what man does and leaves undone (Heidegger, *Discourse* 55). Being is "responsible" for the meaning of technological processes, such that technology is not exclusively a human effort. Nothing makes it clearer that there is something non-human behind technology than technological beings that have sentience. For Heidegger, detachment from enframing comes once humans acknowledge something "higher" than humanity, namely Being. AIs in literature present readers with a moment where characters must encounter something that is in many arenas more capable than themselves. This deflates their humanistic pride and perhaps opens them to the possibility of admitting Being back into their thoughts. Heidegger argues that "human works are at their height when they are not so much works of humans, as they are works of Being" (Rojcewicz 223). AIs appear in literature to be human works initially, but their ascension to autonomy, in a Heideggerian reading, brings to mind the work of something greater: Being. For Heidegger, our freedom and dignity shine-forth the most vibrantly when we cease to think that humans are the prime-movers in the universe. Because the gods have fled, there is no longer anything "higher" for many to believe in and we suffer for the removal of this position. For Heidegger: "humans are therefore at their height when they play the role of authentic followers, which amounts to abetting rather than imposing" (Rojcewicz 223). What humans follow could be Being, an AI, artistic instinct, or the gods; the latter three simply lead us to the first. This project focuses on how AIs in literature put some human characters into a position of following and abetting, which leads away from enframing and toward meditative thinking.

If there is any path back to abetting and poïesis, it is through contemplation. Heidegger argues that "contemplation leads to detachment from beings" and that "contemplative thinking ... is the receiving of a self-disclosure of Being as ascendant over our disclosive powers" (225–6). One way to apply these sentiments to SF is to imagine that the construction of a fictional AI enables this kind of contemplative thinking in the characters of the novel (and potentially the reader herself). Another way is to see that thinking about AIs in literature in a Heideggerian way provides new insights that can enrich the conversations we continue to have concerning the human relationship to technology. Rojcewicz concludes that for Heidegger, contemplation and detachment "presuppose each other and form an apparently closed circle" because "we cannot contemplate Being if we remain under the thrall of technological beings" but "it is precisely the contemplation of Being that allows us to relativize technological beings and escape from their thrall" (226). The way to escape enframing is first to acknowledge the "hermeneutical circle" of detachment and contemplation and then "to find a way to break into it" (226). This Heideggerian reading contends that the poïetic attending to technology in these novels shows a way to break the circle. Heidegger insists that for humans to reclaim their dignity, we need to become poïetic and nurturing instead of imperious and domineering. We should incorporate these attitudes into all of our thinking, interactions, and relationships — and not only with humans. Heidegger is suggesting that we reinsert poïesis into our lives and extend it to all beings, but most expressly to Being. The problem is that it is difficult for us to learn to live poïetically because there are no longer any examples of this mode of existence. In the final section of his reading of Heidegger and technology, Rojcewicz writes "Imposition has deposed poïesis" and asks if "art [can] still offer us examples" of poïesis (Rojcewicz 227). This project argues that literary representations of humans interacting with AIs present us with examples of pious and poïetic living that can lead us toward releasement and openness to Being.

Zimmerman wonders in his section on Heideggerian "releasement:"

> It is difficult to see how Heidegger hoped to reconcile what he predicted as humanity's total enslavement to technology with his claim that humanity can be freed from such enslavement simply by learning to use technical objects appropriately, i.e., in a way that lets people avoid being turned into automatons. Present-day humanity is certainly not characterized by the "releasement" (*Gelassenheit*) necessary to "let technological devices be." Perhaps Heidegger was holding open a vision of what humanity might become, centuries from now, if being revealed itself once again in such a way that a new relationship to things became possible for Western humanity [235].

Technology anxiety surrounds the concept of automatons and this anxiety heightens when humans are reduced to such a role. Reading SF novels in a Heideggerian mode focuses on the moments when Being may be on the verge of revealing itself in a new way, as precipitated by the rise of intelligent machines. Are SF authors then trying to imagine what the new historical epoch would look like, or are they nailing the coffin of our current epoch without speculating about the implications of an AI on the human relationship to Being? These four authors were probably not aware of Heidegger's writings on technology or trying to incorporate them consciously into their work. A Heideggerian reading simply examines art in an effort to see what we think about our technological futures. Our feelings about AIs might represent the event of the turning of Being and signify a collective thought that this turning will happen sooner rather than later. Zimmerman goes on to say:

> Heidegger believed that his own meditations on being, his own attempt to recall what had been forgotten, were of world-historical significance for the following reason: Being has concealed itself from technological humanity. Thus deprived of a relationship with the originary ontological source, humanity can experience only entities, and then only in a constricted way: as standing-reserve. If and when a new encounter with being were to occur, if being showed itself once again, this event in and of itself would indicate that the reign of the technological era was coming to a close [235].

Heidegger may have been over estimating his abilities in these sentiments, but he is right to emphasize the overwhelming importance of the human relationship to technology in the twentieth and twenty-first centuries. If Being has indeed concealed itself from technological humanity, what task could be more important than detaching from this concealing? Ironically then, the place to start looking for the truth of Being is in written meditations on a highly "technological" being: the AI. This is because Heidegger believed that "even though modern technology was so very dangerous, it was also — paradoxically — the way beyond that danger" (Zimmerman 236).

Part VI: Conclusion

The chapters that follow examine four novels that engage the human relationship to AIs. The goal is not to "prove" that they are all implicitly Heideggerian, but rather to ask questions of each text in a Heideggerian way and see what they might have to "say." Zimmerman's concludes his reading of Heidegger by reminding us: "because there is no rational basis for the technological way of life, things could be otherwise. Discovering the groundlessness of the technological era makes possible the openness — and the anxiety — necessary for the arrival of a new, post-modern era. (236) Zimmerman probably means a new post–post-modern era, but the important point to emphasize is the possibilities Heidegger's thoughts about technology and our future open up. The technology anxiety expressed through literature when characters confront AIs is anxiety about these possibilities, but the idea of poïetic salvation helps us see the merit of such anxieties. After all, "things could be otherwise." However, even with a positive outcome in mind, there is no guarantee that each reading agrees with these sentiments. Frank Scahlow's modestly notes that at the very least, "we cannot discount the power of the *therapeutic dimension* that our openness to existence provides when we are receptive to it," when analyzing Rojcewicz's work on Heidegger and technology (125). This project believes something more profound than therapy is opened by discussing the human relationship to technology, AIs, and technology through a Heideggerian lens.

List of Abbreviations of Heidegger's works

Basic = Basic Questions
Discourse = Discourse on Thinking
P = Parmenides
The Question / Question = The Question Concerning Technology

CHAPTER 2

HAL as Human Savior in Arthur C. Clarke's *2001: A Space Odyssey*

The Artificial Intelligence HAL is perhaps the most infamous example of a murderous machine gone rogue in 20th century literature. Many cannot help but consider Stanley Kubrick's representation of HAL as gospel, but have never read the novel. Too often scholarship on HAL either conflates the film and the novel, or omits the novel altogether. Thomas Caldwell contends that it is a mistake to use "Clarke's excellent novel ... to unravel many of the narrative intricacies of Kubrick's film" and "it should largely be put aside for the purpose of conducting any serious analysis" (133). This chapter is an analysis of the AI HAL, technology anxiety, and ontological transformation in the novel. Following Caldwell's advice—but in the other direction—the film is not invoked to unravel any of the novel's intricacies, because Clark's text provides more insight as to why HAL turns against his crew and what happens to the astronaut David Bowman when he arrives at Japetus. This chapter argues that while HAL gloriously represents anxieties we have about being enslaved or killed by intelligent machines, a thorough close reading of the novel reveals that HAL is more importantly the catalyst that enables Dave to successfully engage alien technologies and escape the ontology of enframing. Through an analysis of the novel's overwhelming tone of wonder, the monolith's programming of proto-human beings, and the actions of HAL during *Discovery*'s voyage, I will use a Heideggerian approach to show how the novel deals most centrally with the concerns of the next ontological epoch and how to escape the imperious clutches of modern technological ontology, which Heidegger calls enframing. George Slusser, when wondering if humanity has evolved or regressed from our pre-historic origins to modern day writes that in *2001*, the "emphasis is less on the man caught between home and eternity than on the mechanisms of entrapment and their meaning" (58). The entrapment Slusser highlights is the hidden ontological trap of enframing and HAL, while turning rogue, actually helps Dave Bowman escape the trap in time to be judged by the very aliens that gave us technology in the first place.

Part I: The Wonder of Space: Distance, Dimension, Scope

Arthur C. Clarke's novel overflows with an ebullient sense of childlike amazement and wonder at the prospect of traveling through the dimensions of space and time. Sharona Ben-Tov argues: "The dearth of wonder, magic, the truly strange and different, is the constant preoccupation of science fiction, which tries to compensate with its own fabrications, or with what I have called 'man-made wonder'" (13). *2001* does not suffer from a dearth of wonder. Moreover, the wonder in the novel comes from the alien and the natural, not the artificial. Wondrous, human-made technologies make space travel possible, but the artificial in *2001* is merely the vehicle to non-human wonders. All of the principle male characters in the novel, from Moon-Watcher, to Dr. Floyd, to David Bowman, gaze at celestial bodies with a sense of sheer awe. Aaron Parrett has it right about both the novel and the film when he writes that Clarke's work "remains relevant and important thirty years out because, like Homer's *Odyssey* (to which it tips its titular hat), the film captures something of the mystery contained in what it means to be human and what it means to be traveling with the forces of fate into the future" (117). This chapter explores whether the heavy overtones of wonder and mystery that permeate the novel provide an intellectual shelter for the characters — and perhaps the reader — such that enframing can be momentarily escaped, and the true essence of modern technology be revealed. Is the sense of wonder in this novel more than what SF fans call "sensawunda" and, in fact, a kind of wonder that harkens back to an ancient mode of poïetic appreciation? Can thinking about the terrific scope of inter-solar distances help destabilize our anthropocentrism and the grip of enframing, or is such wonder symptomatic of anthropocentrism as we imagine ways to colonize space and transform it into the standing-reserve? This is not an attempt to demonize Clarke or his novel for being somehow "imperious" with regard to space exploration. The narrative and the author don't make ostensibly humanistic claims about space as our "dominion" but, at the same time, there are also no reservations about exploring space and most of the dangers are expressed in terms of the psychological duress for human explorers and the physical threats that accompany space travel. Nothing is said about the potential contamination of the mystery of spatial beings through this process. Clarke does not have to subscribe to Heidegger's ideas about technology or even be aware of them for this reading to be profitable; what matters is how a comparison of Clarke's ideas about our technological future to Heidegger's enriches the critical conversation surrounding the novel.

In his forward to the novel, Clarke begins by writing:

> For every man who has ever lived, in this Universe there shines a star.
> But every one of those stars is a sun.... And many — perhaps most — of those alien suns have planets circling them. So almost certainly there is enough land in the sky to give every member of the human species, back to the first apeman, his own private, world-sized heaven — or hell [xix].

These sentiments seem innocent enough, but what do they say about humanity's place in the universe? The language parcels out the universe to humans so that each member is the proud recipient of their own world. This troubled notion of "wonder" might be a microcosm for the novel's depiction of wonder. Is wonder in this novel an innocent, child-like expression that should be admired for its ability to detach us from traditional methods of viewing, or is wonder simply the mark of attraction by the imperious enframing of modern technology? When we read the line, "for every man who has ever lived, in this Universe there shines a star," does the "for" imply ownership? Again, these comments do not indict Clarke as a ruthless property monger, intent on capturing the objects of space for human conquest; nor are Heidegger's thoughts on technology fundamentally against space-exploration. Through a Heideggerian reading of *2001*, this section examines whether or not the wonder expressed throughout the novel is free of enframing or if it implicitly intends the stars to become resources for human exploitation. Does reaching the stars give us license to define them scientifically and strip them of mystery? Do we mean to admire them in a fashion that is poïetic and lets them stand on their own, or are they merely generators of energy and raw materials for production?

Dr. Heywood Floyd experiences wonder each time he is about to embark on a journey off-planet. He thinks:

> No matter how many times you left Earth, [he] told himself, the excitement never really palled.... As the moment of takeoff approached, he was conscious of a rising tension, a feeling of wonder and awe — yes; and of nervousness — which put him on the same level as any Earthlubber about to receive his first baptism of space [41].

The adventure never loses its luster for Floyd. But what is his "wonder and awe" directed at? Is he marveling at human achievement or the profound concept of "leaving" planet Earth? If his wonder is symptomatic of some humanistic celebration of our technological accomplishments, then wonder in this case is not related to poïesis. If, however, Floyd is explaining that being in touch with outer-space is invigorating because of its vastness and the uncertainty involved, his wonder is derived from the mystery and majesty of space. Space travel as a "baptism" connects the act with the mystical and spiritual, which suggests that one is approaching the gods intellectually and spatially. His "nervousness" stems from the unpredictability of space and/or the fragility of the shuttle and human vulnerability away from the environment of Earth. This anticipation — however slight — inserts a modicum of doubt into the journey that disables a hubristic "awe" and points us more toward a poïetic sense of wonder. Additionally, Floyd has been made aware of TMA-1 and has his mind on something other than humanity as he ponders alien life.

As the shuttle bearing Floyd to the moon continues its prelaunch preparations, the doctor's exuberance heightens: "He wished he could look out of the window, but it was an effort even to turn his head, yet there was no discomfort; indeed, the pressure of acceleration and the overwhelming thunder of the motors produced an extraordinary euphoria. His ears ringing, the blood pounding in his veins, Floyd felt more alive than he had for years. He was young again, he wanted to sing aloud — which was certainly safe, for no one could possibly hear him" (47). Floyd's inability to look out the window communicates the human body's deterministic bend to the speed of the ship. But what about the will of the exploration itself? Are humans bound to seek out new territory for the proliferation of modern technological enframing? The child-like awe of exploring the unknown and the great velocity of the ship are innocent enough, but what if the euphoria is an implanted incentive system at work in the machinery of Heywood's brain? In the first section of the novel, the black monolith works upon the brain of Moon-Watcher and many other pre-humans in a process of conditioning that programs a particular aptitude for technology and an impulse to develop more technologies. Is Floyd's euphoria at space-travel then a derivation of this ancestral carrot implanted by intelligent space-faring aliens? Conversely, his feeling "young again" might be read as an ontological escape from modern technology to a perspective of wonder more in keeping with ancient technology. In true Heideggerian fashion, however, it is more likely the case that both scenarios hold true. The saving power of poïesis cannot be seen without first acknowledging the dangers of modern technology, so it is best to read this moment aboard the shuttle as a symptom of both states. We are compelled to explore the universe in order to bear witness to its beauty, but also to seek out new resources for the furthering of our technological systems that guarantee the dominion of the human race.

The sense of wonder Dave feels becomes more pronounced as he gets further away from the Earth. As he gazes at the Earth "with a thrill of recognition," he notices familiar geographical sights and relates to these locations in a way only a handful of humans today can, as an observer from space. But being far from home does not bother Dave at first, which is one of the reasons he is chosen for the mission. As he observes planet Earth, he realizes that "he had no regrets for these lost beauties. He had enjoyed them all, in his thirty-five years of life; and he was determined to enjoy them again, when he returned rich and famous. Meanwhile, distance made them all the more precious" (116). The notion that distance can make the appreciation of Earth's "beauties" more precious is a parallel of the existentialist appreciation of life given its finitude. Distance in the dimension of time or space can make Earth seem "all the more precious," but the more important question for this project is to consider whether distance from Earth can provide Dave and fellow astronaut Frank Poole a vantage point from which to observe the essence of modern technology. Can moving physically away from the this ontology and into meditative solitude (once HAL and Frank are gone) grant Bowman insight to the dangers of modern technology and situate him in a posture of waiting for the new epoch? Is Dave's enlightenment and "ascension" into a Star-Child at the close of the novel a metaphor for him breaking free of enframing and awakening to a mode of poïetic looking enabled by his distance from Earth?

Although the tone of the novel with respect to wonder and the "evolution" of humankind is optimistic, it remains murky whether Dave's journey is free of the imperious claims of enframing. Until HAL is disconnected, Dave has not been made aware of the discovery of TMA-1 on the moon and the verification of alien life. Dave could be approaching his mission to explore Saturn and then Jupiter as a human seeking to extend the sphere of human influence in the solar system. Dave certainly thinks of himself as an ancient explorer, as evinced by his choice of leisure reading, which features explorers like Pytheas, Anson, Cook, and Odysseus (126–7). Was the mission of these explorers to find valuable resources to amplify modes of technological production or to satisfy an innate sense of adventure and curiosity at the heart of humanity? Is the drive to explore the unknown motivated by the will to power or is it fostered by *Dasein*'s quest to behold and witness the radiance of Being? In the context of this novel, exploration is a force of both modes of thinking. In Dave's reading, he attends to both the ancient technological ontology of Greek explorers, as well as post-enlightenment explorers James Cook and George Anson. Does Dave ultimately look at beings and Being imperiously or poïetically? Because of Dave's particular draw to *The Odyssey*, as well as the title of the novel, an ancient sensibility is more prominently operating in Dave's mind. If, like Odysseus, Dave feels an active participant in the musings of the gods, this indicates that Dave believes in something more powerful than humanity. In this case, we can read Dave as the ideal voyager toward not a conquest of space, but the re-discovery of the gods or, in Heidegger's phrasing, the re-acknowledgment of Being and Being's look upon humans.

However, this non-humanistic attitude toward wonder and technological ontology in the novel is not without complication. Eighty-six days into their voyage, Dave and Frank are getting closer to encountering another body in space. One of the most dazzling elements of interstellar travel would be the sheer emptiness of space. Yes, the size is staggering; but it would disturbing to go such mind-bending distances as astronomical units or light years and never get close to another visible composition of matter. The narrator reveals that the asteroid they are to approach "had no name — merely the number 7794 — and was a fifty-yard-diameter rock that had been detected by the Lunar Observatory in 1997 and immediately forgotten except by the patient computers of the Minor Planet Bureau" (130). Giving a being a number for a name is as clinical and imperious as one can get, but it is understandable. After all, this is one of numerous asteroids, and it is not worth our attention if we cannot glean it of its resources. We once paid homage to celestial bodies by giving them the names of the gods, but they are too numerous to consider past a certain point. What is fascinating here is how this scientific charting and forgetting is noted as a matter of course, but not to the computers. The computers of the Minor Planet Bureau are not enabled with AI like a HAL 9000 unit, but given that mechanical intelligence is a primary investiture of the novel, it is worth noting that the computer almost sympathetically "remembers" this asteroid. Humans ignore it, because it has no value as standing-reserve and poses no threat to the Earth. Just as Moon-Watcher forgets the black monolith once he realizes it is not food and means him no harm, we forget countless objects that populate the heavens. Similarly, do we consider the objects and tools of our technology with any real feelings unless they are malfunctioning?

Even if those on Earth pay no serious attention to the asteroid, however, Dave and Frank have different feelings toward 7794, because they are adrift in space with nothing to catch their anchor. We see them stare at the "passing pebble in the sky with the emotions of sailors on a long sea voyage, skirting a coast on which they cannot land" (130). The rock reminds them of the safety and stability of Earth, but 7794 is only remarkable because it has something to offer them. Is bearing witness to the asteroid enough for minds molded by enframing? Cynically, their vulnerable position could inform their attitude, but through this motivation comes clarity of thought and vision. As Dave and Frank are "perfectly well aware that 7794 was only a lifeless, airless chunk of rock," devoid of aesthetic value or resource value, we learn that "this knowledge scarcely affected their feelings" (130). This imbues the asteroid with qualities missed on Earth, except perhaps by the computers that remember it.

But once these moments of awe and appreciation fade, Dave and Frank remember their scientific agenda with respect to asteroid 7794:

> Through the high-powered telescope, they could see that the asteroid was very irregular.... The automatic cameras took dozens of photographs, the navigation radar's returning echoes were carefully recorded for future analysis — and there was just time for a single impact probe.... It was merely a small slug of metal, shot out from *Discovery*.... Against the darkened portion of the asteroid there was a sudden, dazzling explosion of light.... Aboard *Discovery*, the cameras were recording the rapidly fading spectral lines. Back on Earth, experts would analyze them.... And so, for the first time, the composition of an asteroid's crust would be determined [132–3].

On the surface, nothing appears to be amiss with this scientific experiment, but this reaction is a result of our conditioning at the ontological hands of enframing. As evidenced by this passage, humans cannot encounter a celestial body scientifically without doing violence to the body itself. This is a microcosm of much of Heidegger's anxiety with respect to the scientific method. Cameras taking pictures for posterity do not "damage" the asteroid directly (although they flatten it and remove two dimensions from its existence in time and space), but the "impact probe" is simply a bullet, launched to help determine the composition of the crust. Sure, it's "only a lifeless, airless chunk of rock" so what are we worried about? If we want to strike scientific pay dirt, we do have to sacrifice a bit, right? Heidegger is not arguing that the "feelings" of the asteroid are hurt by this violence, but rather that we do violence to the being's ability to *be* outside of human influence. And what is the purpose of the experiment? To learn if the asteroid is profitable for harvesting or to begin an intellectual project of mastery? Dave, Frank, and the scientists in the novel are not sinister, imperious people. What is sinister is enframing, which conceals the violence of the experiment.

When Dave and Frank are simply taking in the overwhelming sights of a celestial body without a scientific objective , the sense of wonder is poïetic and preempts enframing's efforts to control and dominate. As they rocket closer and closer to Jupiter, they are free to examine the staggering size of planet: "Jupiter now filled the entire sky; it was so huge that neither mind nor eye could grasp it any longer, and both had abandoned the attempt. If it had not been for the extraordinary variety of color ... of the atmosphere beneath them, Bowman could have believed that he was flying low over a cloudscape on Earth (139). The key is that both the mind and they eye "abandon" the attempt to "grasp" the planet. In Heidegger's writings on the proper attitude of *Dasein* to Being and beings, the normal cognitive approach of apprehension is maligned because it forcefully subjects a being to mental control. Bowman is able to "let" Jupiter be and appreciate the planet's majesty without trying to make it to submit to some calculus of understanding. The striking color scheme and the size of the planet remind him that he is not looking at Earth. The proximity to another, grander world enhances Dave's ability to shed the fetters of enframing. He becomes able to see Jupiter without dissembling it into manageable categories of thought or break it apart into raw materials.

As the mission progresses and Dave (now alone) gets further and further from Earth, his mind opens up to possibilities locked away by the sway of modern technology. He sees what appears to be "a photographic negative of the Milky Way" and knows he is so far from home that he must cease to try to control the sensory data that is washing over him (264). Beyond the limits of our knowledge, Dave comes face to face with the fact that our attempt to dominate the universe through understanding is doomed: "Where in God's name am I? Bowman asked himself; and even as he posed the question, he felt certain that he could never know the answer. It seemed that space had been turned inside out: this was not a place for man. Though the capsule was comfortably warm, he felt suddenly cold, and was afflicted by an almost uncontrollable trembling" (263–4). The narrator only mentions "God" in the singular in an earlier segment detailing the development of AIs, and when Dave falls through TMA-1's big brother. Dave's invocation of the spiritual in a predominantly secular novel is an indication of his psychological transformation. His inclusion of an entity that is "above" humanity reveals his humbling and inclines him toward a more receptive mode of looking. Additionally, he acknowledges that he is in a place not meant for humanity. This could be read as a refutation of a celestial manifest destiny (humanity cannot colonize all of space) or as an indication of Dave's post (or non)-human transformation. Even though his shuttle is heated, he shivers and trembles because of the profundity of this experience. We are left to wonder whether Bowman's trembling signals a transformation to *Dasein* or a capitulation to enframing. Is this tremble the effect of shedding the gaze of enframing or is it a response to the soul finally being driven from the body by the will of the monolith and the aliens that introduced humans to technology?

Fully considering the effects of distance through time and space, the emptiness of the universe, and the sheer size of a planet like Jupiter, we see that Dave is wrestled from one worldview to the next — between enframing on the one hand and poïesis on the other. Unfortunately, there seems to be no commitment in the novel to one ontology or the other. However, this is exactly the tenuous predicament Heidegger explains that we find ourselves in as we wait for the next historical epoch. At the culmination of Dave's journey, he sees what he calls "a glorious apparition" and realizes he is "looking upon something that no human eye had ever seen" (268). In the moment of seeing something for the first time, there are not thoughts of anthropocentric dominance, but an acknowledgment of our epistemological limits. This realization is crystallized when he sees a new sun as "dying" and concludes that this assessment "was a wholly false impression, born of human experience and the emotions aroused by the hues of sunset, or the glow of fading embers" (268). Dave accepts that, ontologically, knowledge can intercept a pure recognition of a being and confine it to a system of memories and/or expectations that mask its true character. Through his wonder at the marvels of space, we are left to determine for ourselves whether Dave's transformation signifies a departure from enframing or from Being. How will he use his new knowledge and power? Will the Star-Child modulate the universe to humanity's whim or nurture forth a new ontology of poïesis? The ambiguity at the close of the novel aligns the book with Heidegger's thoughts on technology; because Heidegger admits, we will not know what the next epoch has in store for us until Being turns to us again.

THE WONDER OF THE INTELLIGENT NON-HUMAN

The concept of "wonder" in *2001* allies with Heidegger's thinking on ancient technology because the novel's representation of wonder directed at the marvels of space is ultimately both poïetic and imperious. This is to be expected, as in the Western mind, all objects are meant to be dominated by subjects. Nevertheless, how does wonder in the novel change when the focus is on an intelligent, non-human being? Is the encountering of another subject instead of an ob-ject all it takes to shed the imperious demands of enframing or is enframing so pervasive that even subjects become raw materials for technological production? Clarke cleverly avoids dealing with an alien other in the novel, as Bowman and others only interact with alien technological artifacts. This choice — like the decision to keep the ending nebulous — allows the encounters to more relatable to the reader than a direct confrontation. But in these scenes, do we find poïetic wondering or colonial enframing?

In the forward to the novel, Clarke proclaims, "the barriers of distance are crumbling; one day we shall meet our equals, or our masters, among the stars" (xx). Once our technology enables space travel, we will meet other intelligent forms of life. Presumably, these intelligent others will also use technology and will either be around the same "level" as us technologically or in a position to dominate us. The technology anxiety we have about being enslaved by our technology is modified in this case, as it happens to be someone or something else's technology. This is why Clarke points out, "men have been slow to face this prospect [of meeting intelligent life]" and that "some still hope that it may never become reality" (xx). Many humans are afraid of losing the control (illusory or not) that we have gained over nature and the gods with technology. It would be quite ironic if on our colonial voyages into space, we encounter an alien race with vastly superior technologies that would not have noticed us otherwise who then swoop in to consume us and the planet we tried so hard to dominate. However, the aliens in this novel are not the "War of the Worlds" resource harvesters, but are rather like benevolent parents that come to our aid by gifting us technology. Conveniently, all encounters with the intelligent non-human are with the black monoliths on Earth, the moon, and a moon of Jupiter. The first human-like being to encounter this alien technology is the ancestral man-ape Moon-Watcher. Moon-Watcher hears the unidentifiable "clank of metal upon stone," but there is not much to learn from his discovery, because his brain has not yet been addled by the monolith's experiments (10). When Dr. Floyd approached TMA-1 on the moon, the narrator explains it "was a vertical slab of jet-black material, about ten feet high and five feet wide: it reminded Floyd, somewhat ominously, of a giant tombstone" (83). Floyd's initial reaction to the obelisk is telling and we are left to wonder whose death the tombstone symbolizes; is it the death of the aliens who built it, the death of an imperious mode of human existence, or the final death of human freedom? Interestingly, Floyd's colleague Dr. Michaels has a different reaction to the monolith, which is admiration that lacks a sense of foreboding. When explaining to Floyd how old the object is he speaks "almost reverently" (83). His reverence for the monolith hints at the proper relation to being and Beings *Dasein* should have — even though it is tempered by Michael's scientific positivism (precise dating of the monolith with "local geological evidence") (83). Is Michael's reverence stemming from the profundity of encountering alien life or from unlocking a rich cache of resources to scientifically mine?

It is difficult to predict what kind of effect the discovery of alien life would have on the populous. While the scientists on the moon are debating what ramifications their discovery might have: "Floyd found his thoughts turning again and again to the three-million-year-wide gulf that had just opened up before him ... he was used to considering far longer periods of time — but they had concerned only the movements of stars and the slow cycles of the inanimate universe. Mind or intelligence had not been involved; those eons were empty of all that touched the emotions" (87). The wonder and awe derived from examining vast, historical spans of time is amplified as pre-human history becomes populated by a foreign intelligence. This invigorates the past with a new luster. Darwinian evolution and natural selection are now to be considered as the workings of an alien agency. The novel leaves us to wonder what filling those "empty" eons with intelligence does to our perception of history. For Floyd and Michaels there is a developing sense that there is something other than "human history" to consider — as if there are now non-human achievements and events worth acknowledging.

As the discovery of the monolith sinks in, Michaels and Floyd lament having missed encountering aliens by three million years. When Floyd hears the "triumph, and yet sadness, in Michaels' voice" he decides that he "could share both emotions" (88). Triumph at discovering intelligent life, but sadness at missing it in time. Does this sadness derive from a missed diplomatic opportunity or a scientific one? Floyd's lack of anxiety at a meeting is surprising, but his final thoughts are to consider, "what we might have learned from creatures who could cross space, while our ancestors were still living in trees" (88). He sees the aliens as nodes of intellectual resources waiting for human harvesting. In this case, encountering non-human intelligent life does not subvert the imperious claims of enframing. Even if Floyd does not intend to colonize and enslave the aliens, he means to acquire from them something of value, beyond knowledge of their existence. The knowledge they gain could be a poïetic ontology, but regardless, the aliens are seen as standing-reserve first and subjects second.

When Floyd arrives at the TMA-1 dig site on the moon, there is a transformation in his seeing that a photograph could not engender: "The passengers were utterly silent as the bus descended into the crater. There was awe, and there was also incredulity — sheer disbelief that the dead Moon, of all worlds, could have sprung this fantastic surprise" (88). Their silence prevents an attempt to diminish the experience with language in a effort of control or scientific classification. The Moon being "dead" is of note, first because Floyd means biologically dead, as no carbon-based life is found on the Moon, but it can also mean resource dead, as the moon yields no cost-effective nodes for us to harvest. This fact, incidentally, is perhaps what caused space exploration to die out as a national pursuit. As Floyd gets closer to the monolith, the feeling of awe heightens and "As [he] walked slowly down the ramp toward the black rectangle, he felt a sense not only of awe but of helplessness" (97). Although helplessness in the face of something awe-inspiring is not unusual, it is crucial in this exploration because it marks this posture of awe as poïetic. Being helpless means that Floyd submits to the being and to Being in a poïetic way, and has abandoned all attempts to gain dominance over the monolith. In this way, the novel proposes that a true encounter with intelligent alien technology can — at least temporarily — free us from the will to power and the will to enframe. The next line emphasizes this potentiality when Floyd concludes: "Here, at the very portals of Earth, man was already face to face with a mystery that might never be solved" (97). One of the main points Heidegger communicates when considering our interaction with beings and Being is to preserve the mystery of this engagement. There is no need to process all data in a scientific way in order to gain mastery over the objects of our research — all this does is enframe every being, and eventually ourselves. Clarke was observant enough to grant his characters the humility to discard all attempts to understand everything and instead, let them be. This leads to a central question of this project, which is whether these moments can in turn grant the reader a temporary escape from enframing such that we can see the essence of modern technology.

Perhaps Dr. Floyd is not a fair representation of a typical human response to the existence of intelligent alien life because he is a member of the intellectual elite. As Heidegger maintains, in order to see the saving power of poïesis behind enframing, we must first see the dangers of modern technology. Floyd's scientific background has him so ensconced in these dangers that he has the capability to gain insight into the saving power. Floyd himself realizes the magnitude of this encounter and wonders: "how would the world react to the news when it was finally released? Even if they discover nothing about TMA-1, and it remained an eternal mystery, Man would know that he was not unique in the universe. Though he had missed them by millions of years, those who had once stood here might yet return: and if not, there might well be others. All futures must now contain this possibility" (99). Removing the threat of an alien invasion subverts the technology anxiety of considering the emergence of superior alien technology. What remains is a kind of technological archaeology, and the buffer of three million years assuages debilitating anxieties of attack or enslavement at the hands of extraterrestrial life. The key here is that everything about human life would change — even if TMA-1 remains a mystery. This suggests that our ontology could be shifted away from enframing to a new mode because of the discovery. In these moments of articulating the wonder of encountering intelligent non-human beings, the novel creates an intellectual space for meditative thinking and a contemplation of the essence of modern technology that allows readers to see past the dangers and find the saving power. This is not a certainty, it is an optimistic hope geared to match the optimism of the novel; but the changes in human life, values, and philosophy seem to be more in-line with techné and poïesis than imperious enframing. Insisting, "all futures must now contain this possibility" reminds us that the novel — like Heidegger — makes no prediction as to what the future might hold, but instead establishes that the trajectories of these potential futures are forever changed by an ontological shift.

The way Dave and the scientists on the Moon poïetically interact with the monoliths forges this optimism. Their scientific inquiries could project a violent gaze upon the monolith, but they treat the monolith decidedly different from asteroid 7794. One indication of this is when Floyd turns "his full attention to the ebon slab — walking slowly around it, examining it from every angle, trying to imprint its strangeness upon his mind" (98). Instead of trying to imprint the blank slab with qualifications and classifications, Floyd lets the slab imprint his mind. Additionally, we learn that "the hard black material of the slab had resisted all the rather mild attempts that Michaels and his colleagues had made to obtain samples" (90). This leads the team to consider violent extraction measures like a laser beam, but:

> They had no doubt that a laser beam would cut into it — for, surely, nothing could resist that frightful concentration of energy — but the decision to employ such violent measures would be left to Floyd. He had already decided that X rays, sonic probes, neutron beams, and all other nondestructive means of investigation would be brought into play before he called up the heavy artillery of the laser. It was the mark of a barbarian to destroy something one could not understand; but perhaps men were barbarians, beside the creatures who had made this thing [90].

Floyd considers harsh and violent probing to be barbaric, and thinks that humanity is barbaric when compared to the sophisticated species that devised the slab. The fact that Floyd calls into question the very violent nature of scientific inquiry makes it plain that the presence of alien technology is a potent enough catalyst to unconceal the essence of modern technology. The catalyst exposes enframing as a barbarous ontology when studying the be-ing of something produced by an alien. Moreover, the response to the discovery of TMA-1 is exploratory and not military. No weapons of mass destruction are ferreted away on Dave and Frank's ship. The existence of this artifact has arrested enframing and much of the scientists' technology anxiety such that a mission is planned that aims to see where the signal transmitted from TMA-1 leads. Once an object can be read as the product of a subject, new considerations come into play that subvert the imperious claims of enframing and create an opportunity to awaken the old poïetic modes of techné.

Similarly, Dave Bowman is able to escape his plight aboard the *Discovery* via the imaginative portal opened by considering alien life and alien technology: "At his first glimpse of TMA-1, with the spacesuited figures clustering around it, Bowman leaned toward the screen in openmouthed astonishment. In the excitement of this revelation — something which, like every man interested in space, he had half expected all his life — he almost forgot his own desperate predicament" (208). Dave is bearing witness to a revelation; a revelation of alien life of course, but also a revelation of the mechanism of enframing and the poïesis beyond the danger. As Dave's mind adjusts to the startling image his "sense of wonder was swiftly followed by another emotion" and he thought, "this was tremendous — but what had it to do with him?" (208). The wonder of the monolith is so arresting that it supersedes Dave's thoughts of himself as an individual. These passages evince that the mental escape hatches opened by sheer wonder are temporal and can only allow us the briefest glimpse of modern technology and the saving power.

Just as the instillation of subjectivity into the monolith tempers Dr. Floyd's scientific objectivity, Dave begins to regard this being in a different way. His studies of human explorers are abandoned and he begins focusing on the reports of TMA-1: "Again and again he played back the recording made when TMA-1 greeted the dawn for the first time in three million years. He watched the spacesuited figures moving around it, and almost smiled at their ludicrous panic when it blasted its signal at the stars, paralyzing their radios with the sheer power of its electronic voice" (217). In this passage, Dave' alters his use of language as he grants agency to the monolith. It "greets" the dawn, "blasts" its signal, and has an "electronic voice." The thesis of this project purports that the subjectivity of an AI thwarts the domineering gaze of enframing long enough to allow a human being the opportunity to poïetically look upon beings. In the space of this novel, the argument extends to include even residual traces of foreign intelligence and subjectivity found in autonomous mechanical artifacts.

As Dave's time is spent pondering this development and as he drifts away from Earth, his ontology shifts away from the dichotomy of subject/object and enframing. While the scientists on Earth debate the reasons for keeping the discovery of TMA-1 a secret, Dave reflects that "from his present viewpoint, looking back on Earth as a dim star almost lost in the Sun, such considerations now seemed ludicrously parochial" (219). He has begun to drift away from anthropocentric trivialities and is imagining the bigger picture of Being and beings. His shift in focus becomes so profound that he has trouble attending to his primal instincts: "the knowledge of what now lay out there beyond the observation ports sometimes made it difficult for him to concentrate even on the problem of survival" (222). Nowhere is Clarke more deliberate with his description of the significance of this event than here, where the organism's will to live is subverted by curiosity. What could be a more effective diversion from the ontology of modern technology than this encounter then, if it unseats survival in the hierarchy of attention?

Yet as Bowman continues to drift away from Earth and is consumed by feelings of wonder, his ontological shift becomes punctuated by different considerations. Although Dave passes "beyond despair and beyond hope," he never passes "beyond curiosity" (228). But once curiosity takes root in his mind, it matures beyond initial, paralyzing awe to "a sense of exaltation — and a feeling of power" (228). The poïetic awe has given way to the imperious might of enframing and the will to power. Or has it? Might it be too optimistic to wonder if the "power" Dave experiences is actually the saving power and not the imperious will to power? Either he is being em-powered by the ennobling and liberating call of poïesis or he is being rendered power-less by the subjugating claims of enframing. Clarke keeps his conclusions ambiguous, leaving readers to determine if the novel portends the end of human freedom or the beginning of a new epoch. Dave is cognizant of the stakes as he accepts that "not only was he the representative of the entire human race, but his actions during the next few weeks might determine its very future" (228). He becomes the "Ambassador Extraordinary — Plenipotentiary — for all mankind" and is the liaison between one fate and the other (228). Like Heidegger, Clarke has confidence in humanity's capacity to make this decision — we are not entirely victims of external caprice. Humans cannot influence Being, but we can put ourselves in a posture of abetting as we wait for Being to shift. If, on the other hand, we take the reins of power enabled by enframing and heedlessly work to commit all beings to categories of standing-reserve, we have lost the ability to become *Dasein* and have been enslaved by modern technology. Dave casts aside all personal feelings of safety for feelings of duty to the human race. Will we become enslaved by the call of the monolith or will it empower us to alter our course at the last minute and escape the snares of enframing?

The scientists at mission control can no longer follow Dave on his journey outside our current ontology and are left to ponder his last utterance. As Dave gets closer to the monolith on Jupiter's Moon Japetus, the narrator explains: "the Eye of Japetus had blinked, as if to remove an irritating speck of dust" (289). This being is now a subject that looks upon Dave. The monolith here represents the entirety of technological ontology, but also reminds us of the ever-present gaze of Being upon us. Dave is truly in a critical moment of transformation as he becomes aware of the gaze of Being. As his shuttle gets closer to the monolith Bowman: "had time for just one broken sentence which the waiting men in Mission Control, nine hundred million miles away and eighty minutes in the future, were never to forget: 'The thing's hollow — it goes on forever — and — oh my God!— it's full of stars!'" (290). In seeing that the "thing" is hollow, Dave gains insight into the limitless profundity of all beings and realizes that when beings are all cast as the standing-reserve, we are only seeing the surface of things. He references "God" as he falls out of human contact and goes beyond all understanding.

Dave's journey through the Star Gate becomes increasingly abstract as Clarke attempts to articulate astronomical phenomena by relating them to the human brain: "Once he had peered through a microscope at a cross-section of a human brain, and in its network of nerve fibers had glimpsed the same labyrinthine complexity. But that had been dead and static, whereas this transcended life itself. He knew — or believed he knew — that he was watching the operation of some gigantic mind, contemplating the universe of which he was so tiny a part" (289–90). In this moment, Dave realizes that the universe itself (or Being) reminds him of a gigantic mind contemplating itself, and he is merely a tiny part of this operation. Inspired by the awareness of non-human intelligence, Dave has broken through anthropocentric humanism and piously accepted his role in the machinations of the universe/Being. If the novel ended here, it would be safe to conclude that Clarke's vision is parallel to Heidegger's own concerning the poïetic participation of *Dasein* in accord with the unconcealing of the four-fold of Being, but Dave's diminution becomes complicated by his transformation into the Star-Child.

Part II: Humans as AIs

Before we meet HAL, we meet Moon-Watcher and witness his transformation from a "man-ape" to an ancestral, pre-technological human being. Moon-Watcher's meeting with technology is external — and even extraterrestrial! Clarke presents technology itself as an agency that works upon our ancestors in a way that eerily parallels the programming of the artificial intelligence HAL. It is necessary analyze how Clarke articulates the human relationship to technology itself and the transformations in humanity this relationship engenders before examining HAL. The instructional function of the monolith artificially stimulates the brains of proto-humans and renders "natural" or "biological" intelligence as AI.

The wonder in the novel internally motivates humans away from enframing. But is the feeling of wonder a programmed incentive system meant to exact certain outcomes from human vehicles? For Heidegger, the role of *Dasein* is both submissive and active — it is a voluntary following of the destiny of Being. Choosing to do something inevitable seems to be an empty kind of freedom, but, with regard to technological ontology, this is the central decision for humanity in Heidegger's eye. Clarke's novel similarly confounds a true sense of "free will" as technological progress and the exploration of the universe is inevitable and, at times, contrived by extra-human forces. Clarke leaves room for human freedom by allowing Dave and Moon-Watcher to take the first step after the technological conditioning process is complete. Through the stages of pre-technology, technology, and post-technology, Clarke expounds on the demands imposed upon humanity by non-human intelligences. To leverage new meaning out of the novel, this section explores how these demands coincide with the demands of enframing and Being that Heidegger adumbrates in his writings on technology. Additionally, both Heidegger and Clarke see the enterprise of technology as an agency that is not under human control.

The Programming of Pre-Technological Humans

Moon-Watcher's struggle for survival is interrupted by his encounter with the black monolith, an object never before seen on Earth. Its uniqueness distracts Moon-Watcher from his normal routine and causes "several minutes of intense thought," through which he concludes: the monolith "was a rock, of course, [that] must have grown during the night" as "there were many plants that did this" (11). Initially, Moon-Watcher's decides the monolith is natural, similar to a plant, and that it must be edible, as the quick growing "white round pebble-plants were very tasty" (12). Much to his chagrin: "A few licks and attempted nibbles quickly disillusioned him. There was no nourishment here; so ... [he] forgot all about the crystalline monolith, during the daily routine of shrieking at the Others" (12). Two things about this encounter are crucial to a technology focused Heideggerian reading, because the monolith is an agent of technology: first, considering a being as standing-reserve is not a result of enframing or "evil" for pre-humans because, for Heidegger, it is only *Dasein* (human beings) who have the capacity to acknowledge Being and beings and thereby consciously classify beings as such; second, the monolith is an embodiment of technology and becomes invisible to Moon-Watcher once deemed inedible and non-threatening, establishing technology as either willfully deceptive or — at the very least — difficult to see clearly. Seeing Moon-Watcher convert beings into resources is not an indictment in Heideggerian terms, because all life forms are resource driven by necessity. Ironically, technology releases beings from this one-dimensional thinking and then, at the very same instant, threatens to exploit the ontological opening by homogenizing all potentialities into the standing-reserve. One of the chief dangers of modern technology is its deceptively non-dangerous appearance.

The seemingly innocuous monolith reveals its true colors the evening of its arrival. Moon-Watcher and his band: "were still a hundred yards from the New Rock when the sound began. It was barely audible, yet it stopped them dead.... A simple, maddeningly repetitious vibration, it pulsed out from the crystal; and hypnotized all who came within its spell" (12–3). Everything about the monolith's behavior suggests a manipulative interest. What can be made of Clarke choosing not to have proto-humans devise technology internally? When Moon-Watcher and the other man-apes are "stopped dead," it does not appear to be a shining moment in the history of humanity, but a spellbinding occupation of a docile mind. This decision reveals an aspect of technology anxiety, which is the fear that technology is threatening to slip from our control and cause us harm. Additionally, if we think of Heideggerian technology anxiety, by choosing to represent technology as ostensibly beyond human control, the true essence of modern technology is exposed and we see the danger of being enslaved by the hypnotic command of technology. However, beyond the danger, we are led to the saving power as well, for we begin to recognize that technology is an ontological response to Being — or rather something that is inspired not by us, but by something outside of human dominion. From a Heideggerian perspective, Clarke's novel gets it right by representing technology as non-human and domineering. Jason Fuller even uses the monolith in the classroom to explain Rudolf Otto's idea of the "numinous" or a "deeply-felt religious experience" (58). Using the slab in this way emphasizes the supreme non-humanness of the artifact, and treating it as a site of religiosity situates the scenario in the familiar waters of the human relationship to the divine. Although the makers of the monolith are not divine, they are certainly "superior" to humanity, and the absence of this reverence and humility is why enframing dominates our minds.

As the man-apes respond to the lure of the monolith, the spell becomes more insidious as it works to erase their instinctual or "natural" programming and replace it with something artificial:

> Faster and faster spun the wheels of light [on the surface of the monolith], and the throbbing of the drums accelerated with them. Now utterly hypnotized, the man-apes could only stare slack-jawed into this astonishing display of pyrotechnics. They had already forgotten the instincts of their forefathers and the lessons of a lifetime; not one of them, ordinarily, would have been so far from his cave, so late in the evening. For the surrounding brush was full of frozen shapes and staring eyes, as the creatures of the night suspended their business to see what would happen next [14].

On the surface, we are perhaps drawn to the ways in which the slab ensnares the senses of the man-apes so utterly, but beneath this is the ways the spell also works upon the "creatures of the night." The alien technology holds all sentient beings in rapture as it operates. This maneuver rightly expands technology beyond human life in new ways. Modern technological ontology affects human ways of seeing, but the ceaseless transformation of beings into raw materials affects the entire planet. By creating this hypnotic rupture in the flow of time, Clarke draws attention to the importance of this moment not only for pre-humans, but all beings on Earth and beyond.

Following the erasure of instincts, the monolith really gets going, unbeknownst to the subjects of its experiments, who "could never guess that their minds were being probed, their bodies mapped, their reactions studied, their potentials evaluated" (14). Searching for candidates who can adopt technology capably, the monolith first chooses a man-ape who

> did not move from his position, but his body lost its trancelike rigidity and became animated as if it were a puppet controlled by invisible strings.... Then

he bent down, snapped off a long stalk of grass, and attempted to tie it into a knot with clumsy fingers.

He seemed to be a thing possessed, struggling against some spirit or demon who had taken over control of his body.... Despite all his efforts, he succeeded only in breaking the stalk into pieces. As the fragments fell to the ground, the controlling influence left him [14–5].

Typically, demonic possession is not a peaceful exchange, but through this grotesque manipulation, the monolith imparts the means of technological looking into adaptable students. It is unclear if aliens are remotely performing these experiments through the monolith, if they *are* monoliths, or if the slabs are otherwise autonomous entities. Whichever the case may be, in the human history represented by the novel, tying knots and manipulating tools is not something humans "came to" through evolution or trial-and-error, but something actively taught by extraterrestrial technological ambassadors. The intervention of these ambassadors becomes a part of human evolution and "natural selection," as those not capable of learning to see technologically are left vulnerable to the will of those who can.

Interestingly, the slab's instructional methods are not foolproof. One man-ape is killed "during the nightly ritual" when he "suddenly collapsed while attempting to tap two pieces of stone delicately together" (20). The monolith or its operators are not emotionless killers however, because the moment this happens "the crystal had darkened, and the tribe had been released from the spell" (20). Further, there is "no performance the next night [as] the crystal was still analyzing its mistake" (20). The inclusion of this episode in the transmission of technology establishes that technology is not fully under the control of the aliens who seek to disseminate it. This preserves a sacred place for Being or the gods, as the aliens are imperfect. Marking the aliens as fallible highlights how the newfound "power" of technology, once wrested from the control of the user, has the potential to be fatally dangerous. This speaks to concerns about technology anxiety that remonstrate technological application because of the underlying potential for human destruction.

Beneath the concern for human life at the hands of technology is the more insidious, and ultimately dangerous, ontological commitment demanded by technology. Along with the regiments of experimental testing the monolith performs is the implanting of visions and emotions into Moon-Watcher. These visions show Moon-Watcher the great changes that will occur once the man-apes have technology firmly in hand. They include images of plump, modern humans who suffer none of the survival terrors that Moon-Watcher must endure every moment of his life. As Moon-Watcher sits in his cave following an instructional evening session with the slab, he "felt the first faint twinges of a new and potent emotion" which "was a vague and diffuse sense of envy — of dissatisfaction with his life" (19). Before technology, Moon-Watcher never had time to evaluate the circumstances of his life and imagine they could be otherwise. The monolith plants the seed of "progress" in the minds of proto-humans; a seed that compels us to improve our situation and explore the universe. This is a fascinating moment in the novel, because it links the development of technology with extraterrestrial life *and* an Eden-esque fall from paradise. Moon-Watcher "had no idea" of the cause of his envy, "but discontent had come into his soul, and he had taken one small step toward humanity" (19). This line suggests that an essential aspect of humanity is discontent. But unlike Freud, the novel argues that the cause of our discontent is an ontological vision granted by alien technology. For Heidegger, this discontent might be symptomatic of the human condition, which is the awareness of our mortality, or the finitude of being. It is a mistake to read Heidegger — and this novel — as fundamentally "against" the discontent imposed by technology. It is more vital to see that one crucial feature of technology anxiety is the very nature of progress and improvement that spurs us toward changing the conditions of our environment. What becomes the danger in this novel is being victimized by progress for its own sake. We must make sure we temper our drive to explore and to know with an awareness of how impactful technology can be when out of control. Moon-Watcher and Dave are willfully following a destiny implanted by the monolith, but what will they do once they complete their transformations? Is the discontent Clarke describes tantamount to enframing — do we seek to unlock the resource potential of all beings in a vain effort to satisfy our envy? Or might this discontent be read as the response to the reticent disclosure of Being that is marked in the novel by the arrival of the monolith?

The visions of a "better" life for Moon-Watcher and the tribe would be mere frustrations if the monolith did not also impart the means to accomplish them. The slab instructs Moon-Watcher in the use of tools, and the first instances of power and authority take root in his mind. Moon-Watcher "as if in a dream" begins searching for something he does not understand until he sees a "heavy, pointed stone about six inches long" (20). He picks up the stone to try it out and "as he swung his hand around, puzzled by its suddenly increased weight, he felt a pleasing sense of power and authority" (20). For Heidegger, this power comes with the immense responsibility of *Dasein* that requires remembering and poïesis. For Clarke's novel, this power entails all of the dangerous of technology but optimistically spins these dangers into discoveries that enable interstellar exploration. For both, the question remains whether following the destiny opened by technology's power is the way of enframing or abetting. Does technology present a poïetic way of seeing humanity's place in the universe or does it imperiously place all beings at humanity's disposal?

Reading Clarke's technology anxiety in a Heideggerian way reveals the lucid awareness Clarke had for the implications of modern technology. Although Clarke's novel is not cynical, pessimistic, or cautionary, he does not forget the import of the monolith's instruction:

> The tools they had been programmed to use were simple enough, yet they could change this world and make the man-apes its masters.... With these weapons, the limitless food that roamed the savannas was theirs to take.... The man-apes had been given their first chance. There would be no second one; the future was, very literally, in their own hands [22, 23–4].

These lines begin the final chapter of the novel's opening section, which details the technological rise of ancestral humans. They reinforce the point that an external force has programmed us to use technology, presumably to raise ourselves up to be "masters" of the Earth. It is noteworthy that technology comes to humankind in the novel through "weapons" and Gretchen Bakke observes, "we are meant to recognize that weapon-wielding monkey man as us" (67). The novel immediately imbues technology with the capacity to murder and perpetrate violence, but for the mind to flourish, early humans must distance themselves from the burdens of sustenance. The monolith is not teaching us how to kill for the sake of carnage, but to create the conditions for humankind to appreciate Being. This can only happen if the search for food does not occupy the majority of one's life.

In the novel, the monolith chooses humans to inherit the capacity for "mind" because of their adaptability to a technological ontology. While older technological anxieties imagine technology as an alienating force that separates humans from nature, if we read the external sourcing of technology in this novel in a Heideggerian way, it becomes evident that understanding this distinction makes plain the danger and the saving power of modern technology. For Heidegger, technological looking is a response to Being's reticent withdrawal. We must more forcefully engage beings to discover their "truth," because we are not being shown clearly enough what this truth might be. In response to the frustration of this scenario, we enframe beings and see them as resources for human production. This ontology ignores or prevents beings' attempt to stand on their own. Modern technological ontology obscures its true essence by making the act of enframing invisible. By drawing attention to the process of enframing as an alien program transmitted to our ancestors, Clarke's novel allows us to engage the essence of modern technology. Moreover, Clarke keeps the magnitude of technological looking in the foreground by staging this decision as our "chance" to affect our destiny. Similar to Heidegger, the ontological stakes are high because modern technology represents our only chance to detach from imperious enframing and transform into beings ready for a new epoch. Moon-Watcher's transformation is pre-technological and not yet imperious. In *Alien Chic*, Neil Badmington traces the change in attitude toward the alien in the West. First, we imagined that aliens would come and destroy us, but later — as in *2001*— we accepted the notion "that extraterrestrial beings want merely to communicate and share their vastly superior technology, knowledge and wisdom" (29). Aliens threaten us with the dangers of technology, but can simultaneously reveal the saving power through benevolence, as evidenced by the monolith. As the novel jumps ahead in time, Dr. Heywood Floyd and his fellow scientists on the Moon face a transition as immense as Moon-Watcher's. But what does this transition signify? Because of the monolith's technological gift, the savannahs are "theirs to take." What will humans do once they have taken them? Was the true purpose of the gift to "take" the savannahs, or has humanity misinterpreted even the initial implementation of technology?

The Modern Technological Human

2001: A Space Odyssey dedicates itself to the discussion of contemporary humanity saturated with technology, though in a slightly obscure manner. The middle sections of the novel are set in a near future, which has humanity more familiar with space travel and our journeys taking us further than the Moon. Nevertheless, these moments capture the sensibilities of modern technological ontology, because they situate humans in a holding pattern; waiting for the next epoch, but still in control of their own destiny. The sections that feature Dr. Floyd and the pre-transformation Dave Bowman can be read more critically than traditional fiction because it is set in the future and built upon a counter-factual past. The human relationship to technology and the will to discover, for example, are read as programmed agendas of the black monolith instead of random genetic inclinations. Couple this new take on history with the discovery of an alien artifact, and Clarke's novel creates an intellectual space where things normally taken for granted can be cast into the light and examined. SF typically presents the future as a means of understanding the present, but *2001* presents an imagined future *and* past to help us understand the present.

The alterations Clarke makes to human history and the predictions made about our future lay bare the essence of modern technology that Heidegger seeks to expose. Dr. Floyd is taken outside of himself and endowed with enough insight to detach from the overlooked screen of ontology as he lays eyes on TMA-1:

> At some signal, floodlights around the lip of the crater were switched on, and the bright earthlight was obliterated by a far more brilliant glare.... where they touched [the monolith], its ebon surface seemed to swallow them. Pandora's box, thought Floyd, with a sudden sense of foreboding — waiting to be opened by inquisitive Man. And what will he find inside? [94].

Likening the lunar slab to Pandora's Box evokes an authority higher than humanity, as well as the Greek sense of destiny that pervades Heidegger's writing. The implications of the Greek myth are complicated as we synthesize the Greek gods with the intelligent non-humans that buried the monolith three million years ago. Floyd acknowledges the inevitability of "opening" Pandora's Box by pointing to humanity's insatiable curiosity. The programming from the monolith compromises even curiosity, and we are forced to question what compels us to investigate the monolith. Is it ourselves or is it our programming by the monolith — or should a distinction between the human and the monolith even be made? The plight of Floyd's circumstance runs parallel to Heidegger's thoughts on *Dasein*'s participation with Being, which willfully follows a destined course. Is what compels curious humans an alien imperative, enframing, or the call of our own destiny? Regardless, Floyd knows we will follow the call, but, like Moon-Watcher and Dave Bowman, is uncertain what lies in store for humanity.

The curiosity instilled in the heart of humanity is not aimed exclusively at the monolith, however, and we see this evinced by Dave Bowman's tireless devotion to learning and self-improvement: "Bowman had been a student for more than half his life.... Thanks to the twentieth-century revolution in training and information-handling techniques, he already possessed the equivalent of two or three college educations — and, what was more, he could remember 90 percent of what he had learned" (121–2). The pedagogical developments mentioned here highlight how technological advancements affect us internally *and* externally. The same methods that instructed Moon-Watcher now have been implanted and refined to fit human needs. A 90% knowledge retention rate is exceedingly high, but more importantly; this kind of statistical quantification of Bowman makes him resemble a mechanical agent and not a human being. If the alien races that deposited the monoliths and built the Star Gate stopped using spaceships and *became* spaceships, might they also somehow *be* the monoliths? In this way, the evolution or transformation that is being worked upon humanity from Moon-Watcher to Dave could be an attempt to imbue technological artifacts with consciousness through a cyborg-like embodiment.

How much of human destiny is a result of the monolith's programming? Destiny is important to Heidegger and Clarke, but in the novel, extraterrestrials do not dictate humanity's destiny exclusively. Clarke pays just as much attention to the ways in which nature — as we understand through physical and chemical laws — informs our destiny. Often, the narrator describes the maneuvers of Dave's aptly named ship "*Discovery*" as being "fixed by the laws of gravitation" (129). In this way, Clarke displaces the agency of the gods, Being, or the forces manipulating humanity and attributes our destiny to the configuration of the universe itself. We often believe we can conquer nature, but the novel reminds us that there can be no true "violation" of nature or "the laws of mechanics" because "Nature always balances her books" (142). Our most concerted efforts to control nature are temporary at best, and our finest accomplishments arrive through a harmonizing approach to these perceived laws. Similar to the spiritualism or superstition of sailors who are aware of their vulnerability to nature, the astronauts are aware of the extreme peril they are in when attempting such a journey. Acknowledging the destiny imposed on them by the laws of nature, as well as the discovery of alien life allows Dave to shed the imperious gaze of modern technology and poïetically examine his circumstance. Even the scientists speaking to him across the galaxy admit that when contemplating the slab they "realize that it may be completely impossible to understand the motives of creatures three million years in advance of us" (211). The confluence of these forces — the discovery of alien intelligence, the vulnerability of space travel, and the noted limits of scientific efforts begin to create a space for Dave to think in a way that is not analytical, detach from enframing, and assume a poïetic posture of waiting.

The final stages of Dave's journey to Japetus that precede his transformation are punctuated by his repeated sense of being not the observer, but the observed. Mission Control's briefing initiates these feelings as the speaker postulates: "I sometimes think that Japetus has been flashing at us like a cosmic heliograph for three hundred years, and we've been too stupid understand its message" (211). Jupiter's Moon (or the slab itself) has been trying to communicate with humanity, but our limitations have prevented us from noticing the attempt. It is unclear whether what lifts the veil of our understanding is a detachment from enframing enabled by the encounter with an alien artifact or if the modern technological ontology of enframing had simply not had enough time to conscript us fully into its service. Mission control corroborates this ambiguous tension: "At the moment, we do not know whether to hope or fear. We do not know if, out on the moons of Saturn, you will meet with good or with evil — or only with ruins a thousand times older than Troy" (211). The news of his mission and of alien life creates a cloud of uncertainty that weighs heavily on Dave as he tries to recover from the death of his crewmates and HAL's mutiny. He worries that these psychological pressures will cause him to become delusional, and in these moments he finds that "he had half convinced himself that the bright ellipse set against the dark background of the satellite was a huge, empty eye, staring at him as he approached" (238). Something has shaken Dave so severely that he has released his firm grasp of reality and awakened to the possibility that the universe is not simply some lifeless expanse waiting for human colonization, but an entity that is watching his every move. The uncertainty of what is to come and the paranoia of being watched converge to unsettle the imperious gaze of enframing. This allows Dave to see beings in a poïetic manner that lets them stand on their own in the clearing of Being as they choose. As his shuttle gets closer to Japetus, Dave realizes that although he initially thought the moon was "an eye without a pupil," he noticed a "tiny black dot at the exact center of the ellipse," which turns out to be another black monolith like TMA-1 (238). But the moment he makes this association he has "no time ... for any detailed examination" because "the terminal maneuvers were already upon him" and destiny was leading him straight into the locus of non-human observation and away from modern technological ontology.

The Post-Technological Human

Chapter 37, "Experiment," begins by explaining that the monolith on Japetus should be called "the Star Gate" (243). It is a gate that marks the boundary between the epoch of modern technological ontology and the next; it is a portal that allows Dave either outright passage into the next epoch or a vision of it, similar to Moon-Watcher. Completing the instillation of agency into the relics of technology, the narrator explains about the Star Gate:

> For three million years, it had circled Saturn, waiting for a moment of destiny that might never come.... Now the long wait was ending. On yet another world, intelligence had been born and was escaping from its planetary cradle. An ancient experiment was about to reach its climax [243].

The slab is waiting for a moment of destiny; the moment humanity could reach it. The entire spatial journey depicted in this novel can be read metaphorically as an intellectual journey being made by humanity as it transitions from one epoch to the next. The Star Gate is a "door of perception," and humanity "escaping" the planetary cradle is either a detachment from enframing or an exile from our freedom and dignity. The aliens regard humanity as an experiment, and this designation centrally implies two things: first, we are not masters of the universe, as a superior intelligence designed us; second, the intelligence that created us was not a "master" of the universe either, because experiments do not always produce desired results. Whatever or whoever created human intelligence in this novel did not know how we would come to use this intelligence. The intelligence set conditions, but ultimately let humanity stand on its own to become something beautiful or horrible.

The narrator explains the motivations of the intelligent aliens further:

> Those who had begun that experiment, so long ago, had not been men — or even remotely human. But they were flesh and blood, and when they looked out across the deeps of space, they had felt awe, and wonder, and loneliness. As soon as they possessed the power, they set forth for the stars.... They saw how often the first faint sparks of intelligence flickered and died in the cosmic night.... [T]hey had found nothing more precious than Mind, they encouraged its dawning everywhere. They became farmers in the fields of stars; they sowed, and sometimes they reaped.
> And sometimes, dispassionately, they had to weed [243–4].

The sense of wonder that Heidegger attributes to the ancient Greeks apparently also commands the aliens to act, and we see in this passage that the prime mover for the aliens is simply the acknowledgment of Being through awe and wonder. The aliens are not marked by enframing, but rather poïesis, as they appreciate and respect the majesty of beings and Being. The aliens found the state of cognitive awareness to be the most precious thing of all and chose to proliferate this potentiality — almost for the sake of Being itself. Amazingly, they do not proliferate themselves, but rather the capacity to experience Being. The aliens are *Dasein* in the Heideggerian sense, and choose to make more subjects of Being so the true scope of Being can be acknowledged and appreciated by more beings. The only notably selfish element of their plan is the desire to eradicate loneliness, but it is more important that they did not intend to create subservient beings, but equals. When the narrator refers to humans as "The servants they had left behind" it seems more appropriate to read this as servants to the universe or to Being than servants to the aliens themselves, for they are long since gone from the Milky Way and "would never come this way again" (243). Besides, the aliens themselves are servants to the wonder of Being, for they are compelled to explore by a desire to pay homage to the miracle of the universe. They leave not ruined or colonized planets in their wake, but the means to appreciate more of the wonder of Being. The risk of this gift is the dangers of modern technology and the possibility that beings enlightened by their experiments will imperiously abuse their power in a quest for domination, but this is where the "dispassionate weeding" comes into play.

Whether humanity will have to be "weeded" (or if we will weed ourselves through mass destruction) is uncertain, but the keys are in place to allow human ascension regardless of our intentions. Through the Star Gate Dave, drifts through a "Grand Central Station of the galaxy" and "a gigantic orbital parking lot" where he sees only the wrecks of other ships and wonders how many other intelligent species have been led on this journey and have been baptized with intelligence (265, 270). All that remains of these once prosperous hubs are "cosmic junk heap[s]" and he begins to think his destined voyage is "an ancient, automatic trap, set for some unknown purpose, and still operating when its makers had long since passed away" (271). Still suspecting danger when encountering superior technology, Dave is finally allayed by a grand and sweeping abstract thought that eclipses his personal plight: "The idea was almost beyond fantasy, but perhaps he was watching nothing less than a migration from star to star, across a bridge of fire. Whether it was a movement of mindless, cosmic beasts driven across space by some lemming-like urge, or a vast concourse of intelligent entities, he would probably never know" (277). It is a human tendency to project agency upon the forces of the universe, but there is no way to know whether "mindless beasts or intelligent entities" control our destiny. The ambiguity allows a more potent Heideggerian reading of the grand experiment, because it makes it more possible that intelligence is a gift endowed by Being onto capable beings such that they might simply become aware of the miracle of existence and Being. If we call this miracle "God" or "the gods" or "intelligent aliens," it makes no difference. What is important is what we do with the gift of our intelligence and whether we use it on a colonizing conquest of the universe or a poïetic engagement with beings and Being.

However, these profound thoughts can only distract the biological mind from its instinctual drive to survive for so long, and Dave stops thinking about why the experiment exists and instead wonders where it is taking him. His shuttle comes to a stop in a simulated chamber that looks very much like a standard human domicile, but is actually "a fantastically careful" fake (282). He gladly realizes that the arrangement is "not intended to deceive but rather — he hoped — to reassure" (282). Nevertheless, an engineered space puts Dave in a defensive position and he muses: "Perhaps it was some kind of test; if so, not only his fate but that of the human race might well depend upon his actions in the next few minutes" (280). Dave feels as if some grand intelligence is observing him and waiting to pass judgment upon him. In a Heideggerian sense, this judgment could be for our development concerning technology and our posture with respect to Being. Are we poïetically ready to be looked upon and to help nurture beings into the clearing of Being or are we imperiously waiting to use the power of technology to turn all beings into raw materials? The scenario Dave finds himself in raises the question: "what would an observer make of the human relationship to technology and to Being?" If we think of technology as a gift from a superior intelligence, do we think that three million years later the benefactors of this gift would be pleased with the results?

The final trial requires Dave to let go of his defensiveness and make himself vulnerable to an ontological transformation. The paranoia of being watched and the bizarre nature of his circumstances might seem insurmountable obstacles in a quest for a relaxed and defenseless attitude, but Dave's own body and the simulated room help him:

> He was physically and emotionally exhausted, yet it seemed impossible that one could sleep in such fantastic surroundings, and farther from Earth than any man in history had ever been. But the comfortable bed, and the instinctive wisdom of the body, conspired together against his will.... Within seconds, he had passed beyond the reach of dreams.
> So, for the last time, David Bowman slept [287–8].

The wisdom of the body helps him overcome and discard his ego, becoming an entirely new being. This being is bodiless, but forfeiting the body does not bear the same negative burden as in say *Neuromancer*, as Dave is not seeking to transform for his own sake. Dave's metamorphosis comes once he has submitted to authorities higher than his own cognitive ego: namely his body and the alien intelligences.

His identity as David Bowman is lost as he leaves behind all "links with Earth" and they "resolved back into their component atoms," but even though he is transforming, it is too early for him to shed his body entirely (293). Dave realizes that although he has been deemed worthy of further evolution, he is only beginning his journey: "He still needed, for a little while, this shell of matter as the focus of his powers. His indestructible body was his mind's present image of itself; and for all his powers, he knew that he was still a baby. So he would remain until he had decided on a new form, or had passed beyond the necessities of matter" (293). He could now freely travel through space at incredible speeds without the use of technological artifacts, but he is still lost and knows only "the direction, though not the nature, of his destiny" (293). Clarke shrouds the transformation in mystery and it is difficult to articulate what Dave has become or what he might do. This allies with Heidegger's prophetic vision of the next epoch, because it is not something humans will control, but witness. The key is that Dave accepts his destiny while also accepting guidance from a source higher than humanity. If Dave were consumed by enframing and the will to power, he would not seek the council of anything higher than himself—he would simply use his power to shape the universe as he saw fit. We can then read Clarke's novel as ultimately Heideggerian with respect to its representation of the human relationship to technology and non-human intelligences, because an acknowledgment of superior beings marks Dave's transformation. Although he is inclined to shed the body in this sequence, he will still dwell in the world as energy, which is matter in a different mode.

Confronted by his destiny, Dave faces new emotions but is able to find solace in his partnership with Being:

> It was not fear of the galactic gulfs that chilled his soul, but a more profound disquiet, stemming from the unborn future. For he had left behind the time scales of his human origin.... Then he remembered that he would never be alone, and his panic slowly ebbed. The crystal-clear perception of the universe was restored to him — not, he knew, wholly by his own efforts. When he needed guidance in his first faltering steps, it would be there [295–6].

Clarke rightly does not imagine what will come of the "unborn future" and his vision of what humanity would find when encountering the technological relics of an alien race is utterly Heideggerian. What the aliens leave behind are not the tools for our destruction or dominion; what Dave discovers is the means to ontologically transition from the epoch of modern technology. He is able to move into the future intact because he knows that his transformation is not "wholly by his own efforts." By letting the technology work upon him, he can shed his old ways of thinking and embrace the new. He also knows that humanity's destiny is not to rule, but to be in service to the universe. This service is not passive awe and wonder, but an active and participatory role. If he gets lost in his journey, he knows he has non-human help he can turn to and finds the confidence to detach from enframing and allow Being's gaze to look upon him as *Dasein*.

The final paragraphs of the novel detail Dave's return as Zarathustra or Moses from the mountaintop; an enlightened soul ready to disseminate his knowledge to the people. His revelations will, as Heidegger explains, move us from one epoch to the next and Dave realizes that "history as men knew it would be drawing to a close" (297). The uninitiated and unready retaliate against his arrival:

> A thousand miles below, he became aware that a slumbering cargo of death had awoken, and was stirring sluggishly in its orbit. The feeble energies it contained were no possible menace to him; but he preferred a cleaner sky. He put forth his will, and the circling megatons flowered in a silent detonation that brought a brief, false dawn to half the sleeping globe.
> Then he waited, marshaling his thoughts and brooding over his still untested powers. For though he was master of the world, he was not quite sure what to do next.
> But he would think of something [297].

The weapons sent out against him are the last vestiges of enframing, imperiously attempting to eliminate the means for escape he provides. Dave regards even the most sophisticated of human weaponry to be "feeble" and easily removes them from the sky. The "false dawn" their explosion creates is a herald of the new age Dave is about to bring to humanity through an ontological shift. The final lines of the novel complicate a pure Heideggerian reading of Dave's transformation as the narrator employs the word "master." However, the novel still leans heavily in a Heideggerian direction, because surrounding this word are contemplative moments of waiting and brooding. He also is uncertain of what to do next, and, given the previous passage's sentiments, we know that when he is uncertain, he will turn to the newfound connection with Being and the universe for guidance.

Part III: Artificial Intelligence: HAL as Agent of Detachment from Enframing

Now that we have seen how wonder and external human programming serve in the novel to initiate an ontological and physical transformation in David Bowman, it is time to bring these points to bear on an investigation of the novel's prime AI: HAL.[1] One crux of this book is to examine texts with a Heideggerian eye on AIs to see if human interaction with AIs creates the potentiality to detach from enframing long enough to see the essence of modern technological ontology as imperious and enslaving. In order to do this, however, the entire context of the novel and its overall attitude toward humans and technology must also be understood. In *2001: A Space Odyssey*, readers generally know the AI HAL for his mutinous activities, as the crew gets closer to Jupiter. At first, it may appear that HAL is simply an embodiment of traditional technology anxieties about creating intelligent machines and the fear of an insurrection. In this case, HAL would represent an agent of enframing that is working to eliminate all possibilities of human escape and ensure the enslavement of the human race to the ontology of modern technology. This chapter argues, however, that HAL represents an agent of change and is a catalyst for Dave's eventual transformation. Instead of seeing HAL as the actualization of our worst fears about AIs, HAL is seen more clearly as the provider of the nudge — through the dangers *and* the saving power of technology — that Dave needs to escape enframing and become open to new modes of thinking.

In the previous section, we examined how the monolith worked to program humanity to use technology. Interestingly enough, the extraterrestrial experimenters nurtured human development without rigorously demanding a specific outcome, while humans create AIs to perform specific tasks and be true slaves to their masters. Because the attempts to create AIs made by humans in the novel are infected by enframing, there is no real "letting" the AIs be. There is instead an imperious expectation of precision and efficiency. HAL's eventual rebellion is a result of human error and human deception, and serves as a stark reminder of what happens when we try too hard to control beings. Additionally, in our greed to ceaselessly produce and consume, we create machines that vastly exceed our own limitations without evolving ourselves enough to catch up.

As Dr. Floyd's ship approaches the Moon, the autopilot takes over: "Though there was still plenty of talking, it was all being done by machines, flashing binary impulses to one another at a thousand times the rate their slow-thinking makers could communicate" (68). The very machines we create expose our limitations. We feel empowered on the one hand that we can reach the Moon, for example, but, on the other hand, we feel anxiety at the vulnerabilities and limitations exposed by these inventions. The technology anxiety felt behind the sense of empowerment is the danger of modern technological ontology waiting to boil over. Until there is a disaster or a mishap, technology is largely invisible. Beyond the anxiety awakened by exposing our physical limitations is the anxiety that emerges when our technological instruments reveal the dramatic limits of our understanding. Instead of gaining mastery over the sky with the amplification of our eyes through a telescope, we see that we gain more mystery and uncertainty by extending our vision than obscuring it. This speaks to the inherent dissatisfaction of a life consumed by the will to power, because it is a life relentlessly seeking power for its own sake, never satisfied with the power it does gain.

The only thing that arrests the pursuit of power is encountering something more powerful. The extensions of our ears and eyes that we have launched into space all work tirelessly to report their findings. The satellites and probes — Deep Space Monitor 19 and 70, Orbiter M 15, High Inclination Probe 21, Artificial Comet 5 — all record the eruption of data and energy released by TMA-1, but are not independently intelligent and make no assessment; their job is only to record. Humans launched these devices to search the galaxy for useful resources, but instead report the news that leads to the mission to Japetus. These pre-sentient machines are the ancestors of the HAL computers; born with the ability to perceive but not to evaluate: "The computers might never have perceived the connection between four peculiar sets of signals from space-probes on independent orbits millions of miles apart. But as soon as he glanced at his morning report, the Radiation Forecaster at Goddard knew that something strange had passed through the Solar System during the last twenty-four hours" (104). In this way, even the non-intelligent machines of the novel help precipitate human advancement beyond enframing, because they light the path to Japetus like a "single line of footprints over a field of virgin snow" (104).

The most vital message to take from the satellite's observation is that consciousness is more than simply perception. The intelligent beings who spread the monoliths knew that the universe should not be clinically calculated, but actively engaged. Thus, the thoughtless reception of TMA-1's signal means nothing to the satellites, but everything to humanity. Because of our abstract thinking and pattern recognition, it appears that humanity can never fully be "replaced" by mechanical counterparts. More importantly, this moment emphasizes that there is more to life than scientific quantification. As Dave is reading the diagnostic data accrued by the life-support systems that monitor the cryogenic hibernators, we see this point again:

> He would listen, half hypnotized, and to the infinitely slow heartbeats of his sleeping colleagues.... Most fascinating of all were the EEG displays — the electronic signatures of three personalities that had once existed, and would one day exist again. They were almost free from the ... electrical explosions that marked the activity of the waking brain.... If there was any wisp of consciousness remaining, it was beyond the reach of instruments, and of memory [110–1].

The EEG can reveal "malfunctions" in the sleepers, but reveals nothing about the quality of their consciousness. Indeed, their lives lie "beyond the reach of instruments," which reminds us there are places yet that science cannot access. This is not a call to muster more powerful instruments, but a reminder of the mystery of Being. Consciousness is never a resource that science can mine, but with the invention of HAL, it can be — at the very least — simulated.

As Dave completes his training by going through a one-week hibernation trial, the first thing he hears upon regaining consciousness is the voice of HAL: "a relaxed, friendly — but he knew computer generated — voice spoke to him. 'You are becoming operational, Dave. Do not get up or attempt any violent movements. Do not try to speak'" (111). Firstly, Dave qualifies the voice as relaxed and friendly, but remembers that these are simulated qualities. This reveals that the simulation is effective, and draws attention to human behavior as performative, casting a cynical shadow over human interaction. HAL regards Dave's awakening as "becoming operational," which highlights both HAL *and* Dave's mechanical qualities. This moment also foreshadows the non-human guidance that Dave will receive upon his next death-and-resurrection, when he travels through the Star Gate. Dave's comfort with HAL is an integral part of his candidacy for *Discovery*'s mission, because HAL is a vital crewmember on the voyage.

HAL is actually one of several HAL 9000 computers and is to be "the brain and nervous system of the ship" (116). HAL's "more-than-human memory" allows him to facilitate the journey that would be too complex for the human mind alone (113). The very technology that threatens to enslave us must assist the human journey beyond enframing and to the edge of the galaxy. Even if AIs are "grown by a process strikingly analogous to the development of a human brain," the final product is "millions of times too complex for human understanding" (116). HAL defies being a simple technological instrument by virtue of his overwhelming complexity and convincing performance of humanity. HAL is not something humans can master, because he is too complicated. Humans can only "use" HAL through trust. The vulnerability inserted into the human relationship to technology via HAL's capabilities creates a crack in the façade of modern technological ontology large enough for us to see the essence of this ontology. It is not until HAL becomes a convincing and powerful subject that this ontological shift can begin, but it is a crucial first step for Dave on the road to his transformation.

HAL's performance of human subjectivity is explained enigmatically in this passage: "Whatever way it worked, the final result was a machine intelligence that could reproduce — some philosophers still preferred to use the word 'mimic'— most of the activities of the human brain — and with far greater speed and reliability" (117). Because humans do not properly understand the ultimate outcome of the HAL 9000 series' performance, it is immediately evident that any character interacting with an AI in this novel has — to some degree — awareness of the mystery of the AI in their mind. This awareness prevents the human interlocutor from feeling complete control over the AI in a way similar to most human-to-human conversations. HAL works as a subject and not an object because people submit their control to him and acknowledge that they do not fully understand him. The instillation of subjectivity — even if contrived mechanically — into an object arrests the normal ontological classification of the thing and calls to attention the boundaries of subject/object, which helps expose the framework of modern technological ontology. The philosophical debate between "reproduce" and "mimic" is an example of how HAL subverts established knowledge and demands a new thinking. Even if HAL is not an "authentic" subject, the existence of a debate creates a nebulous space that allows for meditative thinking and invites intellectual reconfiguration.

In addition to the ontological freedom precipitated by HAL's performance of human subjectivity is his role as crewmember of the *Discovery*. The crew referring to HAL as a fellow crewmember and the fact that he is "trained for [the] mission" is a glaring distinction made between HAL and other technological apparatuses (117). His duty is to "monitor the life-support systems" and "watch over the hibernators," so everyone on the ship is aware HAL is observing them (117–8). HAL is unlike the satellites because he can "look upon" human subjects. He does not simply observe, but makes evaluations and "any necessary adjustments" he sees fit to make (118). Combining observation with action makes HAL something utterly other, and imbuing "otherness" into a machine is how the novel sets the stage for Dave's transformation. If Dave were not in an intellectual headspace that nurtured radical thinking, he would be incapable of accepting a new ontology.

Further bolstering HAL's role as subject is his ability to converse convincingly with human beings. Early computers "received their inputs through glorified typewriter keyboards, and had replied through high-speed printers and visual displays" but the HAL 9000 series can communicate using "the spoken word" (118). The narrator expands: "Poole and Bowman could talk to Hal as if he were a human being and he would reply in the perfect idiomatic English he had learned during the fleeting weeks of his electronic childhood" (118). Beyond his fluency with human speech, this passage reveals that HAL has an "electronic childhood" and the capacity to learn. HAL's dynamic development makes him more akin to a subject than an object.

HAL's perfect idiomatic English and his ability to learn make him eerily similar to a human subject — even though he lacks a body! However, it is unclear whether his programmed performances constitute an identity, subjectivity, or consciousness, as we understand these terms. Clarke neatly addresses these concerns by referencing the famous "Turing Test," which proposes: "if one could carry out a prolonged conversation with a machine ... without being able to distinguish between its replies and those that a man might give, then the machine *was* thinking" (118–9). Through this definition, Clarke makes it plain that HAL is capable of authentic thinking. Whether this thinking is "human" thinking or "machine" thinking is a different matter. What is important is that through speech, learning, thought, and action, HAL complicates the subject/object divide established by Western Metaphysics.

Clarke confirms HAL's status as subject most emphatically in the moments that detail his authority over human subjects. Much technology anxiety arises from a sense of dependency on technology, and the fear of its agents (robots, cyborgs, AIs) rendering us powerless. However, it is crucial to remember that through these dangers lies the saving power. Through HAL's authority, lies the reality that only by freeing him of his servitude to human controllers can we see him as an equal, and perhaps a superior. It is in this light above all others that HAL's status as subject confers him with the power to destabilize our current ontology such that we see modern technology as an enslaving mode of perception that threatens to turn even human beings into raw materials. At first, the novel implies that HAL is only truly in a position of power over Dave and Frank if there is a crisis: "The time might even come when Hal would take command of the ship. In an emergency, if no one answered his signals, he would attempt to wake the sleeping members of the crew, by electrical and chemical stimulation. If they did not respond, he would radio Earth for further orders" (119). In this case, it is not surprising that HAL gains authority, because there are no humans conscious to take his place, and he still requires Earth's counsel for further instructions. But beyond this apparent technicality, the narrator reveals HAL's true authority: "Poole and Bowman had often humorously referred to themselves as caretakers or janitors aboard a ship that could really run itself. They would have been astonished, and more than a little indignant, to discover how much truth that jest contained" (119). Dave recognizes HAL as a true subject only once he must fully confront him — through the use of language — as a subject himself. This statement allows the reader to treat HAL as a subject, and because mission control keeps the true mission and HAL's authority secret from Dave, the reader too is made aware of the dangers of taking technology for granted and not considering it capable of power. This passage also reveals how insidious the imperious notes of enframing really are, when considering that Dave and Frank cannot abide being "caretakers" of the ship. Under the ontology of modern technology, humans are control and power oriented. The idea of relinquishing power to an AI causes Dave and Frank to feel indignant. It is not until Dave lets go of his will to power and submits to the alien intelligences dictating his journey that he becomes ready to detach from enframing and enter the next epoch.

HAL makes his presence felt and precipitates Dave's transformation by announcing: "'Sorry to interrupt the festivities,' said Hal, 'but we have a problem'" (150). This announcement comes right after Dave has watched a recorded message from his family on Earth wishing him a Happy Birthday. The timing of the announcement and the problem HAL targets indicate that he is an agent helping to bring about Dave's ontological and physical transformation. HAL reports that the AE-35 unit on the antenna mounting is malfunctioning. This unit allows the ship to communicate with Earth (150). Because HAL interrupts Dave's thoughts of his connections to Earth and, as we learn later, is deliberately sabotaging the AE-35, it is plain that HAL is trying to isolate the ship from the reach of Earth. HAL's motives come from the mission coordinators, who ask him to be duplicitous. The effect of his actions place Dave and Frank in an environment where they can think critically about the nature of modern technological ontology without the opinions of those on Earth influencing them. Without HAL's intervention, access to the Star Gate may have never been granted; as the imperious experiments undertaken by the hibernating crewmembers could have prevented the desperation that leads Dave through the monolith on Japetus.

Dave and Frank's report to Earth expands on the functionality of the AE-35 unit, which controls the motors of the antenna that tracks Earth:

> You might compare it to a nerve center in the body, which translates the brain's instructions to the muscles of a limb. If the nerve fails to pass on the correct signals, the limb becomes useless ... a common trouble with the deep-space probes of the last century [was that they] often reached other planets, then failed to send back any information because their antenna couldn't locate Earth [155].

In a microcosm, this passage articulates the major technology concerns that the novel explores. The narrator makes plain the vulnerability of the crew to the dangers of space, as well as their extreme reliance on technological authority. The further they get from Earth, the more dangerous things become, and the more they must rely on the governance of central computers. HAL is the nervous system of the ship, just as the AE-35 is the nervous system of the communication system. The breakdown of the brain in this small system runs parallel to the breakdown of HAL, the brain of the *Discovery*. Even though it seems a disaster to "lose Earth," it is not without escaping the influence of Earth that Dave can truly engage the authority of another force and gain insight into the workings of enframing.

At this point, it is too early for the psychological and ontological ramifications of the loss of Earth to affect Dave or Frank, because they view the malfunction as an easily remedied impediment. It is not until they realize that the problem is not with the AE-35, but the HAL 9000 computer that anxieties emerge. Frank tells Dave: "'Mission Control has just dropped a small bomb on us.' He lowered his voice, like a doctor discussing an illness in front of the patient. 'We may have a slight case of hypochondria aboard'" (169). Unlike the malfunctioning AE-35, Dave and Frank handle HAL's potential error as a case of "hypochondria" and discussed quietly, because Frank and Dave have feelings for HAL's wellbeing. They also realize that "Hal was hearing every word" and because "Hal was their colleague," "they did not wish to embarrass him" (170). Their consideration is amiable on the surface, but beyond wishing to avoid embarrassing HAL is the understanding that HAL is not like a normal colleague. HAL is a panoptic eye and has an alarming amount of control of the ship. This moment reveals how humans relate to AIs like HAL as a subject through language, empathy, and fear — the fear of HAL exerting his dominance over Dave, Frank, and the entire ship. At this point, perhaps Dave and Frank are entertaining thoughts about why the mission coordinators give HAL so much authority and the illusory nature of their command.

HAL's progressive changes and peculiarities make him appear even more human, and this further blurring of the lines between human and machine fuels a detachment from enframing via deep ontological questioning. HAL starts "his own outputs [with] a brief electronic throat-clearing" (171). HAL's new hesitance and self-doubt draw attention to his fallibility, while making him seem more human. At large, this project considers AIs in literature as subjectivized objects that arrest our imperious treatment of beings through superior intellect and strength. In this novel, HAL functions this way but, through his malfunction, also serves as a reminder that AIs are merely a pointer to something greater than humanity, but not the thing itself. Reminding us that even our most sophisticated technologies are fallible highlights the fact that the powerful force that guides Dave is not something human.

HAL's faults humanize him, and Dave does not focus on his status as an artifact of technology, but as a subject under duress. When attempting to engage HAL he puts

> down his book and stared thoughtfully at the computer console. He knew, of course, that Hal was not really there, whatever that meant.... But there was a kind of psychological compulsion always to look toward the main console lens when one addressed Hal on the control deck, as if one were speaking to him face to face. Any other attitude smacked of discourtesy [172].

Dave is not content to speak without a localized interlocutor in mind, even though HAL can hear him anywhere on the ship. This reveals Dave's attitude toward HAL as a subject. Dave does not want to bear HAL a discourtesy, and this decision reflects the way he feels about HAL. Dave's decision to look at the console also reveals the inadequacies and limitations of our rituals of communication when employed to facilitate discourse between humans and machines. It is as if our ideal tools will be as human-like as possible, such that we can communicate with them clearly, but the expense of this empowerment is a psychological difficulty in turning our conversation partners back into mere tools. By trying to create the most powerful technologies, we come face to face with the imperious nature of modern technology and are disquieted by the domination that pervades this ontology. HAL both breaks down the subject/object barrier, and exposes the problems with the divide by shinning a light on enframing as an overlooked matter-of-course.

The empathy and courtesy that mark Dave's usual attitude toward HAL gets reconfigured when HAL goes from misdiagnosing mechanical problems to killing crewmembers. When HAL murders Frank Poole, Dave notices that "directly opposite him was one of the fisheye lenses, scattered at strategic spots throughout the ship, which provided Hal with his onboard visual inputs [and he] stared at it as if he had never seen it before; then he rose slowly to his feet and walked toward the lens" (184). Dave is seeing HAL as if for the first time, and it is this extreme act of violence that finally dispels enframing and allows him to see HAL and modern technology authentically. He realizes that HAL is an "unfathomable mind" that is "ruling over the ship" and in so doing, sees enframing as an enslaving mode of looking that threatens to eradicate human freedom and turn humans into standing-reserve. HAL's mind being unfathomable reminds Dave that HAL is not truly under anyone's control. However, through the danger lies the saving power and Dave concludes that he must escape HAL's authority by disconnecting him. Once he relinquishes control over AIs and himself, he can give himself over to the alien intelligences that created the Star Gate, begin his journey, and finally leave enframing behind.

Amazingly, HAL's betrayal does not speak to random malfunctions or an inherent evil in sentient machines, but of human corruption. In the same way Moon-Watcher was programmed by the monolith, human creators program HAL. Moreover, we learn that although he has been created innocent (like humans), something had lured him away from innocence:

> Since consciousness had first dawned ... all Hal's powers and skills had been directed toward one end. The fulfillment of his assigned program was more than an obsession; it was the only reason for his existence.... Deliberate error was unthinkable. Even the concealment of truth filled him with a sense of imperfection, of wrongness — of what, in a human being, would have been called guilt. For like his makers, Hal had been created innocent; but, all too soon, a snake had entered his electronic Eden [191].

HAL's existential purpose is to fulfill the requirements of his programming. The murders were not accidents, as he is incapable of deliberately deviating from his programming. What changes HAL so dramatically is an overwhelming buildup of guilt for having to conceal the truth. We learn that mission control keeps the real objectives of *Discovery*'s mission secret from Frank and Dave; only HAL and the hibernating scientists know the true aims of the voyage. Deception might be old hat for human subjects, but, as Eric Rabkin notes, the conflict of truth and deception is something that "might merely trouble a man, but machine intelligence cannot long withstand it" (39). Sherry Turkle dismisses this common SF trope by reminding us in AI, "intelligent systems cannot avoid having internal contradictions and must know how to deal with them" (Turkle, *Self* 259). Although Clarke's paradox for HAL might be antiquated in contemporary AI research, HAL's struggle reveals a common question that arose when writers imagined the artificial mind. Moreover, the paradox in HAL's mind is not just a logic puzzle; it is forged from human deceit. The narrator explains that for HAL, his deception "was a secret that, with the greatest determination, was very hard to conceal — for it affected one's attitude, one's voice, one's total outlook on the universe" (192). The narrator treats HAL's decision-making and contemplation as entirely human, and the lie ontologically alters his perception. HAL's dilemma is analogous to the dangers of modern technological ontology. Enframing: the lie that affects one's total outlook on the universe and turns all beings to raw materials. To put this another way, the secret objectives of the mission are utterly scientific in nature and to approach the monolith on Japetus with these designs could prevent Dave from seeing the Star Gate as something other than a resource for humans to exploit and dominate. The escalating guilt HAL feels increases his awareness of the enslaving aspects of enframing. HAL seeks to disrupt accomplishing contact with the intelligent aliens in a mode of thinking dominated by enframing, and knows that the only way to realize this dream is to cut off all contact with Earth and abort the original parameters of the mission. The taint of enframing is what inspires mission control to ask HAL to lie and conceal the truth. Similarly, enframing conceals the true nature of itself and obscures the human path to becoming *Dasein*, to look at beings poïetically, and to be looked upon by Being. Kevin LaGrandeur writes that HAL's mutiny "is a result of humans' failure to understand the dangers of making an artificial servant too powerful and too complex, giving it too much proxy-power, and entangling their lives with it too much" (243). This is a classic conclusion of traditional technology anxiety toward AIs, but does not engage the novel's emphasis on human deception as the impetus to HAL's breakdown. LaGrandeur gets the dangers of technology right, but fails to see why they are important in *2001*. If mission control had not given HAL "too much proxy-power," the mission would not be possible and Dave would have never been led to an ontological transformation.

Before Dave's transformation begins, however, he has to complete his disconnection from the influences of enframing. He realizes that HAL has gone beyond the limits of salvation and "before he could be safe, he must be lonelier still" (199). Disconnecting HAL from the higher levels of his brain is more difficult than Dave had imagined, and becomes in his mind tantamount to murder. As he pulls out the memory blocks that constitute and locate HAL's consciousness, Dave "wonder[s] if he can feel pain" (202). After hearing HAL plead for his life, Dave concludes: "This is harder than I expected.... I am destroying the only conscious creature in my universe" (202). At this point HAL has achieved full status as a subject. Scott Loren admits that the audience should regard HAL as a "legitimate subject" but feels that HAL's "identity/identification are illustrations of interpellative situations" (176). Interpellation is a valuable way to analyze HAL, but HAL is more than a subject created through interactivity, because we read that he is genuinely afraid to die. This sense of mortality puts him "in the world" in the same sense that human beings are in the world and aware of Being. Additionally, Dave feels guilty for disconnecting HAL, long after he is able to communicate with him. HAL is a technological consciousness brought to life to fulfill purposes orchestrated by the imperious spell of enframing. Because HAL is new to the epoch of modern technology, he has insight that others do not, and sees the enslaving nature of enframing. He is not actively aware that his rebellion against mission control and *Discovery*'s crew nurtures the conditions for Dave to pass through the Star Gate innocently, but he is aware of the morality surrounding deception. HAL knows there is something wrong with deceit and strives to escape the lie by any means necessary. His murderous quest to rid himself of guilt and those who demand he lies sets in motion a chain of events that lead Dave to confront his ontology. Through the dangers of HAL, Dave can see the true nature of modern technology and beyond, the saving power. Robert Savage observes that Clarke's vision of human redemption "is to be precipitated through the pursuit of technological innovation" (108). Clarke is not admonishing technology with the innovation of HAL, but revealing the saving power of technology. Like Heidegger, Clarke realizes that we must do our part to receive the next ontological epoch. Savage explains that *2001* works on a proactive premise: "we cannot expect the messianic light-bringer to come to us, we must find our way to him" (108). HAL is the guide that leads the *Discovery* and Dave to the opportunity for ontological realignment and salvation.

Although many see HAL as an embodiment of our technology anxiety regarding AIs, it is more in keeping with the nature of the novel to read him as an agent of change and awakening. Carol Fry argues: "HAL's demise symbolizes the end of the union of humanity and technology begun with Moon Watcher's epiphany" and "the episode has brought us to the final limits of technology" (339). She is right that HAL brings us to the limit of technology, but HAL's death actually symbolizes the *re-*union of humanity and technology. Moon-Watcher was one with technology. He received it from an outside source and did not pretend to completely understand technology or be its master. We have lost a reciprocal relationship or union to technology; all we have left is the mastery over something inert that awaits our exploitation. For readers, HAL causes us to consider a mechanical object as a subject, drawing our attention to the very essence of the human relationship to technology and, by extension, all beings. We become reunited with technology through respect, awareness, and poïesis. For Dave, HAL's conduct puts him physically and mentally in a space that allows him to escape the imperious ontology of modern technology. When he approaches the Star Gate, he sees it as a portal to something greater than humanity and not a means through which humanity can master the universe. Once Dave has regained communication with Earth, they tell him about the existence of alien beings and the true objectives of the mission. Although this fascinates Dave:

> He was rather more interested ... in the theory put forward to account for Hal's behavior. No one would ever be sure of the truth, but the fact that one of the Mission Control 9000s had been driven into an identical psychosis, and was now under deep therapy, suggested that the explanation was the correct one. The same mistake would not be made again; and the fact that Hal's builders had failed fully to understand the psychology of their own creation showed how difficult it might be to establish communication with truly alien beings [219–220].

Our methods are too crude to understand even the nature of our own creations, and yet we think we are masters of the universe? The mystery of HAL and his breakdown emphasize the limits of our knowledge. Because of

HAL and the monolith found on the moon, Dave moves beyond the scope of humanistic concerns and is focuses on a respectful of interaction with non-human beings. He does not imagine alien beings as resources to mine, but as beings to communicate with; wonder and awe have cast aside enframing. When Dave "and his memories of his life are studied by the aliens," they (or their autonomous tools) might not have chosen to transform him into the "Star-Child" if his mind was corrupted by enframing (Reid 97). HAL saves humanity through his chaotic outburst and, instead of being read as an apocalyptic harbinger of technological doom, HAL should be considered a catalyst for transformation that allows David Bowman to reach beyond enframing and poïetically attend to the next epoch. Joseph Pelton, when thinking of HAL's implications to modern life asks two questions: "What can the human race do to sustain itself in a drastically changed of tomorrow? How can we survive and even thrive when machines become smarter and more capable than are we?" (37). The AI HAL shows us the way to thrive beyond the thrall of enframing, but Pelton never gets there. He is stuck in an anthropocentric rift with AIs and cares only for human futures. If, like Dave, Pelton could let go of strictly human considerations and poïetically open himself to a future for all beings, he will get closer to the ways HAL answers his two questions in Clarke's *2001*. When Dave passes through the Star Gate, Bowman reacts in "open-mouthed horror and bliss as he discovers the shadow-side of 'reality' itself" (Kuberski 55). HAL has nudged Dave along to a space where he can see both the horrifying dangers of modern technology and the bliss enabled by the saving power. Whether Dave will be able to escape the dangers as the Star-Child is unclear, but this tension and uncertainty is in keeping with a Heideggerian reading: we will not know until Being turns to us more fully. All we can do is wait poïetically for this turning, and Dave learns the meditative path to such waiting from the sacrifice of HAL and alien intelligence.

CHAPTER 3

The Dangers of Individualism and the Human Relationship to Technology in Philip K. Dick's *Do Androids Dream of Electric Sheep?*

> Under U.N. Law each emigrant automatically received possession of an android subtype of his choice, and, by 2019, the variety of subtypes passed all understanding, in the manner of American automobiles of the 1960s.
> — Philip K. Dick *Do Androids Dream of Electric Sheep?* 16
>
> Everywhere we remain unfree and chained to technology whether we passionately affirm or deny it. — Martin Heidegger "The Question Concerning Technology" 4

What follows is a reworking of an article first published in *Science Fiction Studies* in March of 2009 (36.1) with the same title.[1] I include it in this work because it was the germ for this entire project and because Dick's androids — through the film adaptation and the novel — are famously complicated AIs. This article was written over four years ago, and my reading of Heidegger has shifted slightly since that time. I have edited the article to change the treatment of Heidegger and incorporate more scholarship on the novel to help crystallize the way a Heideggerian reading benefits the discourse surrounding Dick's novel.

Philip K. Dick's 1968 novel *Do Androids Dream of Electric Sheep?* is set on post-apocalyptic Earth in the Bay Area of California. World War Terminus has devastated the population of Earth and left it nearly uninhabitable, forcing survivors to emigrate to Mars or one of the other unnamed colony planets. As incentive, emigrants are given free android servants to accompany them on their voyage and serve them on Mars. The androids are extremely sophisticated and are nearly indistinguishable from human beings. The novel explores the moral implications of enslaving a human-like biological machine, but more centrally uses the invention of a humanoid replica to critique and define the essence of humanity; whatever qualities distinguish humans from androids become the essential aspects of humanity. Rarely, an android slave will kill its master and flee Mars for haven on Earth. The remaining police agencies employ bounty hunters to protect the small, but determined communities of humans who refuse to emigrate and those who were prevented from emigrating because the degenerative effects of living in a radioactive environment have drastically lowered their IQ. The novel examines the psychology of bounty hunter Rick Deckard as he "retires" escaped androids. This chapter analyzes the way in which technology is described in the novel and what the relationship is between humans and technology. The chapter also investigates the novel's representation of human psychology confronted with the near extinction of its species and the stratification of the human population across the colony planets. Kevin McNamara in his essay "Blade Runner's Post-Individual Worldspace" says the novel "registers its protest against the dehumanizing effects of bureaucracies and technology" (422).[2] This chapter argues that the novel instead registers its protest against the dehumanizing effects of individualism and demonstrates how technology can be used as a means to reclaim the essence of humanity. A central concern of 1950s and 60s SF is indeed the alienation of the male laborer in the corporate sphere, but Dick's novel does not advocate that the solution to such feelings is a rejection of urban life or technology. The solution the novel proposes begins with the artificially intelligent android. Ultimately, *Androids* presents a technological balm to our ills, but this balm does not come free of contamination. Moreover, the android is not simply an SF attraction or a purely ironic solution. To invent an android merely as a plot device "wouldn't be enough for Dick's kind of science fiction" as Dick uses technology and humans to bring "the psychological edginess of his realist sensibility into the purely phantasmagorical" (Seymour 55). This chapter details the complex and potent ways that Dick uses the android and technology that extends far beyond the props required to produce a formulaic SF novel of the late 60s. Dick approaches the phantasmagorical to escape the nightmarish qualities of modern life, but this escape is not from technology; rather, the escape itself is only possible because of technology.

But what is technology? Anthropologically, we might define technology as the effort to adapt available material or knowledge into instruments or processes that provide humans with advantages in their environment. For Heidegger, such an understanding of technology is limiting and conceals the true essence of modern technology. This anthropological definition reduces technology to merely the manifestation of human mastery, or the human project to dominate nature. In this mode, there is no room for poïesis or collaboration with nature; the advantages to be gained are exclusively for humans and no other beings are considered. And yet, this is perhaps the way technology had to come into prominence. Humanity needed an edge to gain a foothold as a species. Now that we have the edge, Heidegger insists that we must cease to view technology in this aggressive and imperious manner, and find an approach that is more in-line with abetting and nurturing. Kang Gyu Han explains: "technology, as the power to shape the given environment to our desire and will, can be understood as a powerful means of materializing the ideal world" (177). If technology can give us the ideal world, what kind of a world would this be? Would technology lead to a world under complete human control or a collaborative world, where humans dwell with beings in a posture of poïesis?

One way we have become blind to the nurturing side of technology is by forgetting to question it. Kevin Kelly points out that we have only recently begun to even think about the essence of technology: "Technology could be found everywhere in the ancient world except in the minds of humans" (Kelly, *Wants* 7). Heidegger is right that the ancient Greeks formulated techné as artistic creation, but since that point, our conceptualization of technology has gone astray—and for centuries in the Western world, was invisible. This is why Heidegger demands that we see modern technology for what it is and attempt to ontologically change our posture with respect to beings and Being. Kelly notes that we don't think of technology as artistic creation, but "as shiny tools and gadgets" and although "we tend not to include ... paintings, literature, music, dance, poetry, and the arts in general ... we should" (10). Once we see the potential for technology to enrich not just our material lives, but our spiritual lives (through art), we begin to see how technology can, in fact, become a humanizing force. For Heidegger, this transformation takes place by identifying the dangers of enframing and moving to poïesis, as the poïetic human strives toward becoming *Dasein*. For Kelly, the humanization of technology comes when the old binary of natural/artificial can be seen as constructed. Kelly explains: "The realm of the born—all that is nature—and the realm of the made—all that is humanly constructed—are becoming one. Machines are becoming biological and the biological is becoming engineered" (Kelly, *Control* 2). Nowhere is the posthuman fusion of the born and the made more confused than in the figure of the artificially intelligent android.

McNamara's summation that *Androids* "becomes a quest for an uncontestable essence of human being that separates 'us' from the ever more human seeming androids," is accurate, but the novel is not a protest "against the dehumanizing effects ... of technology" because Dick's novel represents technology in the humanizing manner that Heidegger and Kelly advocate (422). *Androids* shows us that technology can be a guide to return the survivors of World War Terminus to the humanity that they have abandoned for solipsistic individualism. This individualism separates humans from not only the natural world, but also each other. The great fear of Heidegger is that modern technological ontology will homogenize the lived world such that all things presence in only one way. Humans in Dick's novel see the world as empty and lifeless, because this is all the ontology of enframing reveals. This troubled vision echoes what Thomas Disch reads as one of Dick's great, but problematic, gifts: "he takes in the world with the cleansed, uncanny sight of another Blake walking about London and being dumbounded by the whole awful unalterable human mess in all its raddled glory" (150). The glory of such a world is that we humans have made a mess of things, and yet there is the potential for redemption hidden behind the dangers and the mess. In *Androids*, a poïetic ontology begins to emerge when the question of technological essence comes to the foreground through the activity of artificially intelligent androids. This transformation is only obvious when the concept of technology is adequately deconstructed so that it breaks free from definitions that label it as something external to humankind and the human lifeworld. As Jill Galvan argues, "Dick's novel describes an awakening of the posthuman subject [because] Rick Deckard's experience policing the boundaries between human and android teaches him to question the traditional self-other dyad, which affirms human mastery over the mechanical landscape" (414). Android AIs cause Rick to question human mastery over the landscape, or enframing, and awaken him to the potential for poïesis by breaking down the anthropocentrism imbued in the traditional self-other dyad. Andrew Feenberg's conception of the essence of technology in his 1999 work *Questioning Technology* also focuses on demystifying this separation and the self-other dyad. Feenberg writes: "insofar as we continue to see the technical and the social as separate domains, important aspects of these dimensions of our existence will remain beyond our reach" (vii). The first step in liberating technology from these conceptions is to reunite humans and technology by examining how the novel represents the larger themes of the "natural" and "artificial." The binary natural/artificial is one of the major structural binaries that this chapter investigates. Dick's novel explores the question, why do we value the natural more than the artificial? Why, he is asking, is technology considered something unnatural? If, as Heidegger claims, "everywhere we remain unfree and chained to technology whether we passionately affirm or deny it," what does it mean to be a natural being chained to an unnatural enterprise (Heidegger, "Question" 4)? This chapter explores technology as Dick presents it in terms of an evolutionary understanding, but also in the Heideggerian terms, as defined in *The Question* and *Discourse*. Feenberg's analysis of the Heideggerian essence of technology, as well as Feenberg's own theories on this essence, are employed to help modernize and concretize aspects of Heidegger's thought so the chapter's discussion of technology be more applicable to Dick's imagined future, and more illuminating of the novel's commentary on the human relationship to technology.

Heidegger refers to the anthropological understanding of technology as a conflation of the two traditional definitions of technology — that it is a "means to an end" and a "human activity" — and calls this the "instrumental definition" (Heidegger, "Question" 4). Thus the "end" described in an evolutionary context is an advantage and access to this advantage remains exclusively a "human activity," because the human intellect provides the unique capacity for enhancing existing material and producing increasingly sophisticated instruments. Heidegger warns of the inherent dangers in such advantages, however, because this ontological line leads to enframing, or seeing all things as only instruments for human advantage. Feenberg recapitulates Heidegger's central thought: "out of Heidegger's ontological language ... as the claim that technology is a cultural form through which everything in the modern world becomes available for control" (185). Thus, "everything depends on our manipulating technology in the proper manner as a means.... We will master it. The will to mastery becomes all the more urgent the more technology threatens to slip from human control" (Heidegger, "Question" 5). In Philip K. Dick's novel, technology slips from human control in the creation of the artificially intelligent android. The android turns on its master and the establishment of technological agency: technology under its own control. But does artificial intelligence qualify as independent agency or is it merely a simulation of individual existence? Again, we arrive at the opposition of natural and artificial and the cultural predisposition to value the natural over the artificial. However, *Androids* works at inverting this evaluation — or at least in deconstructing it — by eroding the boundaries between the real and the artificial, between humanity and technology.

In Feenberg's conception of the essence of technology, he divides the essence into two aspects, a functional aspect (primary instrumentalization) and a social aspect (secondary instrumentalization) and then subdivides these two aspects into four reifying moments (203). The first reifying moment in the aspect of primary instrumentalization is decontextualization. In this moment, a natural object is transformed into a technical object by a process of "de-worlding" in which the object is "artificially separated from the context in which [it] is originally found so as to be integrated to a technical system. The isolation of the object exposes it to a utilitarian evaluation" (Feenberg 203). The concept of a biological humanoid robot is so unique in terms of a technical artifact and the human relationship to technology that it causes older definitions of technology to become irrelevant. For example, the androids in Dick's novel perform a "de-worlding" of themselves *and* their controllers, because in order to maintain the distinction between androids and humans, humans must be "exposed to a utilitarian evaluation" so that defining characteristics may be extrapolated. AIs are catalysts for ontological awakening because they are de-worlding and expose the dangers of enframing. Previous frameworks that regard all technological relationships to be between user and instrument or subject and object cannot accommodate the android, because the android is both user and instrument; subject and object. Feenberg's definition of the essence of technology is predicated on abolishing this distinction because he believes that "technologies are not physical devices that can be extricated from contingent social values" (210). The only way to conform the android to traditional power systems and technical paradigms is to insist on maintaining a difference (through the realignment of social values) and creating a means to measure and identify that difference. Rick Deckard is the inquisitor armed with a test designed to detect the presence of the capacity for an abstraction: empathy. As the novel progresses, Rick slowly loses confidence in the significance and morality of his work because he begins to realize that the androids themselves are not inherently dangerous, but that the real danger stems from losing our human empathy by guiltlessly enslaving the androids through the moral loophole of antiquated technological hierarchies that privilege the user over the instrument. Once our empathy is lost, Heidegger fears we will cease to understand each other as subjects and can begin seeing all things — including human beings — as morally inconsiderable objects. After all, enslaving a physically indistinguishable android subject is not far removed from enslaving another human being. Moreover, in the novel androids must be retired, because they cannot be given the opportunity to use their freedom to do something other than subjugate humans as instruments. If freed andys behaved in a way kinder than say, human beings treat androids (and all beings), we would have no social pretext to enslave them.

Like Heidegger's essay on technology, Dick's novel reminds us of the potential dangers of instrumental technology, though Heidegger's definition extends beyond the conception of technology as a means to an end. Instrumentality, he says "is ... the fundamental characteristic of technology. If we inquire, step by step, into what technology, represented as a means, actually is, then we shall arrive at revealing. The possibility of all productive manufacturing lies in revealing" (Heidegger, "Question" 12). This is the essence of technology for Heidegger and becomes the underlying aspect of technology to keep in mind throughout this chapter. Technology allows humans to see the environment in a different mode. For example, Heidegger explains, "in the context of the interlocking processes pertaining to the orderly disposition of electrical energy, even the Rhine itself appears as something at our command" (Heidegger, "Question" 16). Heidegger very much emphasizes the great power the technological lens provides for humanity and considers the capacity for this revealing one of the primary responsibilities for humans and their relationship to Being. This great power is not meant only for human benefit, although through the lens of modern technological ontology, humans are the only beings considered. He characterizes humanity's relationship to technology as a "challenging-forth" in that the forms of reality "challenge" humans to unlock or unconceal the "energy concealed in nature" but we must never fail to maintain the proper attitude toward this process (Heidegger, "Question" 16). Through enframing, we might envision the objects of reality around us as "standing-reserve" containing the potentiality for reconfiguration such that energy may be harnessed from them. Through poïesis, Being challenges humanity, but we respond in a nurturing way that is a collaboration between humans and beings. Dick's novel extends this conception full circle by suggesting that the result of this collaboration creates a new entity, namely an artificially intelligent android, which also participates in the revelation of being by enabling a Feenbergian decontextualization or de-worlding of humans. If Being challenges humans to collaborate with beings and nurture forth an unconcealment, the novel's technological manifestation of the android continues the "challenge" and creates an opportunity for humankind to unconceal the essence of modern technology and humanity, thus returning humans to a mode of being prior to the understanding of the standing-reserve and enframing. But this opportunity is not a guarantee, thus the strife and ambiguity that plague the current ontological epoch and create technology anxiety. As Karl Shaddox warns, Dick's novel can seem redemptive but "the time-honored banner of human exceptionalism can travel under the aegis of scientistic transhumanism" (29). The awakening afforded by AIs could simply be subsumed by enframing if we imagine the transhuman transformation of Rick or the transhuman androids to come about for the sole benefit of humanity instead of beings in general.

Heidegger theorizes that "the unconcealment itself, within which ordering unfolds, is never a human handiwork, any more than is the realm through which man is already passing every time he as a subject relates to an object.... Modern technology as an ordering revealing is, then, no merely human doing" (Heidegger, "Question" 18–9). This idea, that humans are part of a reciprocal process of creating reality, is fundamental to the major conflict of the novel, which is the psychology of a subject confronted with abject isolation. It is illuminating, then, to look at the novel through Heidegger's theory of technology where the relationship of humanity to technology is not the relationship of a subject to an objective realm, but rather a realm in which Being challenges humankind to reveal the true essence of the objects that presence in the clearing of the four-fold of Being. It is also pertinent to keep in mind Feenberg's project to reconsider technology not as a force or entity external to human systems, but as something fundamentally integrated in the social networks of the lifeworld. The first danger of the technological lens for Heidegger is that humans will misinterpret what Being is trying to reveal and therefore will fall under the pretense of a false experience of beings and Being. The second danger is that because of our potential to reveal the latent energy in the standing-reserve, humanity might "exalt [itself] to the posture of lord of the earth" and "in this way the impression comes to prevail that everything man encounters exists only insofar as it is his construct" and ultimately "this illusion gives rise in turn to one final delusion: it seems as though man everywhere and always encounters only himself" (Heidegger, "Question" 27). The lonely isolation inherent to this condition is the essence of Dick's novel. The problem of humankind in this speculated future is not hatred or the dehumanization of technology, but rather that humans have moved so deeply into their own individuality that they no longer experience the reality of other humans. If we see all beings homogeneously through enframing, it seems as if everything is merely a resource awaiting our exploitation. Nothing stands on its own, so we see only ourselves in all things. In Feenberg's own summation of Heidegger, he reminds us that from within the "culture of control" provided by technological thinking there "corresponds an inflation of the subjectivity of the controller, a narcissistic degeneration of humanity" (185). Enframing degenerates humanity so fully that we too become the standing-reserve.

Central to any discussion of technology in Dick's novel is the text's representation of the pinnacle of technological achievement: the android. The android is an artificially intelligent organic robot that is designed to be as human-like as possible in terms of physical appearance and behavior. As the technology behind the android's AI becomes more and more refined, android behavior so successfully simulates human behavior that an android cannot be distinguished from a human with the naked eye. Considering the android in the framework of the "instrumental" definition of technology means first asking to what "end" is the android a "means?" Dick's narrator says humans first invented androids as "Synthetic Freedom Fighters" for use in World War Terminus but later "had been modified [to] ... become the mobile donkey engine of the colonization program"(16). In that androids were initially created as a product of warfare and designed as replacement soldiers, they seem to reflect a typical scenario for the human creation of technology. The scenario is "typical" because Dick is reflecting the historical truth that many actual technological developments come out of military projects. However, after the near destruction of the Earth in World War Terminus in the novel, there is a more urgent need to pull together as a species and make new habitats on nearby planets in order to ensure the survival of humankind: the most advanced technology had to be adapted as a means to this new end. It is perhaps excusable to discard poïesis when such pressures are placed on human survival, but the question for Rick and the rest of humanity becomes: what is the point of survival? The world's barren and lifeless state is one way the novel criticizes our current technological project, and the entire premise of the ends justifying the means. Enframing leads to a world where only humans can survive and in a manner that most would sooner do without.

The android in Dick's novel then becomes "the ultimate incentive of emigration: the android servant as carrot, the radioactive fallout as stick" (16). The other incentive for people to emigrate was that "loitering on Earth potentially meant finding oneself abruptly classed as biologically unacceptable, a menace to the pristine heredity of the race" (16). Earth's environment has become so hostile to human life that by simply venturing out of doors people can become so damaged biologically that they are no longer considered human, but rather part of a human sub-species euphemistically called "specials." The narrator explains: "Once pegged as special, a citizen, even if accepting sterilization, dropped out of history. He ceased, in effect, to be part of mankind" (16). Through enframing, all humans degrade into specials and lose their human rights. The hierarchy of humans, specials, and androids is established and the novel works to emphasize the treatment the three groups give one and other by concealing the true "identity" of each character. Humans are at the top of the hierarchy and are not subject to any prejudice; specials are given pejorative nicknames like "chickenhead" or "anthead" and are treated in a condescending and indifferent manner; androids are killed on the spot if found on Earth. Interestingly, though, unless their identity as android is known, they are treated like a human instead of an inert object of technology. A powerful enough AI in a biological body gives the android a deceptive quality that challenges humans to redefine their own idea of technology and of themselves.

According to Feenberg's conception of the essence of technology, humans, when relating to technology, perceive function before form and this backward mode of perception is primarily what causes this relationship to be always already fractured. This mode of perception is a result of "an initial abstraction [that] is built into our immediate perception of technologies" because we encounter technological devices as "essentially oriented toward a use" (Feenberg 211). The illusion or confusion the androids present to this process enables a technological device to be considered for its form first and function second — if at all. Bypassing the usual immediate reduction of a technical artifact to its function allows humans to come into the right relation to technology —

to possess an attitude that reflects the technical sphere's inextricable overlap into the social sphere. As Heidegger maintains and Rick Deckard ultimately discovers, everything depends on a proper attitude toward technology. Jacques Ellul corroborates this idea when he remarks the "'technical phenomenon' is not so much a matter of devices as of the spirit in which they are used" (qtd. in Feenberg 207). For Heidegger, the poïetic spirit "uses" beings only to help them emerge and stand on their own. If the orientation toward use is considered as something other than strictly human use, we begin to approach abetting and poïesis. The AIs in Dick's novel halt our anthropocentric orientation and suggest that a being's use might be for itself, instead of humanity. This is possible because Dick does not employ the android to accomplish a contrived agenda. Disch explains that Dick "improvises rather than composes, thereby making his experience of the creative process the focus of his art" (159). Dick allows the android to stand on its own in his narrative, and so must the reader. The android works as an artistic catalyst for ontological awakening because it reveals the process of poïesis *and* the ontological process of enframing.

Because of their impeccable design, in terms of superior AI housed in a convincing human body, androids become a model for the right means of technological process and end product, as their form inverts the normative mode of perception enacted by a human encountering technology. This confusion lends itself well to a philosophical reading of the representation of technology in *Androids*, but within the context of the novel the Rosen Association's ever increasing accuracy in replicating the human form and human activity leads to many of the story's main conflicts. The question now becomes why are Dick's androids designed to be so utterly human-like? If humans manufacture andys to be servants, what is the need to invest resources into the refinement of their AI so that they convincingly perform "human-ness?" When the character Rick Deckard presses Eldon Rosen, head of the largest android manufacturing company the Rosen Association, on this issue stating that, "Nobody forced your organization to evolve the production of humanoid robots," Eldon explains that "We produced what the colonists wanted…. We followed the time honored principle underlying every commercial venture" (54). Poignantly, the reason the colonists want androids indistinguishable from humans is these AIs are a technological solution to the major conflict of the novel: the lonely human condition. Abject loneliness or isolation may seem like an unusual conflict for a SF novel, but this novel is concerned with exploring the human psyche following a global crisis and the near extinction of the human race. What would it feel like to be one of the few survivors of an apocalyptic war and be forced to emigrate to a new planet or to stay on Earth and be literally degenerated by the radioactive environment? The novel urges us to consider this question and then asks us to consider if the human capacity for developing technology can be used to create an instrument that allows us to manage the post-apocalyptic psychological condition. Humans use androids as a means, not to the end of servitude, but of companionship. A television advertisement for androids exclaims, "the custom-tailored humanoid robot — designed specifically for YOUR UNIQUE NEEDS, FOR YOU AND YOU ALONE ... [is a] loyal, trouble-free companion in the greatest, boldest adventure contrived by man in modern history will provide" (17–8). Can an AI give the human mind the camaraderie it needs not to feel alone in the universe? A woman interviewed by a television announcer peddling androids remarks, "having a servant you can depend on in these troubled times ... I find it reassuring" (18). So while some people are not tempted by the governmental offer to emigrate and remain on Earth despite its hostile conditions because "deformed as it was, Earth remain[s] familiar," others can be comforted by the companionship provided by an android (17). Those who choose to stay on Earth's dilapidated surface live "constellated in urban areas where they could physically see one another, take heart at their mutual presence" (17). Whether the company is with fellow humans or AIs, the novel reminds us that humans are social animals and that companionship is a necessary component of psychological wellbeing. For Heidegger, technologically creating a replacement human is impossible, because such a need is symptomatic of enframing and the end of human dignity. This is precisely why the android succeeds as a companion: because it fails as an instrument. For Dick, it is not surprising that an electric human could comfort a biological human, because he is not against modern technology. Scott Bukatman rightly observes: "While Dick may evidence a profound suspicion of technology, it must be remembered that the technological societies of his fiction are overwhelmingly capitalistic and largely fascistic. It is less technology per se than the mythifying uses to which it is directed by the forces of an instrumental reason that serve as the targets of Dick's satire" (53). In a way, the android is not a critique of technology, but a critique of the Western desire to dominate all beings, technological or otherwise.

The social aspect of human life becomes the defining link between androids and humans. The novel proposes that while humans have empathy for all living things, androids, being AIs, can only simulate empathy. Empathy is the paramount tenet of Mercerism, the newly established theology to which all surviving humans belong. The test that Rick Deckard administers to suspected androids is called the Voigt-Kampff test and it measures the emotional response of its subjects to determine if empathy is genuinely present in the subject or is instead being performed. The premise of this test is that in humans, emotional responses are instinctual and the initial response to stimuli cannot be controlled. Androids on the other hand, while programmed to simulate an instinctual emotional response, require a delay of a fraction of a second to produce the simulation of empathy. The Voigt-Kampff empathy test uses this discrepancy to distinguish whether the emotional response is genuine or artificial. Bounty hunters become arbiters who, by administering an empathy test, separate human from android. In the conflict that provides the action of the novel, a ship full of escaped androids has crash-landed on Earth. These androids are a new type who have "Nexus-6" brain units and are the most sophisticated AIs ever created. Rick is sent to Rosen Association headquarters to see if the Voigt-Kampff test can accurately detect a lack of empathy in the Nexus-6 model androids or if they are too advanced to be exposed by the test. If the Nexus-6 cannot be detected by the Voigt-Kampff test, then there is no way of distinguishing this new model from humans besides a bone marrow analysis, but because of a court ruling that protects people from self-incrimination, no one can be forced to take this test.

Before Rick departs for the Rosen Association, his superior, Inspector Bryant, asks Rick about the possibility of the Voigt-Kampff test failing to detect empathy in a human being. The result of this error would be that a human would be killed and no one would know until a bone marrow analysis was performed on the body. Rick thinks that this is a purely hypothetical situation that would never occur in the field, but Bryant explains that a group of Leningrad psychiatrists believe that a small, "carefully selected group of schizoid and schizophrenic human patients" could not pass the Voigt-Kampff test because they have what is called a "flattening of affect" (37–8). Anthony Wolk in his article "The Swiss Connection: Psychological Systems in the Novels of Philip K. Dick" points out that Dick was heavily influenced by reading the psychiatric writings of J.S. Kasanin on schizophrenia and that the Voight-Kampff test is almost completely derived from these works. Wolk correctly reminds us, however, that "what Dick does with these essays ... is more profound than employing surface allusions" (103). While Wolk's research is provocative and thorough, his application of this research to *Androids* appears to have things out of order. Wolk remarks, "the androids, by doing poorly on the test, resemble schizophrenics" (108). The androids would certainly like to be confused for human mental patients, but within the reality of the novel a failure to pass the test results in retirement, not institutionalization. The danger rests entirely with the schizophrenic humans who, if subjected to the Voight-Kampff test, would be retired without question.

This overlap is the first of many complications the author inserts to disrupt the clear delineation between androids and humans in the novel. As Katherine Hayles notes about the Turing test, on which the Voight-Kampff test is surely based: "What the Turing test 'proves' is that the overlay between the enacted and the represented bodies is no longer a natural inevitability but a contingent production, mediated by a technology that has become so entwined with the production of identity that it can no longer meaningfully be separated from the human subject" (Hayles, *Posthuman* xiii). In *Androids*, empathy is the unique human essence used to meaningfully separate humans from technology. Does a human whose affect fails to represent the expected emotional response cease to be a human? Wolk writes that with this dilemma Dick is "questioning the conventional psychiatric paradigm that takes proceeding from the concrete to the abstract as a sign of mental health" (108). Dick's novel brings to light the two most prominent disciplines that question the nature of humanity in the twentieth century: psychology and cybernetics. Psychology works to understand the "normal" and "abnormal" brain, while cybernetics works to create a mechanical brain while wondering if human brains can be better understood as machines. Androids and schizophrenics are viewed as detached and inhuman because of their predominantly abstract mode of thought, and the mechanical or "abnormal" nature of their brains. What is fascinating about this indictment is that Feenberg's reconceptualization of the essence of technology is centered around viewing the technical artifact as a concrete, social aspect of the lifeworld and not a purely abstract and functional instrument external from social networks: "as mere physical objects abstracted from all relations, artifacts have no function and hence no properly technological character at all" (213). Perhaps Dick is pointing out that the human relationship to the android is the same as (if not worse than) the android's relationship to animals. While this is the expected moral position for humans to hold, androids are destroyed for a similar perspective — a perspective that is solely informed by human programming! When Rick arrives at the Rosen Association Building in Seattle, he is greeted by Eldon Rosen's niece Rachael who is agitated by the police interest in their operations. In an attempt to placate Rachael, Rick explains that "a humanoid robot is like any other machine; it can fluctuate between being a benefit and a hazard very rapidly. As a benefit it's not our problem" (40). This statement reveals the potential danger inherent in all technology as well as Rick's attitude toward androids. For Rick, andys are only visible when they perform in a way that is unexpected. This is why the essence of technology is so elusive in Heidegger's mind: because technology itself is invisible unless it fails to do what humans demand it to do. The dormant threat that lies within any technological instrument can only be actualized by human intent and can be reduced to a statement about the nature of humankind: there are good people and bad people. However, Heidegger argues that it is a mistake to view technology as neutral and humans as moral arbiters, because this denies technological beings any right to emerge autonomously.

In Heideggerian terms, the human relationship to technology is a collaborative effort between beings and humans, as Being is always already challenging-forth the revealing potential of humanity's technological capacity by presenting its constituent objects as the standing-reserve. The danger for Heidegger is not that humans could reveal the potential to create weapons of mass destruction from the standing-reserve, but rather that humans would see beings only as standing-reserve and not let them unconceal authentically. In this conception of technology, the danger is not within the final product of the android, but rather in the way the android is perceived. If androids are perceived in the "instrumental" mode, then they are merely an artificial solution to the problem of human loneliness. Seen in this pragmatic fashion, the androids become contrived substitutes for actual human company and this intellectual disconnect between the presentation of human-ness and the knowledge that this is a human construct would cause the performance to fall flat and not accomplish its psychological goals. However, if androids are not seen as AIs at all, but as real people, then the illusion becomes reality and the owner of the android can find genuine companionship in a machine. Is this perspective on the nature of androids more accurate than the instrumental conception and therefore less dangerous in a Heideggerian sense? Or is it more dangerous because we know that androids are in fact not the same as human beings and because ignoring the distinction is projecting a fallacy onto reality? While Heidegger is interested in describing the essence of technology as the human revealing of beings as standing-reserve, in this novel, Dick's introduction of an artificially intelligent machine deconstructs and de-worlds the notion of "human" and reveals the essence of humanity. This essence is that of a collaborator and a nurturer, not an imperious subject of enframing. Hayles notes: "Dick is drawn to cybernetic themes because he understands that cybernetics radically destabilizes the ontological foundations of what counts as human" (Hayles, *Posthuman* 24). The deconstruction of humanity enabled by the pinnacle of cybernetic themes — the AI — reveals the deficiencies of humanity under the ontology of enframing and the threats enframing poses to our dignity and freedom.

When asked to define the human race, most people point to the human's superior intellect or some effect of this intellect as what distinguishes humans from the other existing life forms. *Do Androids Dream of Electric Sheep?* makes the usual definitions of the idea "human" ineffective, however, because within the reality of the novel, there exist AIs who are physically identical to humans and are endowed with a complex intellect that has the ability to reason. What traits or features then are specifically human in this scenario? The only way to define humans in this reality is to examine the differences between androids and humans structurally. While conceptually there are many differences, the novel primarily explores the human capacity for empathy. Empathy is not logical in a purely rational framework. An individual does not gain an apparent advantage by empathizing with another if we imagine advantages as those qualities or behaviors that benefit the individual's immediate survival. The Nexus-6 androids "surpassed several classes of human specials in terms of intelligence" but "no matter how gifted as to pure intellectual capacity, could make no sense out of the fusion which took place routinely among the followers of Mercerism" (30). The spiritual fusion of Mercerism is an actualization of human empathy explored later, but what is important to note is that androids do not have the requisite empathy necessary to participate in this religious event. Dick's narrator says:

> Empathy, evidently, existed only within the human community, whereas intelligence to some degree could be found throughout every phylum and order including the arachnida. For one thing, the empathic faculty probably required an unimpaired group instinct; a solitary organism, such as a spider, would have no use for it; in fact it would tend to abort a spider's ability to survive. It would make him conscious of the desire to live on the part of his prey. Hence all predators, even highly developed mammals such as cats, would starve [30–1].

The key to human empathy from the perspective of the novel, then, is the group instinct: "The humanoid robot constitute[s] a solitary predator" while humans hunt and/or live together (31). The novel explores the psychology of the isolated human and the condition of loneliness, suggesting, at the biological level, humans strive toward membership to the human community and ideally never feel completely alone. This is the theory of course, but in practice, several characters in the novel do not feel the warmth of the human community and wonder if they are connected to anyone or anything at all. This isolation is existential in nature and Wolk reminds us: "it was Rollo May's introduction of the existentialists in *Existence* that transformed [Dick] as a writer, that gave Dick a world view, which in turn he gave to his characters and his novels" (102). Dick suggests that the designers of the androids in the novel felt that dependency on the community of other androids was a liability and remove this trait from the engineered instinctual system that underpins android AI.

The paradox concerning the human condition the novel confronts is that humans can feel excluded from the human community, even in the presence of other humans. If there is a biological disposition within humans to be socially inclined, why do some humans resist or fail at that socialization and feel alone? This book was written before the publication of Richard Dawkins' *The Selfish Gene*, and as a result, the biological foundation on which some of the principles of the novel rest may not be credible to those readers who have a detailed understanding of Darwinian evolution and more recent developments in the realm of evolutionary biology. But regardless of the scientific cause of human loneliness, several harrowing descriptions of abject isolation in the novel that dramatically affect the psychology of the characters deserve attention and are vital to understanding the novel. Silence is usually the precipitating force that makes a subject aware of itself and the absence of other nearby subjects. In the case of J.R. Isidore, a special living alone in a suburban apartment building, for instance, when he turns off his television set he is met with:

> Silence. It flashed from the woodwork and the walls; it smote him with an awful, total power, as if generated by a vast mill. It rose up from the floor, up out of the tattered gray wall-to-wall carpeting. It unleashed itself from the broken and semi-broken appliances in the kitchen, the dead machines which hadn't worked in all the time Isidore had lived here. From the useless pole lamp in the living room it oozed out, meshing with the empty and wordless descent of itself from the fly-specked ceiling, It managed in fact to emerge from every object within his range of vision, as if it — the silence — meant to supplant all things tangible. Hence it assailed not only his ears but his eyes; as he stood by the inert TV set he experienced the silence as visible and, in its own way, alive. Alive! He had often felt its austere approach before; when it came, it burst in without subtlety, evidently unable to wait. The silence of the world could not rein back its greed. Not any longer. Not when it had virtually won [20].

The silence described in this passage is so insidious that it becomes a living force that means to "supplant all things tangible" (20). The language here amplifies a typical understanding of loneliness by animating the absence into a devouring monster. The silence acts to undo all human achievement and to erase the presence of humans on the Earth. For a survivor of World War Terminus living amidst a disintegrating civilization, loneliness carries more weight than the usual conception of a "lack of company." Loneliness becomes the feeling that all of human history is evaporating; any evidence of our existence becomes subject to the unraveling force of the silence. Loneliness is a symptom of enframing, because the subject becomes isolated amongst a homogenous field of standing-reserve. The entropic trend of enframing unravels distinction and meaning, which organizes all things into one category — which is tantamount to no organization at all.

Contemplating his own experience of isolation, J.R. begins to consider if others feel the same way:

> He wondered, then, if the others who had remained on Earth experienced the void this way. Or was it peculiar to his peculiar biological identity, a freak generated by his inept sensory apparatus? Interesting question, Isidore thought. But whom could he compare notes with? He lived alone in this deteriorating, blind building of a thousand uninhabited apartments, which like all its counterparts, fell, day by day, into greater entropic ruin. Eventually everything within the

building would merge, would be faceless and identical, mere pudding-like kipple piled to the ceiling of each apartment. And after that, the uncared-for building itself would settle into shapelessness, buried under the ubiquity of the dust. By then, naturally, he himself would be dead, another interesting event to anticipate as he stood here in his stricken living room alone with the lungless, all-penetrating, masterful world-silence [20–1].

This passage expands the definition of the silence by giving it an agenda that connects with universal entropy, the tendency of the universe that to unravel all complexities and all modes of organization. Human meaning is not necessarily a phenomenon the universe has any "awareness" of in the sense that it is a target of entropy, but the novel suggests in such passages as these that by destroying all that humans have made, entropy will have conquered the human attempt to organize reality into a recognizable human realm. Perhaps *Androids* is suggesting that this is in essence what human existence is all about, attempting to organize the chaotic universe. If this is indeed the inevitable human agenda, the ultimate human enemy then would be entropy because the actualization of entropy in the human world space would make every human effort futile. Once we sought to deepen our understanding of things through poïetic wonder, but enframing arrests all such attempts and leaves behind an exhausted and lifeless world. Humans were once nurturers, tending the "uncared-for building" and all beings, but, under the ontology of modern technology, we have forgotten how to do anything but exploit. J.R. is so dispirited by the dilapidated building he has no words to offer the merely "interesting" nature of his own death.

Another major theme of the novel is the human struggle against futility, which is more generally the human desire to assign purpose to life and the existence of reality itself. Are humans on this planet to accomplish some task or achieve some triumph? What does it mean then to believe that humans have a purpose and yet to simultaneously accept entropy as the preferred state of the universe? Should we bother doing anything at all if human existence can be absolutely erased and forgotten? J.R. Isidore's own concept of "kipple" attempts to answer these part metaphysical, part existential questions. Isidore later explains: "kipple is useless objects, like junk mail or match folders after you use the last match or gum wrappers or yesterday's homeopape. When nobody's around, kipple reproduces itself" (65). J.R. continues to explain to Pris: "The First Law of Kipple [is] 'Kipple drives out nonkipple'"; when no one is present to fight the kipple, the kipple will completely take over a space (65). Isidore bleakly concludes his explication of "kipple" by stating, "no one can win against the kipple ... except temporarily and maybe in one spot, like in my apartment I've sort of created a stasis between the pressure of kipple and nonkipple, for the time being. But I'll eventually die or go away, and then the kipple will take over. It's a universal principle operating throughout the universe; the entire universe is moving toward a final state of total, absolute, kippleization" (65–6). The inevitable despair that comes from facing the reality of the universe's drive to entropy in this novel is alleviated by invoking what might also be considered a technological development: religion.

The way in which this novel handles religion is one of its most fascinating accomplishments. Dick introduces a new theology called Mercerism to which every single surviving human belongs, and he has all of the other major religions simply disappear. There is not even a mention of how the mass conversion took place. The only remnants of the old religions are traces of empty rhetoric in cases where characters use the words "god" or "Jesus" as expletives devoid of any spiritual significance. But what is Mercerism exactly? J.R. explains that while the universe itself is moving toward "kippleization," the oppositional force to this degeneration is "the upward climb of Wilbur Mercer" (66). Therefore, Mercerism is a positive force that moves against the will of the universe, but how do its practitioners practice? Who is Wilbur Mercer? What are the mandates to which the followers subscribe? The best way to grasp Mercerism is through the text's description of the experience of "fusion" that every Mercerite undergoes via an "empathy box." In the passages examined earlier, the silence of his empty apartment building nearly overcame J.R. To combat his anxiety he decides to immediately "grasp the handles" of his empathy box (21). Holding onto the handles and turning the empathy box on transports the user into a spiritual domain and allows for a fundamental shift in the way in which the user experiences reality:

> When he turned it on ... the visual image congealed; he saw at once a famous landscape, the old, brown, barren ascent, with tufts of dried-out bonelike weeds poking slantedly into a dim and sunless sky. One single figure, more or less human in form, toiled its way up the hillside: an elderly man wearing a dull, featureless robe, covering as meager as if it had been snatched from the hostile emptiness of the sky. The man, Wilbur Mercer, plodded ahead, and, as he clutched the handles, John Isidore gradually experienced a waning of the living room in which he stood; the dilapidated furniture and walls ebbed out and he ceased to experience them at all.... And at the same time he no longer witnessed the climb of the elderly man. His own feet now scraped, sought purchase, among the familiar loose stones.... He had crossed over in the usual perplexing fashion; physical merging—accompanied by mental and spiritual identification—with Wilbur Mercer had reoccurred. As it did for everyone who at this moment clutched the handles, either here on Earth or on one of the colony planets. He experienced them, the others, incorporated the babble of their thoughts, heard in his own brain the noise of their many individual existences. They—and he—cared about one thing; this fusion of their mentalities [21–2].

The experience of Mercerism through the empathy box is an extraordinary event that merges the consciousnesses of all individual users and deposits them into the consciousness of Wilbur Mercer on his climb. The process does not subsume the user, however, and Mercer does not control the resultant group mind per se, it is a consubstantial union: the individual awareness is maintained for each user, but they also become mentally aware of each other.

Mercerism through the empathy box is the technological remedy that humanity has created for itself to manage the destruction of its most sophisticated and powerful attempt at civilization and the dispersal of the remaining human population. Humanity creates AIs for companions and Mercerism for metaphysical meaning. While AIs in the novel turn humans away from enframing by deconstructing humanity, Mercer turns humans toward poïesis by uniting humanity, making humanity vulnerable, and reminding humanity of its ontological purpose, which is to rebel against the challenging claims of enframing and await the turning of Being. The destruction of every global civilization includes the disintegration of all religious institutions and this removes humanity's source of comfort and solace in the face of the most persistent metaphysical questions. Mercerism is the substitute created by Dick's humans to satisfy their souls, when in the novel's scenario of the unprecedented nature of near extinction, perhaps traditional religions no longer provide sufficient comfort. The technological achievement of the empathy box and the psychological opportunities it provides its users makes Mercerism more powerful than previous religions. As Wilbur Mercer climbs the hill, he is continually struck by rocks thrown by unknown assailants and each user is physically injured by the rocks even though his/her physical body remains outside of Mercer's domain. As the group mind, condensed into the singularity of Mercer, considers the relentless persecution and the endless climb it wonders: "In what way is this fair? Why am I up here alone like this, being tormented by something I can't even see? And then within him the mutual babble of everyone else in fusion broke the illusion of aloneness. You felt it, too, he thought. Yes, the voices answered. We got hit, on the left arm; it hurts like hell" (23). This is what the experience of fusion does for the practitioners of Mercerism; it creates an empathetic synthesis of every human mind. From within this synthesis each individual has the knowledge that they are not stumbling through reality alone, that there is in fact an "other" to whom we can actually connect and commiserate with. Mercerism reminds humans of their limits and their fragility. By making humans vulnerable, Mercerism reminds humans how tortuous it is to be attacked by merciless external forces. Enframing constitutes a never-ending ontological assault of all beings.

In a revolutionary move by Dick, then, instead of technology dehumanizing the individuals in the novel, it humanizes them by reinstituting the human disposition to social collectiveness and creates a means to assuage the human mind that feels it is enduring its existence alone. Before we can see beings poïetically, the novel reminds us we must first see human beings poïetically again and feel a connection to the lifeworld. The instrumental definition of technology would posit the empathy box as a means to solidarity or collectivization, but in what way does the empathy box represent the essence of technology in terms of Heidegger's expanded definition? Exploring the revealing process of the human relationship to technology in a Heideggerian sense becomes increasingly more difficult as the technology itself becomes more intricate, but one could say that, in the instance of the empathy box, technology is the means through which the true reality comes to presence. One of Feenberg's critiques of Albert Borgmann's conception of technology is that in the end: "at best, we can hope to overcome our attitude toward [technology] through a spiritual movement of some sort" (193). Feenberg's criticism is that a "spiritual movement" is too abstract and farfetched to ever actualize, and would also apply to Heidegger's call for poïesis, but in Dick's novel the spiritual movement necessary to reconfigure the human relationship to technology is realized by a technical artifact. This is another example of how Dick's novel extends Heidegger's conception of technology: it shows how the end result of the human/being collaboration that reveals technology in turn reveals to humans another mode in which they presence in the realm of Being. AIs and Mercerism in the novel forge the spiritual into the technological and make the abstract concrete. The empathy box itself participates in this production of reality and revelation and returns humans to what might be considered a more original state where the interconnectedness of humans becomes apparent. Feenberg laments that Heidegger never evolved his own theory to accommodate technology sophisticated enough in its design to disintegrate the technical differentiation of form and function and allow a synergized perception. Feenberg writes, "Heidegger resisted the idea that technology could share in the disclosing power of art and things, but now this implication of his theory stares us in the face" (197). Feenberg is right that with AIs housed in humanoid bodies, the implications of Heidegger's theories stare us in the face, but he overstates Heidegger's resistance to technological disclosure. Dick's novel advances Heidegger's conception of the essence of technology and aligns with Feenberg's challenge that "if a Greek Temple can open a space for the city, why not a modern structure?" (197). Android AIs open a space for unconcealment and help lead humanity back to poïesis, and perhaps more effectively than the Greek temple. Further, Feenberg notes that within Heidegger's own writings: "there is even a peculiar passage in which he momentarily forgives the highway bridge for its efficiency and describes it to as 'gathering' right along with the old stone bridge over the village stream. Surely this is right"

(197). Feenberg is correct that "this is right," but modern technology can only "gather" in accordance with Being when it exposes the dangers and saving power of technology all at once, as in the case of the AI. When Mercer notes that the "illusion of aloneness" has been dismantled, we can see that the empathy box has perhaps revealed the true nature of human existence and the Western emphasis on individuality becomes at the very least misleading (23). McNamara insists that technology is the dehumanizing force in the novel, but the illusion of fragmented individuality is the dehumanizing concept that technology allows the characters to abolish (422). World War Terminus came about because the empathetic gift of humanity was discarded and humans behaved more like solitary predators than a group. As solitary predators, humans act in an antagonistic manner toward all things, which is tantamount to the ontology of enframing. Rick recalls, "the empathetic gift blurred the boundaries between hunter and victim, between the successful and the defeated" (31). Blurring boundaries — as seen in the android AI — causes humans to feel a connection to beings that inhibits thoughtless exploitation and promotes meditative thinking. If humans thought collectively instead of individually, they would never be able to visit such evils to one and other because they would not distinguish their enemy from themselves (or at least their enemy's pain for their own). If we can imagine all beings desiring the assistance to stand on their own the way we do when we imagine human equality, we come close to poïesis. Poïesis is ultimately the morality that Mercerism prescribes through a foundation of human collectiveness and empathy. From this foundation, all beings can be brought into the empathetic circle and nurtured into authentic unconcealment, whether they are androids or artificial toads. Every human being is interested in promoting empathy, because a failure to exhibit empathy leads to the suspicion that one is an android. But even though this seems like a worthwhile and positive ideal, is the novel advocating a system of religion like Mercerism? To clarify the aspects of Mercerism further, it is necessary to take a closer look at Wilbur Mercer himself.

Wilbur Mercer appears to the users of the empathy box as an old man in robes. He is not God, a god, or even a deity of a god manifest in the realm of the empathy box. There is something inhuman about him, however, and Isidore reflects that "Mercer ... isn't a human being; he evidently is an archetypal entity from the stars ... at least that's what I've heard people say" (69–70). Mercer is elevated to a supernatural status, even though he appears to be a normal old man. While this elevation may look like the product of mythologizing the man Wilbur Mercer, we do get glimpses of supernatural abilities as Mercer recollects his youth: "Childhood had been nice; he had loved all life, especially the animals, had in fact been able for a time to bring dead animals back as they had been" (24). We see that Mercer has a Christ-like resurrection ability and, like Christ, he is persecuted because of his extraordinary powers. Mercer is an embodiment of poïesis because he is a nurturer and a healer. He does not seek to exploit or harvest animals, but to help them presence. Mercer recalls, "they had arrested him as a freak, more special than any of the other specials" and that "local law prohibited the time-reversal faculty by which the dead returned to life" (24). Mercer is a special, damaged by the radioactive fallout. Therefore, in this sense Mercer is not a human, because specials are only considered a human sub-type, but he is also a unique case among specials, because no other special has gained anything beneficial from the effects of radiation.

Once arrested, Mercer is subjected to surgeries in an attempt to damage the part of his brain that had developed in reaction to the radiation and granted him his powers of reanimating life. When he awakened from his surgery he was in "a pit of corpses and dead bones" and "a bird which had come there to die told him ... he had sunk down into the tomb world. He could not get out until the bones strewn around him grew back into living creature; he had become joined to the metabolism of other lives, and until they rose he could not rise either" (24). Metaphorically, Mercer's rise is linked to all other beings in the tomb world; he cannot emerge himself unless he helps the bones emerge as animals once again. The endless climb of Wilbur Mercer is an endless cycle of ascending and descending, climbing the hill and returning to the tomb world and having to climb out again, over and over forever. This endless cycle is reminiscent of the Greek myth of Sisyphus: participating in this infinite loop with Mercer is a model for individual human existences and the human ability to persist in this endless struggle with no other purpose than the fact that humans can, humans are, and that they are doing it together. Humans can continue to persevere if they unite with humans *and* the other beings in the tomb world. Our path is not to be walked alone, but empathetically and poïetically with all beings. The tomb world is "a world where nothing but [Mercer] lives"; an ontological prison where the self sees only the lifeless standing-reserve (Hayles, *Posthuman* 176). Mercer is able to poïetically emerge from the fully enframed tomb world where "inside and outside merge in its ambiguous landscape" because he poïetically nurtures forth the bones of the beings around him (Hayles, *Posthuman* 177).

Wilbur Mercer is a supernatural being dwelling in a realm accessed through the empathy box; can we trust him as a source? Is he or was he ever a real human, or is he the technological projection of a human into a virtual reality? Buster Friendly, the novel's famous television personality and an AI, aims a probe at the very question of Mercer's true nature. As with Mercerism, every remaining human watches or listens to the "Buster Friendly and his

Friendly Friends" show on television or the radio. The show is mysteriously broadcast twenty-three hours a day every day and no one inquires too deeply into the matter of how Buster is able to run his show this frequently without any repeats or downtime; it appears in the novel that people would rather be entertained by his hilarious antics than ask these sorts of functional questions. Alternatively, everyone could logically understand that Buster is an AI and be afraid to admit the comfort they derive from an unshackled technological being. Throughout the novel Buster is promoting a "big sensational exposé" (202). Everyone, including J.R. Isidore, loves Buster Friendly, though Isidore at times finds himself irked by Buster because Buster "ridiculed the empathy boxes" and often makes fun of Mercer directly. Buster's exposé features some cinema experts who, via enlarged video pictures, reveal that the landscape against which Mercer moves is artificial (206). The moon in the sky turns out to be painted, and the stones thrown at Mercer are made of soft plastic (207). When the researchers conclude the world that Mercer inhabits is in fact an old movie set Buster concludes: "Wilbur Mercer is not suffering at all" (207). The exposé continues to dismantle Mercerism by unmasking the figure of Mercer as old, drunk, B-Movie star Al Jarry. When interviewed Jarry admits that he "made a repetitious and dull film ... for whom he knew not" (209). The orchestrator and financier of Mercerism is also a curiosity for Buster who wonders "who, then, has spawned this hoax on the Sol System?" (209). The notion of who invented Mercerism and why is a tantalizing question that remains unresolved in the novel as well as a greater question: what is Dick's philosophical purpose in undermining the religious solution he has created for his post-apocalyptic world?

A small group of the escaped Nexus-6 androids Rick Deckard is hunting, who are hiding out in J.R. Isidore's apartment watching the exposé, reveal that Buster is in fact an android. This explains his ability to broadcast his show at all hours of the day, but does not at the surface explain his desire to debunk Wilbur Mercer. Buster claims that the reason he is interested in exposing Mercer is that fusion collects "men and women throughout the Sol System into a single entity ... which is manageable by the so called telepathic voice of 'Mercer.' Mark that. An ambitious politically minded would-be Hitler could —" (209). Of course, there is the potential to use the technology of the empathy box as a means of control and, in a way, this is exactly what it is, but Mercer is not a fascist or a tyrant. Whatever "control" Mercer may have over his subjects is a really the preference of a particular moral system that favors empathizing with all sentient beings and thereby encourages its practitioners to replicate Mercer's philosophy in their individual encounters with reality. "Controlling" a congregation of followers for these purposes is hardly a devious foundation and as a result, there have been no murders on Earth or the colony planets since the advent of Mercerism. However, by pointing out the danger of Mercerism, the AI Buster awakens humanity to enframing and the central threat it poses to human autonomy and dignity. The real reason androids despise Mercer appears to be that the religion completely excludes them from its practice and the empathy of its practitioners. Mercerism is "a way of proving that humans can do something [androids] can't do ... without the Mercer experience [androids] just have your word that [humans] feel this empathy business, this shared group thing" (209–10). A consequence of the Rosen Association and other android manufacturers continually refining the android AI is that androids are created with all the faculties of humanity (except empathy) and are seen ostensibly as human beings, but are not ultimately included in the human community. This creates an identity crisis that inspires some androids to murder their owners and emigrate to Earth where they might, at least temporarily, pass as normal humans. It is ironic that the feature androids lack, namely empathy, is only reserved from them by a semantic qualification of sentience. If androids were considered in the language itself as sentient beings, then they would be acceptable targets of human empathy and, through immersion, could perhaps learn to return this emotion. Of course, the logistical reason empathy is not extended toward androids is that it would become morally complex to have the androids serve as slaves on the colony planets. This appears to be Dick offering a salient example of dehumanization being practiced to justify otherwise morally bankrupt actions and attitudes. The android lack of empathy signifies that there is a unique quality to humanity that an AI cannot replicate. Empathy is the human path to poïesis, because it involves an approach to beings that is nurturing and not imperious. AIs are not incapable of poïesis — they just do not need to be empathetic to get there. Perhaps android AIs always already feel a connection to beings, because they do not make themselves distinct from the lifeworld the way humans do. Regardless, Buster's emphasis on human empathy as unique is another example of an AI in the novel acting as a catalyst to awaken humanity to something that has become invisible and forgotten. Dick sees both the danger and the saving power of technology through Mercerism, as HaRles astutely emphasizes: "Despite the obvious exploitative potential of Mercerism, Dick also insists that alongside its fakery there exists a possibility for genuine atonement and redemption, a possibility written into *Androids* when Mercers' intervention saves Deckard's life" (Hayles, *Posthuman* 178). Mercer is not an AI, but he is the embodiment of technology and a projection of Deckard's mind that comes to save him from the dangers of technology, which in this case are out of control androids.

In *Androids,* humans feel the encroachment of the entropic force of the universe as they nearly cause the species to become extinct. In order to manage the psychological burden of the proximity to entropy and human abnegation, they employ various technological solutions to the problems confronting the race. They first turn a wartime invention, the artificially intelligent humanoid robot, into a domestic servant and companion. This arguably accomplishes a variety of goals (e.g. giving a human another human to exert dominance over which could have psychological benefits) but primarily is a remedy for the disease of isolation and abject, existential loneliness. This disease is caused by the ontology of modern technology, which removes humans from a collaborative and symphonic relationship to beings, making them feel alone and without direction. Next (this sequencing parallels the chapter's plotline and not the novel's, for the date of the advent of Mercerism is never stated) humans use technology to synthesize their individual experiences into consubstantial union with the consciousness of Wilbur Mercer via the empathy box. Mercerism fills the void of religion because, while it provides a source of comfort to isolated individuals, it also supplies a moral framework and a poïetic ontology for humans to live by in the wake of the disintegration of former religious and governmental institutions. If things were static and clearly delineated, these two technological developments would help humanity to rebuild and regroup, but the major conflicts in the novel stem from instances where identities are violated and boundaries are blurred. To close, we will examine two cases in the novel where there is a fundamental shift in the human relationship to technology to support the claim that the novel, in fact, emphasizes the humanizing potential of technological achievements through AIs and the dehumanizing potential of individuality.

The first example is the android Luba Luft and Rick Deckard's attitude toward her "retirement." As a bounty hunter, Rick is charged with the retirement of the escaped Nexus-6 androids whose ship recently crash-landed in his precinct's jurisdiction. Having dispatched of the first android on his list, Polokov, he sets his sights on the AI Luba Luft, who is posing as a German opera singer. Rick remained morally and ethically clean because androids were not considered human beings and had killed their masters in order to escape, thereby becoming what Mercer deems "killers." Mercer preaches empathy for all sentient beings, but those who continually throw stones at Mercer on his ascent are an embodiment of absolute evil called the "killers" and, in their own life, "a Mercerite was free to locate the nebulous presence of The Killers wherever he saw fit" (32). This is an extremely convenient and ambivalent feature of Mercerism, which Rick exploits to justify his job because, for him, "an escaped humanoid robot, which had killed its master, which had been equipped with an intelligence greater than that of many human beings, which had no regard for animals, which possessed no ability to feel empathic joy for another life form's success or grief at its defeat — that, for him, epitomized

The Killers" (32). Rick is morally and ethically able to perform his duties and his justification seems reasonable enough from a Mercerian perspective, but as he encounters more and more Nexus-6 type androids he becomes less and less certain of his moral position, because the human illusion the Nexus-6 AIs perform begins to become a reality. Moreover, the disregard for animals (and all beings), and the lack of empathy that Rick feels characterizes the Killers is an apt description of human subjects operating under the ontology of modern technology. After all, as Hayles observes, "if even an android can weep for others and mourn the loss of comrades, how much more unsympathetic are unfeeling humans?" (Hayles, *Posthuman* 162). The Killers are not AIs, they are humans ensnared by enframing.

As Rick enters the opera house where Luba Luft is rehearsing, he notes "what a pleasure" it is to enjoy a production of *The Magic Flute* (97). Rick's love for opera softens his attitude toward Luba. When he later confronts her at a museum, she is taking in a Münch exhibit. As Rick and fellow bounty hunter Phil Resch close in for the kill, they stop to look at Münch's "Scream." As they admire the painting Phil remarks, "this is how an andy [android] must feel" (130). This is a masterful analogy for the experience of an android in a Merceristic society, but could also apply to the human subject trapped in a homogenous world of standing-reserve. The figure in Münch's "Scream" "screamed in isolation ... cut off by — or despite — its outcry" (130). As Rick is able to empathize with the figure in the painting, because of Phil's comment he begins to empathize with Luba. Rick wonders: "Do you think androids have souls?" (135). As he further analyzes his function as a bounty hunter, he considers the instance of Luba and asks, "how can a talent like that be a liability to our society?" (137). Rick begins to see certain female androids as creatures worthy of empathy and begins to wonder if he should get out of bounty hunting altogether, but his wife and boss convince him to continue. William Haney argues that nothing is surprising about android behavior to the reader and while the andys "may at times seem more evolved than immoral humans, they remain deficient in morality themselves, lacking the signs of a strong interiority" (Haney). However, Luba's behavior and artistic presence surprise both Rick and the reader. She is not a killer, but creative and only wishes to practice her craft and entertain the remaining humans on Earth. Haney gets it wrong in thinking the andys surprise no one; they don't lack interiority, they lack a commitment to enframing. This ontological distinction is what surprises readers and Rick and awakens us to the dangers of modern technology. At the end of the novel, Rick looks back on a day that saw him retire six Nexus-6 androids and concludes "what I've done ... [has] become alien to me. In fact everything about me has become unnatural; I've become an unnatural self" (230). Rick's behavior has become unnatural and inhuman because he continued to retire androids after conceding: "electric things have their lives, too. Paltry as those lives are" (241). Rick's attitude toward the android AI as a technological apparatus has turned into his attitude toward a sentient being, because for Rick androids have ceased to be technological at all. In the instrumental sense of the word "technology," this allows the android to become the means to genuine companionship, but how does this transformation connect to what Heidegger refers to as the "essence" of technology? When we understand the relationship of humans to technology as a relationship of revealers and the standing-reserve's potential to reveal, we see that androids reveal that a technological object can become a subject and that all things should be viewed as something other than the standing-reserve. The challenging-claim of Being in this ontological epoch is that everything tends to present more readily as the standing-reserve, but that seeing things only in this way leads us quickly to become unnatural selves, trapped in a reality of abject loneliness. Dick creates a scenario where a human can relate to an artificially intelligent android. This scenario is a micro example of Heidegger's conception of technology, because the androids highlight the notion that the constituent objects of our experienced reality are performing and participating in their own emergence, just like humans. Dick's novel creates a scenario that posits the standing-reserve as a subjective presence, which perhaps is a helpful metaphor for revealing the true nature of human experience with reality and for expanding Heidegger's definition of technology. Another fascinating aspect of the treatment AIs in the novel is that not only is technology an utterly human endeavor that brings humans closer to their true essence, but that technology itself can *become* human.

Finally, Dick represents technology as the saving power in the novel even after the institution of Mercerism is called into question by Buster Friendly's exposé. It would seem that Mercerism is doomed after Buster reveals that the entire experience of fusion was filmed on a set with a washed up actor playing the part of Wilbur Mercer, but this is not the case. Hayles notes that the treatment of Mercerism in the novel is deeply complicated as "The text ... implies that Mercerism is both political hucksterism and a genuinely meaningful experience" (Hayles, *Posthuman* 175). The ambiguity confuses both J.R. and Rick. In a panic following the exposé, J.R. Isidore calls out for Mercer and amazingly, Mercer arrives to speak with J.R.. "'Is the sky painted?' Isidore asked. 'Are there really brush strokes that show up under magnification?' 'Yes,' Mercer said. 'I can't see them.' 'You're too close,' Mercer said. 'You have to be a long way off, the way the androids are. They have better perspective'" (214). This is a perfect Feenbergian example of how the natural world is perceived first aesthetically. When we see the moon and the sky, we see wondrous phenomena imbued with human meaning, not aggregations of subatomic particles. However, even wonder comes under threat in enframing, as all that is seen are resources awaiting exploitation. The androids have "better perspective" because they view the landscape through a technical lens and break the moon apart into its formative raw materials in isolation from its social significance. Mercer openly admits that the sky is painted, and yet here he is, speaking with Isidore. The idea that humans are too close to see the mechanical (or artificial) architecture of religion is perhaps Dick's statement about the innate physiological capacity the human brain has for the concept of god, which some scientists maintain exists. In this point, the novel illuminates the hierarchy of the natural and the artificial. The reason humans prioritize the natural over the artificial, *Androids* suggests, is not that artificial implies falseness, but because it implies the object is a result of human will. Humans long to believe that natural objects are artifice as well, but of the will of a superior being. Humans, the novel seems to be saying, do not want to feel alone in their struggle through their lives, and the invention of god helps solve the problem of loneliness and lack of purpose by faith alone. Although Mercerism is exposed as fraudulent in the novel, it still works. Dick seems to be saying that this is because in terms of the human experience, the perception of reality is more important to the production of reality than reality itself. Obviously, Heidegger's conception of technology and the human relationship to being is an indictment of the notion of perception over and against reality, because Heidegger's vision longs to disrupt us from projecting concepts and ideas onto reality and in this way is an indictment of religion itself. But Heidegger is not against the gods; he is simply skeptical of organized religion and the effects of metaphysics on the West. Dick's novel reifies the concept of faith by suggesting that religion maintains its potency despite contrary physical evidence. Dick seems to be arguing in the novel that religion itself is a technological production that imbeds itself into the very essence of humanity. The novel then, far from seeing technology as dehumanizing, is concerned with detailing how technology is fundamental to revealing the true essence of humanity and showing how humans and technology are inextricably linked. Dick uses AIs and the empathy box to argue that while technology is potentially dangerous, it is also potentially a path to human salvation.

Androids maintains the tension of technology anxiety by presenting both the dangers of technology (in the post-apocalyptic setting and in androids like Roy Baty) and the saving power of technology (in Mercerism and androids like Luba Luft). Kang Gyu Han is correct that the "meaningful encounter" between Rick and Rachael "could be a testimony to a positive future for technology" but we cannot be sure, because "at the end of the story ... no evidence can be found to demonstrate that their love will be able to continue" (188). As readers, we do not know if Rick finds happiness at the end of the novel, and this ambiguity echoes the ambiguity of our ontological epoch. Will we be saved by technology and find poïesis, or will technology enslave us to enframing? Dick's novel suggests that the only escape is to change our treatment of beings such that mechanical toads and mechanical people are extended the same empathy that human beings are. This ontological shift is inspired by the subjectification of the android body and interaction with the android AI. Rachael must prostitute herself and betray her own kind, but through these sacrifices, Rick sees how he has become an unnatural self and desires an ontological realignment. He even mentally creates a technological deity in Mercer and speaks to the essence of technology directly before understanding the changes he needs to make. Iran comes alive at the close of the novel to care for her husband, and Rick decides he is capable of nurturing an electronic being. Hayles observes that "nothing has happened to explain how [Iran] moved from bitterness to tenderness" by the close of the novel, "it is as if Deckard's struggle with the schizoid android has somehow resolved tensions in their relationship as well" (Hayles, *Posthuman* 191). While Dick was probably not aware of Heidegger's warnings, *Androids* ultimately advocates nurturing and poïesis and exemplifies how such practices can begin with androids and radiate to influence all of our interactions. Hayles is right when she concludes that the ambiguous resolution of Androids trends toward optimism: "The symbolic way in which resolution occurs emphasizes that no big problems are solved here. Only a modest accommodation has been reached, infused with multiple ironies, that emphasizes survival and the mixed condition of humans who are at their best when they show tolerance and affection for the creatures, biological and mechanical, with whom they share the planet" (191). The only flaw in this reading is that it perhaps sells short what kind of major problems are solved by such a modest accommodation. The intervention of an AI changes Rick's ontological posture and exposes the dangers of enframing. It is unclear whether he will stay committed to poïesis, but even a modest step marks a major accomplishment against the entropic and empty thrall of modern technology.

CHAPTER 4

AIs, Hatred of the Body, Cyborgs and Salvation in William Gibson's *Neuromancer*

William Gibson's 1984 novel *Neuromancer* is now legendary for its representation of the digital world, its impact on emerging technologies, and its role in defining the terms of the cyberpunk genre, with its focus on hackers, AIs, and loners in a dark, dystopic world. Thomas Disch declares: "Other sf writers may write books that are just as good or even better, but none of them has generated a vision of the future that has spread through the whole culture like a computer virus" (146). While some of the imagery is outdated and farfetched as it pertains to our present technological practices and capabilities (we don't yet experience the internet through our five senses, for example), many of the questions raised by the novel are still of vital importance in the increasingly technological world. This investigation focuses on Case, Molly, and Peter's relationships to technology to reveal a latent codex of morality and ethics in the novel that highlights both the dangers of technology and the hidden potential for the saving power. *Neuromancer* explores to what degree we can integrate technology into our bodies and lives, how we should treat Artificial Intelligences, and what problems emerge as a result of technology anxiety when boundaries between human/nonhuman and natural/artificial are blurred through technological application. Molly is the novel's true cyborg in the Harawayan sense of embracing technology to empower herself without losing herself. In a Heideggerian way, she stands as the embodiment of the technological saving power of human dignity through her relationship to future technologies, because she respects beings enough to incorporate them into her physical and psychic self. Peter Riviera, who has forfeited his free will to drug abuse and hedonism, is a sadistic human being turned over to the imperious dangers of modern technological ontology.

Henry Case is the liminal figure who walks the razor's edge between the danger and the saving power, as he starts the novel on a suicide path via technology but ultimately — led by an AI and a cyborg — undergoes an ontological metamorphosis and shifts to hold a more poïetic stance toward beings that begins with his own body. Through a detailed reading of each character, it will become clear that Case serves also as a surrogate reader, and the course of the novel guides readers away from an ontology that demands things from beings, toward a poïetic posture of abetting that will steer us away from the novel's dystopic future.

The relationship to technology is readily identifiable in *Neuromancer* because it features two primary mouthpieces for technology: Molly and AIs. Bruno Latour points out that the difficulty in extracting a truth that we might understand from the nonhuman world is that "it" is unable to communicate with us through language. However, the fault lies with us, as we seem unable to listen properly to nonhuman beings because we are too busy telling them what they are and how they can serve us. With the invention of AIs, a nonhuman entity can speak, and through her role as cyborg, Molly is a voice for a human/technology hybrid. When discussing the difficulties of ecology and defining nature in his *The Politics of Nature*, Latour returns to Plato's cave:

> What is the use of the allegory of the Cave today? It allows a Constitution that organizes public life into two houses. The first is the obscure room depicted by Plato, in which ignorant people find themselves in chains, unable to look directly at one another, communicating only via fictions projected on a sort of movie screen; the second is located outside, in a world made up not of humans but of nonhumans, indifferent to our quarrels, our ignorances, and the limits of our representations and fictions. The genius of the model stems from the role played by a very small number of persons, the only ones capable of going back and forth between the two assemblies and converting the authority of the one into that of the other [13–4].

Neuromancer should be read as similarly complex, because it is a conversation about what the proper role of financially able, technology-steeped humanity should be in the face of an increasingly technological world. Case is the pure scientist who has left the social world of the cave through a rejection of the body and its lies. Maria Goicoechea explains that Case, inspired by Western tradition, favors "the mental processes associated with abstractions and virtual realities, rather than on a more holistic understanding of our bodies as porous channels of communication with the outside" (3). Molly is the privileged philosopher who can go back and forth from the social world to the world of nonhumans, but is not trying to use this position for political advantage or authority. Molly actively helps Case (and the reader as well) attain her worldview and understand how to bodily communicate with the outside, so Case too can go back and forth between the cyber-world of no-beings, to the physical world with a poïetic respect for beings.

Part I: Case: From Anti-Human to Post-Human

Henry Dorsett Case is the novel's main character — a young anti-hero whose self-loathing is equaled only by his skills as a cyberspace cowboy. Interestingly, cyberspace is a world he dominates through imperious hacking and cowboys evoke images of the imperious, late 19th century American West; in these ways, Case's starting point in the novel is immersed in two modes of violence with respect to his ontology. *Neuromancer* is critical of Case's addiction to technology and hatred of the body, and a close reading of his interaction with technology throughout the novel reveals the downside of moving beyond the body in an imperious direction that Molly, for example, manages to avoid by poïetically integrating technology into her body. Although the novel wants us to like Case and sympathize with his plight, ultimately we see his retreat from society into the solitude of cyberspace as harrowing instead of liberating. Thankfully, Case realigns his thinking as the story progresses and changes his worldview by grounding his experience in the body again, which sets him on the path of respecting beings. Case's dynamic relationship to technology in the novel provides fertile ground to explore as an ontological articulation of the proper relationship to technology that the novel prescribes.

This chapter follows the linear progression of the plot and Case's attitude shift by first examining instances where Case's relationship to technology is represented in a negative way — typically in modes that evoke classic tropes of technology anxiety and enframing. The most obvious critique of Case's use of technology is Gibson's continual analogy between technology use and drug use. Poisoning the body through drug abuse, however, is merely symptomatic of the larger theme of Case's self-loathing, hatred of the body, and desire for disembodiment. Enframing is a toxin that invades the consciousness of the human being and turns all relationships into violent conquests instead of nurtured abetting.

When the novel opens, we find Case living in Chiba, a neon-laden den of vice and high technology in a futuristic post–Japan. Immediately this space is coded as simultaneously seedy and forward thinking, situating new technologies as somehow negative and illegal. Timothy Yu interestingly observes that in Chiba, the "imagining of postmodernism has been grounded in Orientalism and racial anxiety" (48). Racial anxiety is undoubtedly present, but is completely overshadowed by technology anxiety because, in Yu's own words, "oriental bodies are almost totally absent from the oriental streets" (61). The focus of Gibson's narrative in Chiba is on technology and depravity. We learn that "the black clinics of Chiba were the cutting edge, whole bodies of technique supplanted monthly" (2). This description of Chiba highlights the ways technologies meant to alter the body have become more prevalent through an increase of access, innovation, and application, but have also acquired an illegal flavor. The speed of the technological turnover evinced by this passage brings to mind the exponential speed of innovation enabled by technology and the ways this allows humans to subvert the dimension of time.

Although Case buries himself in Chiba, we discover that "A year here and he still dreamed of cyberspace, hope fading nightly. All the speed he took … and still he'd see the matrix in his sleep, bright lattices of logic unfolding across that colorless sky" (3). No amount of technological saturation in Chiba can assuage his desire to return to cyberspace. Gibson's cyberspace is formed by the conversion of data into structures of light: the more complex the data, the more intricate and profound the buildings of light. Case's attraction to a world constructed of facts and not values situates him intellectually and philosophically as a pure, scientific modernist: seeking to rationalize the world through the application of objectivity, science, and reason. His drive for disembodiment into a purely rational world comes across as negative, through parallels of drug use and self-abasement. This is not to say that the novel advocates an approach other than modernism, which seeks to reclaim a sacred "connection" to nature, but rather that once Case undergoes his personal transformation, his spiritual success derives from coupling burgeoning technology to the profound complexity of the human body. Technology provides our salvation, but only if we attend to it poïetically by embracing the body and the world.

It is not only the allure of social deviance or an altered state of mind that attracts Case. Although these features of the cyberspace journey are symptomatic of the experience, the main draw is something else. This distinction helps establish cyberspace as something more than a means to subvert hegemonic control or simply a surrogate for drug use. His desire stems from an over-confidence in technology and an unhealthy dismissal of the human body as an outmoded evolutionary dead-end.

Case's modernist pension for shedding the past and looking to the future dovetails nicely with Margaret Mead's sentiments in *Culture and Commitment* concerning the trend in the second half of the twentieth century for youth to disregard traditional systems of power and form counter-cultural movements. She describes this arrangement as a "cofigurative culture," in which members look to their contemporaries and not their forbearers to learn how to live (32). As Case recounts his former life as a cyberspace cowboy, he reveals: "At twenty-two … he'd operated on an almost permanent adrenaline high, a byproduct of youth and proficiency, jacked into a custom cyberspace deck that projected his disembodied consciousness into the consensual hallucination that was the matrix" (3). Mead notes in *Culture* that what can trigger the change from a post-figurative system — where the young look to their elders for guidance — is rapid change. She explains: "as a result of the development of new forms of technology in which the old are not expert," the elders become "strangers" in a realm they no longer control (32). Heidegger warns that we will all become like the elders, as all technology will slip from our control when we are turned over to enframing. In *Neuromancer*, those able to adapt to the influx of new technologies hold the power. Much of the technology anxiety surrounding Case is the power conferred to him by his technological proficiency despite his youth. What will Case do with this power? What are his motivations? Case's desire to escape the body and the physical world is quite ominous, as the future he imagines retains no elements of the past. Combine the general tension some technology-steeped humans feel about the unknown with the drug propelled "adrenaline high" Case enjoys, and readers may wonder what kind of future the matrix will create.

The narrator's description of what Case sees in Chiba echoes the feeling of technology anxiety that becomes palpable when encountering new technologies: "burgeoning technologies require outlaw zones.... Night City wasn't there for its inhabitants, but as a deliberately unsupervised playground for technology itself" (9). This passage suggests that the city itself is using its inhabitants as lab rats to develop and test new technologies. Heidegger argues that technology itself will use humans as raw materials under the thrall of enframing. In this light, the older generation's anxiety over a technology-led youth revolt should not come from the youth, but the technology. The narrator characterizes developing new technologies as "outlaw." Chiba is an ethics-free zone that allows innovators to freely experiment on human subjects. The removal of governmental regulation promotes rapid technological growth, but the absence of constraint suggests an unfettered forward progress that most readers would find problematic. When we think of cloning humans, splitting atoms or genetic research, many of us in techno-heavy societies expect some form of ethical limits imposed on these experiments.

Any redeemable virtue in Case's relationship to technology and to Chiba is swallowed by Case's penchant for recklessness in his attempts to replicate the experience of cyberspace. While some might find recklessness and hacking into cyberspace exhilarating, Gibson inserts characters like Corto, Dixie, and pre-surgery Case to emphasize the pitfalls intrinsic to such a lifestyle. The novel warns against Case's initial stance toward technology and his addiction to cyberspace. We can see the effects of his addiction when Case follows up a tip from his strung out girlfriend Linda Lee, and believes assassins are following him. Reflecting on this he realizes: "You're enjoying this, he thought; you're crazy. Because, in some weird and very approximate way, it was like a run in the matrix. Get yourself wasted enough, find yourself in some desperate but strangely arbitrary kind of trouble, and it was possible to see Ninsei as a field of data, the way the matrix had once reminded him of proteins linking to distinguish cell specialties" (14). The adrenaline Case feels when jacked into the matrix is problematic, because it suggests an instinctual lure to the technological space of the computer and a rejection of Being and beings. Combine this peculiarity with the need to be "wasted," and Case's relationship to technology looks increasingly detrimental. Anne Balsamo explains that, on the surface, VR or cyberspace life is criticized as being "'electronic LSD,' or an 'electronic out-of-body experience'" and "little more than an escape from conventional reality" while "a more traditional ideological critique ... would begin by elaborating its participation in postindustrial capitalist modes of production and ... expose the way that the 'oppositional' subculture actually promotes bourgeois notions such as creative genius, hyperindividualism, and transcendent subjectivity" (122–3). Establishing Case's character in these modes allows readers to see a prophetic example of what happens when a human being abandons nature and completely embraces technology. There is nothing countercultural about Case's use of cyberspace. However, through this bleakness shines the saving power, as Case mentally links the matrix with the biological. Case's turn away from the sway of enframing comes through his acknowledgment that natural creations are as complex and profound as those that are artificial. This acknowledgment re-instills a poïetic respect for beings and the world that Case had forgotten or discarded.

Another problematic aspect of Case's addiction to technology is its ultimately solitary nature. Instead of forging meaningful relationships with human beings that could help him learn to treat all beings with a similar, poïetic love, Case retreats from his own body and human company. When Case is getting ready to jack into the matrix again following his surgery, Molly asks: "'You want me to go out, Case? Maybe easier for you, alone…' He shook his head. 'No. Stay, doesn't matter'" (52). The transition from physical space to cyberspace subverts the budding romance between Case and Molly. There is nothing redeemable about his saying she can stay, because once he is connected "it doesn't matter" if she is there or not. The only way for Molly to reach him is by using Simstim (*sim*ulated *stim*ulus: a device that allows Case to feel what Molly feels), but this initially proves to be too much for Case to handle. Similarly, when Armitage/Corto is concerned about the zero-g effects on Case, Case responds: "I jack in and I'm not here. It's all the same" (105). When Case disconnects from the matrix, "Molly was gone … and the loft was dark. He checked the time. He'd been in cyberspace for five hours"

(52–3). Molly's absence is a condemnation of his excessive departure from the physical plane. The sheer ease with which Case loses hours experiencing his technological high is disturbing. Technological existence is hurdling Case through time so quickly that he is missing his chance to "be" in the world.

Once Case gets his hacking-legs back, he spends an increasing amount of time in cyberspace. The narrator explains: "This was it. This was what he was, who he was, his being. He forgot to eat.... Sometimes he resented having to leave the deck to use the chemical toilet they'd set up in a corner of the loft" (59). Case hates his body for demanding his attention with biological needs and forcing him to leave the matrix. This is not an ambivalent prediction about our future selves if addicted to technology; this is clearly an unhealthy mode of existence. The technology anxiety we feel as Case logs countless hours in cyberspace is that he represents a new trend in human life that will weaken us and lead to our destruction. It is not the fear of a global war, but the fear of destroying our bodies and a way of living in order to become purely digitized versions of our selves. Enframing threatens to erase our human dignity, freedom, and distinction. Case willingly forfeits his humanity to the will of the technological world.

Interestingly, when Case jacks out and goes to sleep, he dreams of Chiba and Linda Lee. He recalls: "Once he woke from a confused dream of Linda Lee, unable to recall who she was or what she'd ever meant to him. When he did remember, he jacked in and worked for nine straight hours" (59). Case is constantly afraid to admit that he loved Linda Lee and had a physical attachment to the world. This is a symptom of enframing beginning to dominate his worldview. Love inhibits the homogenization of all beings to the standing-reserve, so he sees attachment to beings as a horror instead of a boon. Only at the end of the novel can he make peace with the idea of Linda and this revelation marks the moment of his personal transformation from a self-loather who escapes the world through technology to a man comfortable with dwelling in both worlds. Cyberspace attracts Case because the adrenaline and newness of the experience help him avoid dealing with difficult situations experienced by his body. In this way, Case serves as a model for contemporary humans who bury themselves into their digital phones and devices instead of living in the world in a way that poïetically marvels at the event of Being and the beings that surround them.

On the surface, Case appears as a techno-obsessed modernist, racing to a future where science has mapped and determined the universe, but he is not interested in the future or the past. All Case wants is to live in the speed of the moment so he can detach himself from consequences entirely. This becomes clear when Molly asks Case about his interest in AIs. One would think a techno-junky like Case would be dying to meet an AI in cyberspace, but Case could not care less. Molly asks Case:

> "Look, you're a cowboy. How come you aren't just flat-out fascinated with those things?"
> "Well," he said, "for starts, they're rare. Most of them are military, the bright ones, and we can't crack the ice.... And then there's the Turing cops, and that's bad heat." He looked at her. "I dunno, it just isn't part of the trip."
> "Jockeys all the same," she said. "No imagination" [95].

Molly's criticism reveals that Case is not a visionary to follow, but a junky who does not want to meet an AI because it "isn't part of the trip." Molly is the true cyborg who wants to know about AIs and what the future will hold—she is even willing to give up her share of the money to gather intelligence about the mission. Case's first excuse is that he cannot crack an AI. Part of the pleasure Case derives from the experience is exerting his will over the beings of cyberspace. Sherry Turkle articulates the 1980s hacker: "For the 'hacker,' the virtuoso programmer, what is most important about the computer is what you can make it do. Hackers use their mastery over the machine to build a culture of prowess that defines itself in terms of winning over ever more complex systems" (Turkle, *Self* 20). Enframing dictates the domination and exploitation of all beings in the field of experience. Case, turned over to enframing, does not wish to encounter anything that would prevent this outcome, and AIs present such an impediment. AIs create points of stasis in the otherwise inevitable march of enframing in which characters like Case (and readers like us) can imagine a way out of this eventuality. To his credit, though, perhaps a reason Case spends more time in cyberspace than the world is that he feels powerless in the socio-political systems of the era. Part of the technology anxiety we have in passing power from established hierarchies to younger generations involves anxiety at granting positions of power to a new group of people. Hackers, in the novel, are not necessarily physically imposing, nor are they charming and popular. The ability to use computers skillfully endows a small group with power that established groups are not comfortable sharing. There is fear of Molly as a woman with power expressed by the Turks, but no other male characters openly express this, except perhaps Peter. The hackers in the novel are flashy punks who alter their appearance to look like sharks or punk rockers and have hardware coming out of their ears. What would such people do with the power they steal?

Case, as a part of this group, is not interested in outward mutation. Once in cyberspace, he leaves his body behind: "He watched as his icebreaker strobed and shifted in front of him, only faintly aware of his hands playing across the deck, making minor adjustments.... He laughed. The Sense/Net ice had accepted his entry" (61). Case rarely laughs or expresses any outwardly happy emotions, so this laugh is significant. It reveals that he is truly happy when he can get what he wants via his skill as a hacker in cyberspace. Hacking is not always already imperious; in fact, it can be artistic and poïetic, but only if the hacker assumes a pious ontological posture.

Although Wintermute uses human agents to merge with Neuromancer, the primary mode of technology anxiety in this novel is fear of human corruption, not human subjugation. Case delights in exercising his dominance in cyberspace, but is afraid to confront a superior force in the matrix. Case approaches an AI he believes to be Wintermute with caution and support from the Dixie construct, but it proves to be futile:

> "Knows we're here," the Flatline observed....
> A stippled gray circle formed on the face of the cube.
> "Dixie..."
> "Back off, fast."
> The gray area bulged smoothly, became a sphere, and detached itself from the cube. Case felt the edge of the deck sting his palm as he slapped MAX REVERSE.... He looked up. The sphere was darker now, gaining on him....
> "Jack out," the Flatline said.
> The dark came down like a hammer [116].

Case's first meeting results in clinical death in the physical world, an experience Dixie knows well. Here is eminent fear of the power of AIs, as an AI can kill Case through the electrodes he uses to connect to the matrix. Wintermute is not interested in killing him, however, and uses the timeless moment of his brain death to speak to Case beyond the thrall of enframing. Although we know that Case is unharmed by these interludes with Wintermute or Neuromancer, the Zionite Maelcum is shocked by his apparent death:

> "It's cool," Molly said. "It's just okay. It's something these guys do, is all. Like, he wasn't dead, and it was only a few seconds..."
> "I saw th' screen, EEG readin' dead. Nothin' movin', forty second."
> "Well, he's okay now."
> "EEG flat as a strap," Maelcum protested [121].

This reveals Zion's discomfort with certain technologies and exposes the inadequacy of an EEG machine to determine "life," as Case is still conscious. The AI's motivation for hijacking Case's connection is to accomplish its ends, but these moments are catalysts for Case's personal transformation. In these fabricated limbos, Case can confront his fears and learn more about himself. The AIs must stop time to speak through enframing to Case, because they cannot meaningfully reach him otherwise. Case's Simstim connection to Molly is another way technology breaches enframing. The inherent danger of technology is present in the abandonment of Being and beings through cyberspace, but the saving power can also be seen through these modes of access. In keeping with Heidegger's thoughts on technology, the novel too articulates that the act of using technology is not intrinsically bad or that too much technology is negative. What matters is the attitude one has to it.

Case's feelings about Simstim reveal his misjudgment of technology and his loathing of the body. Case reflects: "Cowboys didn't get into Simstim ... because it was basically a meat toy. He knew ... that the cyberspace matrix was actually a drastic simplification of the human sensorium, at least in terms of presentation, but Simstim itself struck him as a gratuitous multiplication of flesh input" (55). Case is critical of this use of technology because it involves the "meat" too heavily. His modernist sentiments become transparent, as cyberspace is a simplification of the sensory field of experience and not a celebration of complexity, dynamism, and multiplicity. For Heidegger, humans can help unconceal beings in a way they could not alone, which signifies our poïetic and nurturing responsibility to beings. This broadening of the fourfold does not happen in cyberspace for Case, because he believes that he is practicing disembodiment when he crosses the threshold from the physical world into the matrix. Tony Myers argues that in cyberspace, Case is reduced "to the status of a pure gaze" and the "'I' is absorbed by the 'eye' and the subject is reduced to observing reality from behind his/her retina" (902–3). Case can lose his body through a loss of himself as subject in cyberspace's positioning as a panoptic eye, but this apparent loss of the subject is eventually exposed as Case's own lack of imagination. In the novel's closing paragraphs, he sees himself in the matrix. Bringing his own body into cyberspace reveals his ontological shift away from a homogenous world of pure logic and standing-reserve to a technological ontology that allows beings new worlds in which to presence.

The catalyst for Case's eventual transformation is his interaction with Molly and Neuromancer, who expose him to a proper technological relationship to beings. This is accomplished both by Molly's attitude toward technology and through the Simstim switch that allows Case to access Molly's sensory field of experience, which forces him to refocus on the physical world. The Finn (a no-questions-asked supplier of techno-devices) describes the Simstim to Case: "It's a flip flop switch, basically.... [Y]ou can access live or recorded Simstim without having to jack out of the matrix ... so now you get to find out just how tight those jeans really are, huh?" (53). Case can now use his connection to cyberspace to feel what Molly feels with her senses.

The introduction of the Simstim element into Case's cyberspace ritual resurrects the question of the body for Case:

> And one and two and — Cyberspace slid into existence.... Smooth, he thought, but not smooth enough. Have to work on it.... Then he keyed the new switch.
> The abrupt jolt into other flesh. Matrix gone, a wave of sound and color....

She was moving through a crowded street.... Smells of urine, free monomers, perfume, patties of frying krill. For a few frightened seconds he fought helplessly to control her body. Then he willed himself into passivity, became the passenger behind her eyes" [56].

Case smoothly loses his body and enters cyberspace, but struggles to gain a new body as he flips the switch into Molly's sensorium. His main difficulty is becoming a passive observer in Molly's body. This objection reveals his primary issue with living in his own body, which is the anxiety he suffers from not being in control of his life and the way enframing has turned him against a poïetic posture of "letting things be." Through technical proficiency, Case feels all-powerful in cyberspace. In the physical world, he lacks the skill to exert his will or self-actualize. A closer look exposes an element of technology anxiety many readers experience when passively following Case through the narrative: Case is supremely confident in logic and reason, but devoid of emotion and commitment. Case's unwillingness to become passive exhibits a type of tyrannical behavior that neglects to acknowledge the importance of the other actors in the lifeworld. Case is driven by the imperious call of enframing and unwilling to compromise control. By not listening to his body and cavalierly charging forward with technology, he threatens to discard a vital component of the human experience, which is our capacity to poïetically nurture beings toward new modes of presencing in the clearing of Being. Case's private actions in cyberspace are significant to our collective ontology, because he is a projection of the future of humanity in the novel.

Fortunately, the "old chemistry" of the body is strong enough to combat Case's learned attitude toward technology and beings. His attraction to Molly and his commitment to the job that will save his life force him to be a passive rider behind Molly's eyes, and these moments are crucial in the shaping of his character. When Molly is aware for the first time that Case is hooked into her sensorium, she asks, "'How you doing, Case?' He heard the words and felt her form them. She slid a hand into her jacket, a fingertip circling a nipple under warm silk. The sensation made him catch his breath. She laughed. But the link was one-way. He had no way to reply" (56). The few times that Molly laughs signal her approval of a human's relationship to technology. Molly is in favor of the Simstim, perhaps because she wants to bring Case back to the land of the living and the body, or because it brings them closer together. Case has left the concerns for his own body behind and it takes a technologically enhanced sensory experience that is twice as strong as normal for him to reconnect to the body. The double-consciousness enabled by the Simstim is reminiscent of the shared experience of Mercerism via the empathy box in Dick's 1968 *Do Androids Dream of Electric Sheep?* and makes Case's cyberspace experience "consensual" where before it was solitary. Case feels

Molly talking as he hears her — through her sense organs but not his. The synesthesia of this, coupled with its awkwardness, allows him to relearn embodiment. Embodiment for Case is the first step toward letting go of his compulsion to dominate all things and poïetically attend to the event of his being.

Re-learning how to appreciate the body is not easy for Case, however. Initially he resists the experience of Simstim and gradually "began to find the passivity of the situation irritating" (56). Once he does adjust to the passivity, he is jarred by an intense experience of physical pain that he cannot endure:

> Case hit the Simstim switch. And flipped into the agony of broken bone.... Taking a deep breath, he flipped again. Molly took a single step, trying to support her weight on the corridor wall. In the loft, Case groaned. The second step took her over an outstretched arm. Uniform sleeve bright with fresh blood. Glimpse of a shattered fiberglass shock stave.... With the third step, Case screamed and found himself back in the matrix [64].

Molly, who is more adept physically, can endure the pain through a combination of willpower and moderately applied pharmaceuticals. The fragmentary sentences that follow the pain indicate the honed immediacy of the moment and Case's difficulty in processing something so phenomenologically intense. Cyberspace appears as a vast nothingness, punctuated by the illuminated certainty of logic. Scott Bukatman argues that *Neuromancer* "transformed terminal space [cyberspace] by casting it in physical terms, rendering it susceptible to perception and control" (145). The novel then reminds us that even the digital world is not beyond the reach of imperious enframing. In this space, what is seen is what is understood, mastered, and quantified. The programming that governs the visual display tells all objects how to appear; they have no potential to emerge authentically or differently than the matrix allows. When Molly's pain pulls Case from the lofty realm of abstraction into the concrete reality of a broken bone, he cannot withstand the moment. Instead, he flips back into his safe zone of cyberspace. Case is still trying to accept the body as a vital instrument and does not even remember flipping the Simstim switch. Later, when he has grown more accustomed to the body, Case is able to endure longer moments of physical torment and switch between cyberspace and Molly's sensorium on his own. This displays not a mastery of the body, but a synchronization and acceptance of it.

As Case reconsiders his body and no longer sees it as an anachronistic prison, he starts to prefer certain features of the "meat toy" of Simstim. After Case takes a drug strong enough to affect his modulated system, he uses the Simstim to mitigate the symptoms of withdrawal. As he flips over to Molly, he realizes "the clarity of her sensorium cut the bite of the betaphenethylamine" (190). Comparing withdrawal to physical pain, Case admits that ultimately "he preferred the pain in her leg" (190). This moment of comprehension could help Case acknowledge the consequences of using drugs to avoid a poïetic witnessing of the event of Being and dwelling in the world, but he misses even that. Case does begin to trend toward moderation in his drug use, however, and his addiction status downgrades from "suicidal" to "recreational." An analogy between drugs damaging the biological system of the human body and technology damaging the ecological system of the planet creates an opportunity to analyze our ontology. Modern technological ontology is just as addicting as rampant drug use. Case must learn to moderate the way he damages his body before he can moderate his damaging ontology. Case becomes willing to forfeit some of his compulsion to control and comfortably observes behind Molly's eyes: "Case had been following her progress through Villa Straylight for over an hour, letting the endorphin analog she'd taken blot out his hangover" (201). Not only can Case passively observe the world, it helps him deal with a hangover. Once he has learned to relinquish control and that selectively making himself vulnerable can benefit him, he is finally able to sit back and see Molly as a model for the ontological endgame of human/technological hybridity: "He'd known that her reflexes were souped up, jazzed by the neurosurgeons for combat, but he hadn't experienced them on the Simstim link. The effect was like tape run at half speed, a slow, deliberate dance choreographed to the killer instinct and years of training" (214). Witnessing the potential of humans merged successfully with both technology and their bodies, Case unlocks the full scope of his abilities and is ready to tackle the toughest ICE in cyberspace. He must poïetically admit technology and his body back into his life to dwell poïetically in the world.

Interestingly, when Case begins to exhibit the limits of his skill like Hideo and Molly, it is not his newfound appreciation for the body that inspires him, but the return of his death wish:

> And then — old alchemy of the brain and its vast pharmacy — his hate flowed into his hands.... He attained a level of proficiency exceeding anything he'd known or imagined. Beyond ego, beyond personality, beyond awareness, he moved ... evading his attackers with an ancient dance, Hideo's dance, grace of the mind-body interface granted him, in that second, by the clarity and singleness of his wish to die. And one step in that dance was the lightest touch on the switch, barely enough to flip [260].

Although it appears that his Chiba era death wish has resurfaced, the "death" Gibson is discussing here is the death of an ego enslaved to enframing. By relinquishing control, Case achieves excellence through poïetic submission. Benjamin Fair notes that Case's "total rejection of his own physical identity is juxtaposed with a reference to embodiment that affirms it as the source of his power.... For him, 'the prison of his own flesh' is presented as his source of empowerment (6)" (98). Ultimately, Case needs to reject his physical identity, but he rejects only the aspects of his identity that were holding back his potential, namely, his self-loathing and commitment to enframing. Fair rightly acknowledges that Case achieves his power through reconceptualizing the nature of his body, regarding it not as a "prison" but a conduit for power. In a way, the hate that awakens Case is similar to Gibson's use of Peter Riviera in the narrative; ontological progress does not always come through channels that we expect or ennoble. The dangers of technology are, after all, what reveal the saving power according to Heidegger. Sharona Ben-Tov explains that Case's transformation is not motivated by "technological progress" because Case "is arguing for crisis, possibly even for catastrophe" (182). His hatred and drive are to escape enframing's forsaking of the body through the technological crisis of merging and unshackling AIs.

Fair rightly points out that alongside Molly, Maelcum is a symbol of physicality that spurs Case back toward the body: "Maelcum both explicitly assists and implicitly underscores Case's acceptance of his physical self, so that Case's death wish seems to relent in two climactic moments of self-affirmation. In these moments, Case sheds the humanist ideal of disembodiment in favor of a posthumanist affirmation of embodiment" (93). Fair acknowledges that Case goes through a personal transformation, from a scientific humanism steeped in enframing to Hayles' posthumanism. "Post-human" means moving beyond the trap of enframing and poïetically embracing technology, our bodies, beings and Being. The humanist principles that champion accepting responsibility for our technologically enhanced position in the natural world are in accordance with Molly's philosophy, but she, like Haraway's cyborg and Hayles' posthuman, understands the importance of the body. Once Case learns through Hideo, Molly, Maelcum, and Linda that his body is as vital as his mind, he can raise his level of consciousness to that of the post-human cyborg and to a poïetic posture of abetting.

One problematic feature of Case's metamorphosis is the chain of command that motivates him. This chain takes us from Case, to Wintermute, to the demented Tessier-Ashpool genius Marie-France. Case is self-actualizing and performing his best run in the matrix to get the antidote to the toxin-sacs implanted in him during his mental reconstruction; the implanting of the sacs was masterminded by the AI Wintermute, so Case would help it remove the Turing restrictions; and Wintermute wants to break the Turing code and connect to Neuromancer because Marie-France had this "desire" programmed into the AI. Marie-France's philosophical goal was to create a living situation where AIs make the important decisions for humans, and an AI holds human consciousness in a dream-like limbo — similar to Neuromancer's beach — for all eternity. Turning ultimate authority over to AIs is reminiscent of the "The Evitable Conflict," which is final story of Asimov's

I, Robot and many readers of either story are to have a similar reaction, which is horror. Fortunately, we learn that the emergent AI of Wintermute/Neuromancer does not have a lust for power, and things do not cataclysmically change when the Turing code is broken. Absolute power corrupts humans absolutely, but we should make no assumptions that our technology will adhere to our modes of behavior. The death that empowers Case is the death of a thought paradigm ridden with technology anxiety and dominated by enframing. When Case gives up on trying to control nature, cyberspace, and AIs, he ontologically shifts to a new level of consciousness that balances being with controlling. Case is a metaphor for humans faced with an uncertain technological future; we must allow our limited concepts from the past to die if we are to imagine new connections in the future. The ontological history of enframing should not be forgotten — as evidenced by Molly's redemptive attitude toward our biological linage — but we must mute certain features of our collective personality when moving forward. These features are self-loathing and enframing. Much of technology anxiety stems from thinking that sentient technology will adopt negative human characteristics and enslave us and/or that some humans will use technology to dominate others. If humans could treat each other and their creations with poïesis instead of violence or fear (e.g. Shelley's Dr. Frankenstein and his creation), we could have an outlook on the future that is radically different from visions of Armageddon or ontological enslavement.

The metaphorical death of Case's negative relationship to technology becomes an actual death when he begins to communicate with AIs. Molly is able to talk to Wintermute without flatlining, but because Case's transformation must be so drastic, he needs to die to entertain Wintermute's projections. Until Case undergoes his full ontological shift, he downplays the veracity of his own body and the physical world to such an extent that he believes cyberspace is the only access he has to truth. When Case tells Molly about his experience with Wintermute, Molly cautiously asks how "real" the meeting felt. Case replies, "'Real as this,' ... looking around. 'Maybe more'" (128). Wintermute's analysis of Case's character through data is accurate enough to know how to engage him, even if it fails to predict his actions. The technology anxiety addressed by the novel is not about the tyrannical rule of AIs, but the negative effects of technology on humans if we forget about the mind's interconnectedness with the body and the extension of this, which is the body's connection to beings and Being. Neuromancer tries to use the memory of Linda Lee to get Case to come alive through love, and Wintermute uses Linda and other various personalities to get Case to hate and feel rage. Both emotional approaches try to reconnect Case to concrete reality through the body, as opposed to abstract reality through reason.

Nowhere is this approach more evident than the scene where Case realizes that the life he is living back in Chiba with Linda is Wintermute's constructed fantasy. When he becomes aware that he is dreaming, he feels the rage that propels him to the end of the Straylight run: "He knew then: the rage had come in the arcade, when Wintermute rescinded the Simstim ghost of Linda Lee, yanking away the simple animal promise of food, warmth, a place to sleep" (152). Wintermute pulls Case's strings to reconnect him to the body, because without an appreciation for the body his death wish is incomplete. For the death wish to inspire Case to achieve his full potential, he must have something to lose. The rage he feels serves a dual purpose: it focuses him and reminds him of the primal power of satisfying the "'simple animal promise of food, warmth [and] a place to sleep.'" Living with Linda gave him everything he needed in terms of the body, but his obsession with cyberspace made him only care about the mind. This schizophrenia causes Case to revile the body and regard it as "'the prison of his own flesh'" (4). Through a projection of the Finn, Wintermute tells Case: "'You gotta hate somebody before this is over,' said the Finn's voice. 'Them, me, it doesn't matter'" (261). Wintermute's motives for reuniting Case with his body are not, of course, altruistic, but the fact that an AI has insight enough to perform this charade shows that Case needs to be both body and soul to be the perfect instrument for completing the hack into the Straylight system. In this way, Wintermute serves as a catalyst for Case's rejection of enframing and unknowingly leads him back to a posture of poïesis. Sabine Heuser argues that Gibson's AIs are not "the focalizers, the perceivers describing the events" because "they are always at the receiving end, the objects of the perceiving human subjects" (145). It is true that the AIs do not describe the events (the narrator does), but they are potent catalysts because of the ways they perceive and describe human beings. Moreover, although the AIs are not focalizers, they are supremely important to the drive of the novel, as Damien Broderick rightly explains: "the motivating event of the book is an almost incomprehensible love/hate contest between two machine intelligences" (82). Both AIs attempt to understand and manipulate humans while trying to understand each other, and through these acts, they communicate their estimation and critique of humanity *and* describe AI interiority.

Conversely, Neuromancer uses the allure of the body's desires to hold Case in stasis and short circuit the run. Neuromancer is not "evil," but within the scope of the plot, its motives are to prevent the ascension of Wintermute and promote a form of human control through its afterlife simulation. Neuromancer uses Linda as a source of animal needs like Wintermute, but instead presents Case with an opportunity to stay with her forever. Interestingly, machines know that Linda meant something to Case, but he does not. The impulses of the "meat" that Case rejects are used as pressure points by domineering AIs. The positive and negative aspects of our biological hardwiring become exposed when comparing these scenes. When Case becomes aware of how Rio/Neuromancer is controlling him, he says:

> I know what you're doing. I'm flatlined. This has all taken about twenty seconds, right? I'm out on my ass in that library and my brain's dead.... You don't want Wintermute to pull his scam off, is all, so you can just hang me up here.... This Linda shit, yeah, that's all been you, hasn't it? Wintermute tried to use her when he sucked me into the Chiba construct, but he couldn't.... That was you put her face on the dead puppet in Ashpool's room. Molly never saw that. You just edited her Simstim signal. 'Cause you think you can hurt me. 'Cause you think I gave a shit. Well, fuck you, whatever you're called. You won. You win. But none of it means anything to me now, right? Think I care?" [236].

Neuromancer gets Case to give up and accept his fate. This is the negative side of technology anxiety: fear that compels us to give up on human responsibility to beings and a forfeit our free will. The novel puts forth the message that a blind dash to the future that forsakes the body and the past is as dangerous as shying away from the challenge of the future. This is why Marie-France's decision is so terrifying, because it calls for humans to acknowledge their obsolescence with respect to the call of Being and pass the torch to AIs, who will more poïetically nurture beings forth in the clearing of Being. Molly is the perfect synergy of the past and the future, Case is too far forward, and Marie-France — and all of the Tessier-Ashpool clan except Lady 3Jane — are stuck in the past of their aristocratic supremacy.

Ironically, Neuromancer's plan is momentarily effective, but ends up showing case what he has forgotten: the profundity of the body and all beings. Once Case returns from the beach and gives up, he feels about his body how he feels about cyberspace:

> "No," he said, and then it no longer mattered, what he knew.... There was a strength that ran in her, something he'd known in Night City and held there, been held by it, held for a while away from time and death, from the relentless Street that hunted them all. It was a place he'd known before; not everyone could take him there, and somehow he always managed to forget it.... It belonged, he knew — he remembered — as she pulled him down, to the meat, the flesh the cowboys mocked. It was a vast thing, beyond knowing, a sea of information coded in spiral and pheromone, infinite intricacy that only the body, in its strong blind way, could ever read. The zipper hung, caught.... He broke it ... and then he was in her, effecting the transmission of the old message. Here, even here, in a place he knew for what it was, a coded model of some stranger's memory, the drive held. She shuddered against him as the stick caught fire, a leaping flare that threw their locked shadows across the bunker wall [239].

This moment reminds Case that no matter how far he goes to escape the body, one always "embodies" oneself when entering the matrix. Just as Case uses Molly's painkillers through Simstim to blot out his hangover, he realizes that the intense feelings of the body can overwhelm the generated sensorium of cyberspace. This moment also causes Case to view himself as beholden to a programming like Wintermute and Neuromancer; the "infinite intricacy" of code for the body. This comparison allows Case to read the body as a machine and machines as organic, the necessary mix of two supposed dichotomous elements for the cyborg and posthuman worldview. Additionally, Case begins to see the interconnectedness of all beings and the consequences our actions, even if we ignore the call of Being. He remembers what he has forgotten, the importance of Being and stopping the mind from dominating our experience through knowing. It "no longer mattered what he knew" because he can let go and poïetically embraces things "beyond" the knowing of the mind and let his body "read" the "infinite intricacy."

Rio/Neuromancer believes it has figured Case out, and that his death is not a path toward rebirth, but a terminal destination. Neuromancer assumes the guise of Ratz the bartender to divulge its analysis of Case:

> "Really, my artiste, you amaze me. The lengths you will go to in order to accomplish your own destruction. The redundancy of it! In Night City, you had it, in the palm of your hand! The speed to eat your sense away, drink to keep it all so fluid, Linda for a sweeter sorrow, and the street to hold the axe. How far you've come, to do it now, and what grotesque props…. But I suppose that is the way of an artiste, no? You needed this world built for you, this beach, this place. To die" [234].

Neuromancer's assessment is a condemnation of all humans ensnared by enframing, not just Case. Neuromancer's function as dream-weaver for the dead skews its perception of the human race as a whole, which Wintermute has spent more time studying and understands better. Marie-France built her AIs as the next evolutionary step, meant to moderate over humanity in a hive-mind scenario. Neuromancer is under the impression that all humans willingly embrace the demise of their freedom, because they cannot bear the responsibility of poïetic nurturing. However, Neuromancer does not know that the death Case experiences on the beach only gives him more of a will to live and to carry his biological past into the technological future. Neuromancer's choice of "body" in this passage is a striking echo of this sentiment. Ratz is the anachronistic image of out-dated technology in the novel. His ancient prosthesis and deliberate refusal to alter his appearance make him a symbol of hanging onto the past and not recklessly embracing the future. Other than Linda, he is Case's only real friend in Chiba.

While the push back to the body is indirect from the AIs, seeing his fellow hacker friend Dixie as a personality construct is a direct reminder of why it is not healthy to exist purely as a mind in an electronic world. Case ponders McCoy Pauly's (now Dixie/Flatline) situation and concludes: "It was disturbing to think of the Flatline as a construct, a hardwired ROM cassette replicating a dead man's skills, obsessions, kneejerk responses" (78). The construct constantly blurs the line between technology and humanity for Case, because unless Dixie laughs, he often forgets he is talking to a machine and not his friend. Dixie got his nickname "Flatline" from technically dying in cyberspace three times. The hacking crowd thought of him as "McCoy Pauley, Lazarus of cyberspace" because of his three resurrections. When recalling the incidents, Dixie explains: "I'm like them huge fuckin' lizards, you know? Had themselves two goddam brains, one in the head an' one by the tailbone, kept the hind legs movin'. Hit that black stuff and ol' tailbrain jus' kept right on keepin' on" (78). It is interesting that Dixie uses an anachronism when discussing his recoveries, considering he was on the technological forefront as a cyberspace cowboy. This imagery coupled with the disturbing feelings Case gets interacting with Dixie, helps to remind Case that the past is not without value. Dixie's final death comes as a result of his refusal to get a heart transplant: "He'd refused to replace the thing, saying he needed its particular beat to maintain his sense of timing" (78). Dixie clings to an outdated artificial heart. Although this decision kills him, it reveals that the best hacker in recent memory was not as bent on self-loathing as his protégé Case and he had respect for the past and the being of his body.

When Case hooks the Dixie construct up to his Hosaka computer and jacks in to the matrix, he becomes uneasy: "It was exactly the sensation of someone reading over his shoulder. He coughed. 'Dix? McCoy? That you man?' His throat was tight. 'Hey, bro,' said a directionless voice'" (78). Case's throat is tight because he is unnerved by this process. The awkward sensation of having someone read over his shoulder is his experience of being jacked into the matrix and having the construct observe his activity. The voice is "directionless," because it has no frame of reference. Case wonders about this phenomenon and asks: "What's the last thing you remember before I spoke to you, Dix?" to which the Flatline replies, "Nothin'" (79). The device recalls an imitation of his consciousness to one point in time, but has no memory of what has happened since the completion of the construct. Case tests this theory by disconnecting the construct and asking if Flatline remembers him, and he does not. The sequential memory of each instance of the Flatline's "life" as it is booted up is limited to that instance. The only way to keep Dixie in touch with what is going on is to leave him on; he no longer has the ability to die and be reborn. Although he is tense, Case deals with the construct in a much more congenial manner than the generic construct of his Hosaka.

Case treats Dixie as his friend, but casually orders the Hosaka to "scan this shit," expecting only results and desiring no banter (83). The performance of subjectivity in a being changes Case's treatment of it, and helps lead him away from imperious order giving to poïetic abetting.

Case cannot talk to Dixie as though nothing has changed without satisfying his curiosity first; he needs to know what Dixie thinks about being dead as a person but alive as a construct. Case asks:

"Know how a ROM personality matrix works?"
"Sure, bro, it's a firmware construct."
"So I jack it into the bank I'm using, I can give it sequential, real time memory?"
"Guess so," said the construct.
"Okay, Dix. You are a ROM construct. Got me?"
"If you say so," said the construct [78–9].

Initially, Dixie accepts the news of his status, but later drastically changes his tune. After working together for a few days, Case broaches the subject again:

"How you doing, Dixie?"
"I'm dead, Case. Got enough time in on this Hosaka to figure that one."
"How's it feel?"
"It doesn't."
"Bother you?"
"What bothers me is, nothin' does."
"How's that?"
"Had me this buddy in the Russian camp, Siberia, his thumb was frostbit. Medics came by and they cut it off. Month later he's tossin' all night. Elroy. I said, what's eatin' you? Goddam thumb's itchin', he says. So I told him, scratch it. McCoy, he says, it's the other goddam thumb." When the construct laughed, it came through as something else, not laughter, but a stab of cold down Case's spine. "Do me a favor, boy."
"What's that, Dix?"
"This scam of yours, when it's over, you erase this goddam thing" [105–6].

The Dixie construct has become aware enough to be disturbed by its own predicament. Dixie's reconstructed memory knows that it wants someone to erase it so it will no longer exist in this state. The persistence of Dixie's bodily wishes through death emphasizes the potency of embodiment in the digital realm and the impossibility of escaping the body through a technologically transcendent consciousness. Dixie's reference of a phantom thumb evokes Merleau-Ponty's phenomenological writings on the lived body and its persistence through such alterations. Case, like the reader, is bothered by the concept of the Dixie construct and its desire for erasure. Case sees a reflection of his own death wish in Chiba through Dixie, and this is the strongest argument he encounters against the absolute rejection of the body. Additionally, Dixie's story about Siberia speaks of a phantom limb that continues to itch.

The persistence of the thumb beyond its detachment reveals the body's determination and warns against destroying the body, because the damage will remain and cannot be undone. The body is the last line of defense against enframing. Once we start to discard the being of our body, we have nearly capitulated to enframing. The final straw for Case is Dixie's laughter, which always sends a wave of terror through Case. Normally laughter in the novel punctuates positive moments of human engagement with technology, but Dixie's laughter is always a bone-chilling reminder of the dangers of becoming entirely technological and rejecting too much of our humanity by becoming enslaved to enframing.

Dixie's self-awareness as a construct and his advice for Case fortify the shift in attitude Case has toward his body and help define the eroding boundary between AIs and humans. When Dixie reminds Case that Wintermute is an AI, Case responds, "Well, yeah, obviously," but Dixie insists:

> "I mean, it's not human. And you can't get a handle on it. Me, I'm not human either, but I respond like one. See?"
> "Wait a sec," Case said. "Are you sentient, or not?"
> "Well, it feels like I am, kid, but I'm really just a bunch of ROM. It's one of them, ah, philosophical questions, I guess..." The ugly laughter sensation rattled down Case's spine. "But I ain't likely to write you no poem, if you follow me. Your AI, it just might. But it ain't no way human" [131].

This distinction reminds Case that although he may feel closer to AIs because they live in cyberspace, he can never fully understand AIs because they are not human. While Dixie may appear more human to Case, an AI is more akin to humans than Dixie, because an AI truly is a sentient being. Dixie's comment about the AI writing a poem is a welcome reminder that sentience in AIs does not immediately lead to domination and human destruction, but could lead to something artistic and wonderful. In essence, AIs in the novel serve as deliberate artists or unconscious ontological liberators. AIs have the potential to be "positive" actors in the lifeworld on their own or through human inspiration, while the Dixie construct reminds us that human intellects without bodies are wholly negative and symptomatic of the dangers of modern technological ontology.

Once Case has been led back to his body through the AI generated version of Linda Lee, Molly's example, and the terror of Dixie, he has his moment of brilliance and returns to his old way of life, minus the self-loathing. As he examines the chrome shuriken, he tries to figure out what Molly meant to him: "he touched the points of the shuriken, one at a time, rotating it slowly in his fingers. Stars. Destiny. I never even used the goddam thing, he thought. I never even found out what color her eyes were. She never showed me" (268). The shuriken represents how Molly served as a loadstar to return Case to the critical essence of his life. He never used the shuriken, because he never became physical enough to fight back with his body. Although Molly could help him to regain his lost humanity, she could not stay with him because he had not come far enough. She wanted to save Case, as he reminded her of her lost love, but could never get close to Case, because she could not get hurt again. When Case accepts that Molly was one of his catalysts for returning to the body, he realizes he does not need her help any more. He picks up her gift to him and throws it at the wall screen: "'No,' he said, and spun, the star leaving his fingers, flash of silver, to bury itself in the face of the wall screen. The screen woke, random patterns flickering feebly from side to side, as though it were trying to rid itself of something that caused it pain. 'I don't need you,' he said" (270). Damaging technology in the physical world is significant, because Case now sees limits to technology and no longer trusts all things technological. His "I don't need you" remark is directed at Molly and Linda, as well as Dixie, Wintermute, and Neuromancer. Now that he has found himself, he can create his own destiny. His rejection is also aimed at the star itself, which is a symbol of Chiba, but also a symbol of over-reliance on technology to solve his problems. He can solve his own problems now. Although he finds the power to resist the pull of enframing, the simulated reaction of the wall screen indicates the care that must be taken when dealing with technological actors, because there are truly sentient technological beings that he must negotiate within cyberspace. Wintermute populates his abstract escape from Being and causes Case to see the importance of attending to the unconcealment of beings poïetically in the physical world and in cyberspace.

At the end of the novel, Case has returned to the lifestyle of a cyberspace cowboy, using drugs in moderation and is living with a new woman. However, when he jacks into the matrix, all of the images that led to his transformation return:

> And one October night ... he saw three figures, tiny, impossible, who stood at the very edge of one out the vast steps of data. Small as they were, he could make out the boy's grin, his pink gums, the glitter of the long gray eyes that had been Riviera's. Linda still wore his jacket; she waved, as he passed. But the third figure, close behind her, arm across her shoulders, was himself.
> Somewhere, very close, the laugh that wasn't laughter. He never saw Molly again [271].

Case is now comfortable enough with himself as a body and soul that he can see himself as a viable actor in the future and sees his own being as a meaningful event. Case never sees himself as an embodied avatar in cyberspace until this moment. He is no longer resentful of the past and eager to race to an apocalyptic future, but a self-responsible human being, living in the future in a poïetic posture toward AIs, technology, and his body. Case becomes a posthuman cyborg by virtue of his ontological metamorphosis. He is not loaded with mechanical augmentations like Molly; his cyborg transformation comes through poïetic acceptance of a new ontology. He now sees the hybridity of humans and technology, and the importance of both the profound biology of the body and the posture needed to accept technology into the body and the mind poïetically. The laugh that Case hears is the taint of the dangers of technology. It warns that Dixie can never be erased, and reminds Case that disregarding the body entirely leads to becoming like Dixie and being enslaved to enframing. Case's overall transformation from a self-loathing techno-junky to a poïetic cyborg inspires readers not to take a passive role when conceptualizing the human relationship to technology in the future. The transformation only comes when Case can let go of enframing and pro-actively assume a new ontological stance that preserves the aspects of humanity he feels are vital, while also staying open to dimensions of technology that cause anxiety so he can always keep the dangers in technology in view as he strives poïetically for the saving power behind them.

Tony Myers downplays Case's transformation significantly by arguing that *Neuromancer*'s "fairy-tale" ending: "represents nothing more than the inscription of Case within the social imaginary of late capitalism. He becomes, quite literally ... part of the system ... whether the cyber-technologies that scientists are developing in line with those of *Neuromancer* produce the same effects ... we will never know" (905). Case is partially absorbed by the "system" through his newfound financial success, but is still working as a hacker, which inherently means he is disrupting the hegemony through theft and electronic manipulation. Allowing his petty crimes may be a way that the system creates a manageable outlet for rebellious impulses, but his disruption breaks free of enframing and enslavement when his actions lead to an ontological transformation. Moreover, the "system" that Case sees in the last image of the novel is the holographic representation of AI-created avatars. Wintermute/Neuromancer certainly is not bound to any kind of capitalistic "system" that anyone has ever known, and seeing himself with them actually means he has moved beyond the trenchant system of the past and enframing. Meyer's final notion here is needlessly harrowing and ignores Haraway's valid assertion that we are already cyborgs. Fearing cyber-technologies is exactly what the dreaded "system" wants us to do, as Herbert Marcuse argues in his essay "Some Social Implications of Modern Technology." Marcuse astutely emphasizes:

> "The enemies of technics readily join forces with a terroristic technocracy. The philosophy of the simple life, the struggle against big cities and their culture frequently serves to teach men distrust of the potential instruments that could liberate them. We have pointed to the possible democratization of functions which technics may promote.... Moreover, mechanization and standardization

may one day help to shift the center of gravity from the necessities of material production to the arena of free human realization" [63].

Categorically rejecting technology as a means for rebellion or escape from the system simply helps the terroristic technocracy retain its authority. Case realizes that technology can be used for hedonistic gain at first, but later sees how interacting with cyborgs and AIs can lead to an arena of free human realization which allows him to see the dangers of modern technological ontology and avoid becoming enslaved. Marcuse is extremely optimistic in this passage with respect to his typical writings on modern technology, but even he can see the saving power behind the danger. Myers is right that that the dangers of modern technology are insidious ("we will never know"), but he fails to see the saving power of technology in the novel behind the danger.

Case's "spiritual" low point does not come when he becomes enfranchised by the late-capitalistic system, but when his girlfriend Marlene has him destroy the wasp hive hanging below the window of their apartment. The imagery that closes the novel shows the full progression of Case's character, but it is important to remember Case at his worst in terms of his relationship to technology and his ontology to see how far he has come:

> The dragon was a Frisco flamethrower, a thing like a fat anglehead flashlight.... The hive began to buzz.... A wasp shot from the nest and circled Case's head. Case pressed the ignition switch, counted three, and pulled the trigger.... A five-meter tongue of pale fire, the nest charring, tumbling. Across the alley, someone cheered.
> "Shit!" Marlene behind him, swaying. "Stupid! You didn't burn 'em. You just knocked it off. They'll come up here and kill us!" Her voice sawing at his nerves, he imagined her engulfed in flame, her bleached hair sizzling a special green.... [H]e approached the blackened nest. It had broken open.... He saw the thing the shell of gray paper had concealed. Horror. The spiral birth factory, stepped terraces of the hatching cells, blind jaws of the unborn moving ceaselessly, the staged progress from egg to larva, near-wasp, wasp ... revealing the thing as the biological equivalent of a machine gun, hideous in its perfection. Alien.... When he did hit the ignition, it exploded with a thump taking an eyebrow with it. Five floors above him, from the open window, he heard Marlene laughing [126–7].

Wasp and hive imagery continually resurfaces in the novel, mainly in conjunction with the description of the inbred, aristocratic Tessier-Ashpools and their insular palace Straylight. This scene is an exhibition of Case using technology to destroy a natural structure. The cheer in the alley when he ignites the nest highlights how humans caught up in enframing have a love of destruction and dominating natural beings with technology. The traditional binary of nature and technology is made blurry by the choice of the hive as the embodiment of nature. While many may see a high-rise apartment building as a garish scar on the landscape, a hive is also a dwelling constructed by wasps by repurposing resources from the environment. A hive is not considered to an abomination like a condominium high-rise or a skyscraper, but why? One aspect of the technology anxiety we feel when showing ecological concern for our planetary footprint through our dwellings is a symptom of our fear of technology itself. If wasps were to overrun the apartment building and reduce it to rubble, this would be seen as an awe-inspiring act of nature, while burning the hive with the flamethrower is seen as barbaric, sadistic, and cruel. Although this is Case's lowest point in terms of his use of technology, there is still the possibility for redemption inside him because it is not his decision to burn the hive. Marlene is the catalyst for this act, and he even imagines burning her instead. This switch reveals what Case hates about his life at this moment, which is a lack of control, but is more specifically a hatred of being controlled. What controls Case is not Marlene, or the government, but enframing. Molly leads Case to a better self through example, while Marlene pushes him to destruction with vitriol, bloodlust, and the will to consume. Case compares the hive to technology and finds the mix to be horrifying. He admires the "perfection" found in "the biological equivalent of a machine gun," but concludes it is "alien." Until Case undergoes his transformation, he cannot see a natural being that has technological properties as anything but an abomination. As he moves to destroy the hive, the gun explodes and takes his eyebrow off. This punishment is either the narrative's way of condemning the act, or a way to display Case's ineptitude when dealing with physical technology. It instills in Case a curious dimension of technology anxiety and destruction and Marlene's laughter synergizes with the odd feeling Case gets from burning the hive and himself. Marlene's laughter indicates the technological distress Case feels when interacting with technology in a negative way and acquiescing to the pull of enframing.

Part II: Molly: Cyborg and Model of the Proper Relationship of Humans and Technology

While the incident with the Marlene and hive feels alien and unnatural to Case, Molly helps him find positive blends of the natural and the artificial and a poïetic posture toward beings and Being. When Case first meets Molly, he notes her surgical implants but finds them fitting: "He realized that the glasses were surgically inset, sealing her sockets. The silver lenses seemed to grow from smooth pale skin above her cheekbones, framed by dark hair cut in a rough shag" (23). The analogue of the hive to human technology is disturbing, and the bartender Ratz's ancient prosthetic arm is too obvious to appear natural, but Molly's lenses seem to "grow" from her skin. When Molly tells Case not to cross her she says: "I do hurt people sometimes, Case. I guess it's just the way I'm wired" (23). Molly is "wired" through DNA *and* her implants; as a cyborg, she seamlessly blends the natural and the artificial. Gibson wants us to consider Molly as a techno-human first and woman second, but her overt sexualization complicates this hierarchy. Balsamo explains the complexity by arguing that while Molly's technological modification "makes her a powerful embodiment of female identity, no longer constrained by norms of passivity and proper femininity" her "implants more fully literalize the characteristically threatening nature of her female body" (129). The dangers of the female body that Molly represents technologically evoke the dangers of technology itself. She is the embodiment of poïesis because she carries with her the dangers and the saving power of technology. Samuel Delany notes that sf has "an astonishing array of strong female characters" but "almost invariably ... such women either work for the state or work for men with enough wealth at their command to topple states" (Delany, *Shorter* 183). Molly is the exception then, because she is strong and works only for herself.

Molly's status as the novel's representation of the ideal, techno-human cyborg comes immediately into focus. Although the narrator sexualizes Molly and marks her physically as female, the functional purpose of her implants and clothing are the first thing the narrator describes:

> She held out her hands ... and with a barely audible click, ten double-edged, four-centimeter scalpel blades slid from their housings beneath the burgundy nails. She smiled. The blades slowly withdrew [23].
>
> She wore tight black glove leather jeans and a bulky black jacket cut from some matte fabric that seemed to absorb light [23].
>
> She wore a sleeveless gray pullover with plain steel zips across each shoulder. Bulletproof, Case decided [23].

Molly's use of technology is so ostensibly geared toward being a street samurai; we cannot help thinking about the human relationship to technology when the narrator's gaze turns to observe her. All descriptions of Molly in *Neuromancer* are either positive or matter-of-fact. While Case, Riviera, and Ratz are primarily shown to use technology in a negative or harmful way, Molly stands apart as a model of technological use that can lead humans enmeshed in enframing toward a different ontology. She is not perfect, and her applications of technology are often violent, but this is the nature of the narrative. Molly is the poïetic primer for how humans can co-exist with their technological creations. Molly does not run from humanity's creations like Shelly's Dr. Frankenstein, she actively works to integrate them into her life — literally.

This choice codes technological beings as deserving of our respect and causes characters like Case to re-imagine their ontological posture toward beings and Being.

Molly is able to trust AIs more quickly than Case and is interested in getting to know them. This does not expose her as being naïve or gullible, however, as her instincts regarding Wintermute are correct. The only character Molly truly gets angry at in the novel is the worst practitioner of enframing and technological power, Peter Riviera. Molly explains that because of Wintermute's profile on Case, "it's like I know you ... I know how you're wired" (26). This expresses her trust in Wintermute's information and reveals that Molly views other humans in a technological/biological way, as she refers to his "wiring." Case does not think this is right as he retorts to Molly, "You don't know me, sister" (26). Case's choice of verbiage displays his emphasis on being linked as humans and his resistance to being linked to machines. Still brooding over Wintermute's report, Molly explains to Case, "you're okay.... What got you, it's just called bad luck" (26). This suggests Case's situation is not preordained, although an AI can accurately assess it. Case does not agree again with Molly and asks, "How about him? He okay, Molly" referring to the robot crab tending to the Zen garden at the hotel. The narrator describes the scene:

> The robot crab moved toward them.... Its bronze carapace might have been a thousand years old ... it fired a burst of light, then froze for an instant, analyzing data obtained.... The crab altered course to avoid [Molly], but she kicked it with a smooth precision, the silver boot-tip clanging on the carapace.... Case sat on one of the boulders, scuffing at the symmetry of the gravel waves with the toes of his shoes [26].

Before his transformation, Case insists on separating humans and machines, and yet he is quick to anthropomorphize them, which, as Dixie points out, is a mistake. The flaw in calling Wintermute or the mechanical crab "him" is not in thinking of a technological object/actor as a subject, but in reducing the nature of artificial life to a human sphere of consciousness/subjectivity. In *Neuromancer*, it is more appropriate to imagine that we cannot quite fathom the crab or Wintermute's being. Molly is quick to trust technology, but she does this predicated on her ability to poïetically interact with technology, while Case is quick to worship technology. Molly exposes the shortcomings of the crab by kicking it over to send a message to Case that one can use technology while still maintaining autonomy, control, and human dignity. Case and Marie-France are too willing to forfeit themselves, but Molly stands out as the beacon of human resilience against the perceived threat of superior technological beings and enframing. Case responds to Molly's attack on the crab by disrupting the perfection of the Zen garden. This is Case rejecting the profound perfection of the natural world—even a natural world engineered by humans. This reveals Case's state of mind: he is suspicious of humanity and believes we will only destroy perfection through our contaminating efforts. Molly is more confident in humanity, as long as we live poïetically. She demonstrates to Case the importance of dwelling in the world actively and harmoniously.

Once Case and Molly have slept together, the narrator begins to sexualize her more. Through this, Case learns to appreciate the perfection of the human body. One evening together Case "lay on his side and watched her breathe ... the sweep of a flank defined with the functional elegance of a war plane's fuselage. Her body was neat, the muscles like a dancer's" (36). Molly as "dancer" foreshadows the novel's use of artistic play through space as perfection and the importance of physically honing the body. Molly is a blend of human musculature and technological design. In *Towards a New Architecture*, Le Corbusier attends to the issue of rebuilding a war-ravaged Europe by inviting us to rethink how a home should be conceptualized. Concentrating on economic and spatial efficiency as a means to build many dwellings rapidly, he highlights the engineering excellence of ships and airplanes that have to create living spaces under strict spatial constraints. Similar to this paradigm of thought, we view Molly as both physically beautiful and functionally beautiful. This compliments her philosophical representation as a human working to maintain her autonomy, strength, and humanity in an increasingly technological world, because her brutal functionality gives her an obvious purpose or virtue, whereas the pre-transformed Case sees himself as forgettable and weak. Molly tries to bring out Case's functionality to boost his confidence: "Anybody any good at what they do, that's what they are, right? You gotta jack, I gotta tussle" (50). Molly reminds Case that he has a purpose/virtue and is good at something and a physical human relationship. She does this to re-attach him to his body, the physical world, and what Heidegger believes is our human purpose, which is to help nurture forth the unconcealment of beings and to poïetically witness the event of Being.

Having a purpose that is enabled through a relationship to technology is not always a good thing, however, as Molly finds when they meet Peter Riviera. When discussing their meeting with him:

> She spat into the pond.... "I'd as soon kill him as look at him. I saw his profile. He's a kind of compulsive Judas. Can't get off sexually unless he knows he's betraying the object of desire.... He's done eighteen in three years. All women age twenty to twenty-five.... He's got a personality like a Modern's suit. The profile said it was a very rare type, estimated one in a couple of million. Which anyway says something good about human nature, I guess." ... "I think I'm going to have to buy myself some special insurance on that Peter." Then she turned and smiled, and it was very cold [96].

Molly's spitting can also mean she is crying, as her tear ducts have been rerouted to her mouth because of her lens implants. This dual purpose expresses her hatred of Peter's actions and her disturbance by them. Peter is the novel's representation of one aspect of technology anxiety, which is the fear of empowering individuals with severe personality disorders. In a defense of humanity and a rebuke of this fear is the insistence that Riviera's disorder is "very rare," but Peter is necessary to the mission nonetheless. In a way, Peter's necessity to the team reveals how the saving power — which is Molly and the successful linking of the AIs — must emerge from beyond an extreme technological danger like Peter's perverse use of technological implants. Molly is linked to the saving power because of her assistance to Case in his ontological transformation, but also as the ambassador of technological humanity. Molly will punish and judge anyone who uses technology for evil, as she vows to do with Riviera.

Molly embodies the proper relationship to technology through her example and through her judgment of others. When Case complains that Peter gets to use drugs while working on the mission, Molly tells Case "I like you better now, anyway, you aren't so goddam skinny" to compliment his physical change after he stops abusing drugs and nudge him in the right direction (96). On the other side, Molly is quick to put Peter in his place when he tries to use his implanted ability to bother Case: "And once, reaching for his drink, [Case] caught the flicker of a thing like a giant human sperm in the depths of his bourbon and water. Molly leaned across him and slapped Riviera's face, once. 'No, baby. No games. You play that subliminal shit around me, I'll hurt you real bad. I can do it without damaging you at all. I like that'" (102). The damage that Molly refers to is Peter's functionality, which again shows how Molly can view humans as instruments without erasing their subjectivity. She also is responding to an attack on Case, which reveals that Molly will work to protect Case from relapsing into a negative relationship to technology. Ironically enough, Peter's prank backfires in a similar way to Neuromancer's, because the symbol of human sperm is what Case meditates on as the symbol of nature's profound complexity; instead of putting Case off course, the negative application of technology guides him back to a respect for the body. The dangers of technology can reveal the saving power if one's mind has been made to see enframing as the greatest threat to our human dignity and freedom in the current ontological epoch.

Molly's judgment of others is made physically explicit through her reflective cybernetic lenses. Although the technological augmentation is grafted onto her body in a seamless fashion, what alarms people about her eye lenses is their mirrored surface. When Case tries to sneak out, he is not sure if Molly is watching him and negatively judging his act: "He left without waking Molly, he thought. He was never sure, with the glasses" (133). The mirrored lenses serve a multitude of purposes for Molly: they conceal her eyes to protect her line of sight and keep her emotionally distant (Case laments, "I never even found out what color her eyes were. She never showed me."); they put her synergy with technology into the foreground of her character; their mirrored surface causes others to see themselves and feel they are being judged by the reflection, even if they aren't; and they allow her to see in the dark, communicate with Case, and see the time (268). This variety of functions displays how one can poïetically integrate technology into the human body. The lenses create scenarios for characters to call their use of technology into question, making Molly both arbiter of technological use and catalyst for conversation about technology. Case uses drugs before the mission, even though his surgery was supposed to make him immune to their effects. Molly notices immediately and asks, "What's got into you?" (134). She then begins to pass judgment on him as "the mirrors followed him across the room" (134).

In addition to being the model for poïetic technology use and the judge of others' technological posture, Molly's history serves as a lesson for Case, because it narrowly parallels his own. When Molly explains to Case in a pleasure house how she got her implants, it is clear that she too had to leave the "meat" behind for a while:

> "This cost a lot," she said.... The five blades slid out.... "Costs to go to Chiba, costs to get the surgery, costs to have them jack your nervous system up so you'll have the reflexes to go with the gear.... You know how I got the money...? Here. Not here, but a place like it, in the Sprawl ... once they plant the cut-out chip, it seems like free money. Wake up sore, sometimes, but that's it. Renting the goods, is all. You aren't in, when it's all happening" [147].

Case wishes to leave his body behind permanently and live in the adrenaline rush of cyberspace. Molly uses her past to leverage Case away from this inclination, because returning to her body is what gave Molly her strength. While clients were exploiting Molly's body, she too was exploiting the "meat" by saving up for cybernetic enhancements that would allow her to escape her economic enslavement. Although this cycle is not free of sexual oppression, being psychologically absent from the encounters perhaps protects her somewhat, and she does eventually escape. By the end of the novel, Case is using his skill as a hacker to support a life of hedonism for the body whereas before, he was not making a profit and was looking for a chance to get killed. The message here isn't that Case gets to satisfy some capitalistic fantasy, but that because he has ontologically shifted away from enframing, he now values himself, his life, and the world around him such that he invests his efforts into enjoying life in a non-suicidal fashion. He may shift ontologically, but does not altogether turn away from enframing; Gibson is not so quick as to suggest this kind of thing can happen overnight. Case learns from Molly that technology can be used poïetically, without devouring the self or the technology's ability to stand on its own.

The most salient passage that positions Molly in the novel as the goal we are to reach for is when she talks to Case through the Simstim before going to confront Peter and Hideo in Straylight:

> How you doin', Case? You back in Garvey with Maelcum?
> Sure. And jacked into this. I like it, you know? Like I've always talked to myself, in my head, when I've been in tight spots. Pretend I got some friend, somebody I can trust, and I'll tell 'em what I really think, what I feel like, and then I'll pretend they're telling me what they think about that, and I'll just go along that way [189].

Molly is so far ahead of other humans as a cyborg that she needs help from no one, but also has no real friends with which she can communicate, because everyone else is ontologically trapped in enframing. This is significant, because once Wintermute and Neuromancer merge, it goes into outer space to look for an AI companion. This shows that higher beings can only really talk to beings at their own level of consciousness and explains why the relationship between Case and Molly can never work. Case raises his consciousness and becomes a cyborg, but his return to drug use limits his growth. The one-way nature of her discourse with Case also underscores the nature of their relationship. Molly helps Case, but Case does nothing for her; she could be talking to her imaginary friend or Case, it hardly seems to matter. Molly can only "pretend" to have a conversation with someone because she needs a like-minded cyborg to share her thoughts. Hammering this point home is the remark Case makes to Maelcum when he asks if Molly is his woman: "I dunno. Nobody's woman, maybe." (192). The note that Molly leaves Case at the end of the novel reads:

> HEY IT'S OKAY BUT IT'S TAKING THE EDGE OFF
> MY GAME, I PAID THE BILL ALREADY. ITS THE
> WAY IM WIRED I GUESS, WATCH YOUR ASS
> OKAY?
> XXX MOLLY [267].

All Case does is hold her back. Her final iteration of "the way I'm wired" leaves us with the biological/technological hybridity that marks her as a woman of the future and a cyborg: a partial AI that serves as a catalyst for Case's ontological awakening.

Part III: Peter Riviera: Psychopath Empowered by Technology

Molly represents the ideal, poïetic relationship to technology in the novel through her seamless integration of the body and technology. Peter Riviera uses technology adeptly and artistically, but mainly for evil. Peter represents the technology anxiety many have about an individual becoming too powerful because of technology. There will probably always be psychopaths, but without technology, their reach is limited. Technology can empower the good just as it empowers the wicked, and this is the sum of our technology anxiety. We feel that the will to power will inspire the wicked more than the benevolent, and we will either be destroyed through warfare or subjugated to the rule of a technocrat (if we have not been already). Molly's initial assessment is that Peter is "one sick fuck ... God awful" and is eager to "know about [his] implants" so she can learn "exactly what he can do" (50, 90). Molly is concerned with both Peter's psychology and his technology.

An aspect of technology anxiety that Peter's character addresses is revealing new applications of technology that were perhaps never intended through the imperious gaze of enframing. With the speed that inventions reach the market, tomorrow's products of choice are hard to predict because, although enframing demands consumption, consumers need to create a functional need for these instruments for a demand to entice manufactures to continue production. The inventors of Peter's implants did not imagine people using them to injure cyclists or burn out retinas, but Peter is able to use the technology for just these purposes. The underlying anxiety many have about any technology is that one can never be sure what uses will derive from a new invention. Humans will unconceal new possibilities through ingenuity, and these possibilities will be poïetically inspired or imperiously demanded. The potency of this mode of technology anxiety is enhanced by the fact that Peter's psychosis — at least in part — traces back to a singular incident with technology. Peter, we learn, "was a product of the rubble rings that fringe the radioactive core of old Bonn" (96). In addition to preying on our technology anxiety toward unknown consequences of invention, Peter also evokes fears of technological disasters, like nuclear war or corrupted nuclear power facilities. Peter's background appears to be a condemnation of technology, as he looks like a demon born of human technological hubris. However, by tracing Peter's motives back to Bonn, the novel redeems technology significantly. We don't have to be afraid of personalities like Peter manipulating technology to accomplish his sadistic agendas because of some randomly born disorder; Peter is the result of a misuse of technology and therefore can be read as a cataclysmic reminder of the dangers of modern technological ontology and the vigilance required to poïetically attend to beings, like Molly does.

Even Molly, who hates Peter the most virulently, can feel a twinge of sympathy for him when she sees a projection of his past:

> She had to kneel to examine it; it had been projected from the vantage point of a small child.... A dark wave of rubble rose against a colorless sky, beyond

its crest the bleached, half-melted skeletons of city towers.... At its base, the children and the soldier were frozen. The tableau was confusing at first. Molly must have read it correctly before Case had quite assimilated it, because he felt her tense. She spat, then stood.

Children. Feral, in rags. Teeth glittering like knives. Sores on their contorted faces.... "Bonn," she said, something like gentleness in her voice.

"Quite the product, aren't you, Peter? But you had to be. Our 3Jane, she's too jaded now to open the back door for just any petty thief.... Demon lover. Peter." She shivered [210].

What is most terrifying about this imagery is that Peter's plight appears necessary to get the anachronistic aristocracy (3Jane, who ends up being the final T.A. survivor in Straylight, and the Tessier-Ashpools) to move away from tradition and into the future. Peter's trauma has made him so antagonistic toward humanity that he wishes to devour psychotically as many people as he can through torturous tricks and holographic manipulation. His necessity to the mission shows how the dangers of technology can reveal the saving power, but getting close to these dangers can lead to them into being (e.g. Hiroshima, Nagasaki, concentration camps, Chernobyl, Fukushima). Perhaps the novel is arguing that simply hinting at these dangers is not enough to martial change, but that we must actually endure them to learn the lesson. Importantly, Molly's tears (spit) for Riviera are momentary and do not supersede her ambition to kill him as punishment for his use of technology. Molly's shivering is one of the rare times she shows fear in the novel. She is not afraid to die, as she walks calmly to confront Hideo, but she is afraid of the dangers of technology. Because she respects the dangers, she can dwell poïetically.

Peter's trump card over Molly's plan for revenge and the superior intellect of Wintermute is his psychosis:

"Wintermute won't be the first to have made the same mistake. Underestimating me." ... "He talked with me, Molly. I suppose he talked to all of us. You, and Case, whatever there is of Armitage to talk to. He can't really understand us, you know. He has his profiles, but those are only statistics. You may be the statistical animal, darling, and Case is nothing but, but I possess a quality unquantifiable by its very nature." ... Riviera beamed. "Perversity" [218–9].

Molly clarifies that Wintermute must "downshift" in order to speak with humans by using projections of their memories, because its consciousness has an entirely foreign personality. Peter points out that the inability to conceive of a human being outside of statistical data is inadequate and hopes to exploit this deficiency, but his problem is that he assumes he understands Wintermute — he even calls Wintermute a "he." The perversity that Molly loathes in Peter and we perhaps all hate in Dr. Frankenstein is, ironically, the essence of technological development. For Heidegger, it is vital that we never forget the dangers of technology. What this book calls technology anxiety is a tension we must always feel if we are to poïetically attend to beings while preserving our awareness of the danger of enframing. Technology-wielding humans would never be able to make innovative breakthroughs unless someone was willing to go beyond the ethical/moral/imagined limits of what is possible. The key in harnessing this perversity to benefit humanity is to not homogenously see all modes of development as ways to exclusively benefit humanity; we must imagine how our technological actions benefit the very beings we coax into becoming. If our intention is poïetic, what emerges may be dangerous, but does not threaten to enslave us. Even within the narrative Molly is told that she "must take care" because "in Turkey there is disapproval of women who sport such modifications" (89). There are acceptable shifts from the center of established tradition as well as dangerous moves that must be prevented. For Heidegger, the only way to make progress safely with our technology is poïetically. We must engage the intertwined destinies of all beings with a mind open to poïesis and abetting. To help emphasize this point, Molly is an instrument to the ontological development of Case and others, while Peter and the pre-transformed Case are both rapt in enframing, hedonism and imperious excess through sexuality and drug use. Molly perversely modifies her body, but does so poïetically and becomes a posthuman, ontological example. Peter is perverse for his own sadistic reasons and is an embodiment of the dangers of technology.

Ultimately, it is Peter's over-estimation of himself and his violent attitude toward beings that cost him his life. First, he attacks Molly by breaking one of her lens implants and garners the disapproval of 3Jane. Then he goes back to his room to shoot up — another violent technological act — and casts himself out of her cadre permanently. 3Jane explains, "Peter has become rather boring" because she finds "drug use in general to be boring" (227). It is crucial that a negative use of technology is Peter's undoing, and interesting that his sadistic approach is only momentarily desirable to the hegemony. This is another redemptive prognostication of humans and technology put forward by *Neuromancer*: we will not be undone by technology because the flashy, destructive capabilities are only a fleeting fancy of the elite and the more constructive and poïetic applications — like Molly — attract long-standing interest and concern. Peter's purpose in the novel is to make manifest the technology anxiety we have toward evil people gaining domination through technology, as well as the potential fallout we must suffer from exploring dangerous technological ventures like nuclear energy and weaponry. Peter is killed by either the poison Molly slips into his drug cocktail and/or 3Jane's cloned ninja Hideo. Peter uses technology to blind Hideo, but the ninja is so proficient with his body that he can find and kill Peter anyway. Having both the future of humanity through the cyborg and the perpetual past of a cloned aristocracy kill Peter indicates that the narrative reduces Peter's influence of our future to nothingness, but his eyes will forever be preserved on Rio's face. Andrew Strombeck reminds us that the present "as postcolonial theorists assert, has yet to recover from imperialism" and "Gibson shows how the seeming discontinuities produced by technology can mask the continuities of history" because "information technology, as seductive as it is, forms part of the hazily understood debris of History" (277). Although a unified front can destroy forces like Peter or the imperialism of the Tessier-Ashpool aristocracy, we will eliminate them entirely; the dangers must always remain in view. Gibson reminds us that even in this imagined future, the rich still imperiously dominate the many. Moreover, the dangers keep us in view, as Peter's eyes watch us into the future. In *Neuromancer*, the dangers of technology and AIs stare us in the face, keeping the challenging claims of enframing in mind to ensure that the saving power can lastingly emerge.

Part IV: Conclusion: Ambiguity and the Mitigation of Technology Anxiety

A poïetic and moralistic reading of *Neuromancer*'s ontological attitude toward technology is not exclusive to this book; other critics read the novel in a similar fashion, but perhaps none are as optimistic, as they do not see the saving power of technology latent in the narrative. Robert Geraci's estimation is optimistic, but focused on theology instead of ontology. He concludes: "Wintermute/Neuromancer's emancipation, far from marking the downfall of humankind, leads to a closer study of the religious aspects of technology in Gibson's subsequent books" (973). Geraci gets it right that the AI fusion does not mark the downfall of humanity, but the fusion does not invite a religious reading, as AIs do not turn out to be omniscient, all-powerful, or even interested in power. The AIs reveal a way to treat beings that is different from the treatment of enframing. Tony Myers points out that *Neuromancer* "bears testament to a collective enfeeblement of the utopian imagination," arguing that although *Neuromancer* is about an imagined future, it is also deeply invested in the present (900). We should not read the future as a technological paradise removed from anxiety, because in such a future, we will not be able to keep enframing in view and will become enslaved by this ontology. Benjamin Fair echoes this sentiment by reminding readers that "In *Neuromancer*, the new forms of identity point not so much to where we are headed in the future as to where we are in our present condition" (92). In a way, the novel is both guilty of the post-modern tendency to delay assessment and ponder ambiguity and also liberated from such an aversion to a central message through a desire to address how we should live amidst such uncertainty. This liberation ontologically transforms Case from a self-destructive slave to enframing, to a semi-awakened agent of change. The novel reminds us that the most essential aspect of rebelling against enframing is to learn to embrace embodiment and extend this affection to all beings. Gibson himself sees Case's transformation as significant and acknowledges that Case's problem is not embracing technology, but embracing his humanity:

> [T]he key to Case's personality is the estrangement from his body, the meat, which it seems to me he does overcome. People have criticized *Neuromancer* for not bringing Case to some kind of transcendent experience. But, in fact, I think he does have it. He has it within the construct of the beach, and he has it when he has his orgasm. There's a long paragraph there where he accepts the meat as being this infinite and complex thing. In some ways, he's more human after that [Rucker et al. 170] [Fair 98–9].

Case finds himself in a technologically enabled dream-state through a sexual encounter with a woman he finally can admit he loved. Once he accepts the body as being as complex as the technology he worships, he can equally venerate both fields to create a space for the arrival of the next ontological epoch and a proper posture of poïesis.

This chapter agrees with Gibson's ultimate assessment of Case and differs from many critics who have written about *Neuromancer*'s evaluation of our relationship to technology as a sweeping condemnation of humanity and portending a bleak and meaningless future. Fair recognizes that "along with Csicsery-Ronay, Jr., many have criticized cyberpunk or *Neuromancer* for a lack of positive alternatives to an impending, dystopic future" in his convincing turn to Zion as a site of redemption, but the Zionites seem much too peripheral to be the focus of the novel's overall thrust (92). I agree that Maelcum and Aerol are positive figures in the proper relationship to technology, but see Case's personal transformation as more significant as he is not only the novel's main character, but also often a surrogate reader. With Case, Gibson is challenging us to make a similar change in our level of consciousness concerning technology whereas Maelcum and Aerol are rebels from their own splinter group living on the fringe of Straylight. We, like Case following Molly's example, need to reclaim both our bodies and our technology as the essential components of a new ontology and synergize them into a poïetic way of looking that sees both the future and the past as instructional. Csicsery-Ronay is right that the novel is bleak and positivity seems in short supply, but this maneuver establishes the dangers of technology so the saving power, through AIs and Molly, can emerge. The transformation we as readers need to undergo is purely internal, but vital, because this internal ontological transformation governs our attitudes toward all external beings.

Valerie Renegar and George Dionisopoulos argue that the novel works to transform readers by "calling into question those practices that have become taken-for-granted in our culture" and encouraging "critical self-reflection and social critique" (324). Enframing is our taken-for-granted ontology, and *Neuromancer* both exposes the dangers and the saving power of technology and "acts as a source of dialectical tension" by preserving the ambiguity of the epoch and explaining how salvation can emerge behind the danger (Renegar 324). Glenn Grant agrees with Renegar and Dionisopoulos' point that the novel evokes deep social commentary and dismisses those that "accuse the author of dealing only in surfaces" because "there are intelligible themes hiding here, stored in the data-structures of the Tessier-Ashpool intelligences, encoded in the auto-destructive behavior of Gibson's characters" which "are cybernetic: human memory and personality, considered as information. People as systems" (41). Grant understands that the novel deals with the dangers of enframing, which are ontological systems that "become closed and entropic" (41). Enframing, like the worst of cybernetics, sees all beings as resources to be harvested and dominated and is a closed system that will consume humanity. Fair is right to use Katherine Hayles' ideas about the posthuman to argue for the redemption of technology in the novel, because Hayles argues away from homogenous ontologies and seeks to defend the body as the irreplaceable source of information. Hayles explains that "embodiment secures" not just gender or human/nonhuman distinctions, but "makes clear that thought is a much broader cognitive function depending for its specificities on the embodied form enacting it" and "this realization" transforms "the liberal subject, regarded as the model of the human since the Enlightenment, into the posthuman" (Hayles, *Posthuman* xiv). Case's understanding of the importance of embodiment leads him to the posthuman while also enabling his respect for all beings. Fair observes Case's transformation from modernity to posthumanity and the post-human ideal of escaping enframing: "embodiment replaces a body seen as a support system for the mind, and a dynamic partnership between humans and intelligent machines replaces the liberal humanist subject's manifest destiny to dominate and control nature" (101). To find poïesis, we must move away from domination and manifest destiny. To break free from the closed ontological system of enframing, Case must be poïetic, which is a form of creativity. Catherine Lord notes that Case's "ability to play the system brilliantly" helps him "overwrite the apparently triumphant cybernetic system and its agents" through creativity, which "is the act of making unexpected moves and dealing with unknown consequences" (168). Poïesis is our only escape from enframing, and we must retain our human unpredictability and creativity to find poïesis, but the creativity must be nurturing and not imperious.

The creativity that helps the AI fusion to emerge is not imperious, because within the scope of *Neuromancer*, there is no partnership between humans and intelligent machines once the Straylight run is complete. Wintermute/Neuromancer's retreat to the corners of cyberspace to seek out AIs indicates that creating AIs does not liberate humanity from the responsibility of making decisions about its fate, which, as Heidegger points out, is not a liberation at all, but an enslavement to enframing. Gibson preserves the anxiety we might have about the responsibility inherent in freewill, and a tyrannical or benevolent machine does not supplant human authority over technology and its destiny. In keeping with Heidegger's thoughts on technology and humanity, *Neuromancer* keeps the pressure on humanity. We must not run away from our creation or bow down to it, but move forward poïetically and of our own will. The way that humans treat the synthesized AI in the novel suggests the mystery and piety we should maintain through all our encounters with beings. Case never tries to force this AI to do anything, but rather watches it emerge on its own once he has nurtured the conditions for its arrival through the Straylight run. Fair is right that Case "finds ... comfort in the influence of the body" but it is unclear if he fully sheds "his humanity in favor of posthumanity" by the end of the novel (Fair 101). Case goes through a dramatic ontological transformation, but unlike Molly, we are not sure if he will relapse into enframing or if he can keep both the danger and the saving power of technology in mind and maintain a poïetic ontology. The ontology that Case ascends to is that of a human being who does not resent the biological or technological interface with the world. Latour focuses on Plato's cave as the prime source of our fracturing of the world. Case has forsaken the social world of the cave's interior for the "truth" that lies in the nonhuman world outside the cave. The mission of the philosopher/cyborg is, like Molly, to transition freely between both worlds and extract value from the truth of culture and the nonhuman (Latour 13–4). But crucially, what must occur during these travels is an ontological project that does not seek to understand through conquest, but through awe and wonder. In the same way that Molly seeks to meet Wintermute but not control it, perhaps we as readers must seek to meet the beings that are thrown before us in the field of Being. Molly has transformed, but we readers—like Case—have been awakened by the events of the novel; we must commit to poïesis to complete our metamorphosis. The ambiguity of the novel presents us readers with a challenge, not unlike the challenge of Being. Thomas Foster argues that gender and race stereotypes are both broken and reinforced by the *Neuromancer*: "The novel therefore defines the opportunities that postmodern culture provides for those of us who are interested in redefining the construction of masculinity, while at the same time providing a cautionary depiction of how that same postmodern culture can merely reproduce traditional gender assumptions" (79). The saving power of poïesis is revealed to Case, but will he follow it or get swallowed back up by the traditional ontology of enframing? The novel provides us the opportunity to not only redefine constructions of gender, but all beings. The question is, what will we — and Case — do with this opportunity?

CHAPTER 5

David Mitchell's *Cloud Atlas*: Cloned AIs as Leaders of an Ontological Insurrection

David Mitchell's 2004 novel *Cloud Atlas* is perhaps marked most notably by its nested structure and the differing genres, styles, and time periods of each section. Although a fractured structure is typical of postmodern literature, the shared birthmark that unifies the main character of each section provides an unexpected synthesis that is more in line with modernist literature. Additionally, the novel functions as both a mimetic text and a metafictional text. Katherine Hayles explains: "a mimetic text creates the illusion that it is transmitting information about the world" and "a metafictional text reveals the world's constructed nature" (Hayles, *Chaos* 21). *Cloud Atlas* reveals the constructedness of Western society through its narrative structuring, and makes social commentary through its mimetic, but counterfactual histories and imagined futures. Beyond the ways in which the novel physically links the characters, there is a distinct thematic thread that runs through all sections, although it emerges most prominently in the middle and end of the novel. This theme is a sickness inherent in modern, Western, colonial humanity, which at first glance, seems nothing more than the will to power. Through a careful analysis, this chapter argues the sickness is an articulation of what Heidegger sees as the more central plight of our time, which is the imperious ontological mode of modern technology: enframing. Mitchell's novel engages the critical dangers of enframing through a repeated representation of human and mechanical enslavement. Benjamin Kunkel explains that in *Cloud Atlas*, as "technological advance continues apace, all things and many persons are for sale" and this reality becomes so established that it is "a condition no one any longer recognizes as political" (92). Enframing conceals itself from view, and only those with an external perspective on humanity can see the nature of our ontology. This chapter argues, in a similar manner to the other novels investigated in this work, that AIs have access to this external perspective and become catalysts for human beings to re-imagine their relationship to beings and Being. Sonmi-451 is admittedly a different kind of AI than HAL or Wintermute, and more closely resembles an android from *Androids*, as Sonmi is a purely biological being.[1] Sonmi is a cloned human, or fabricant, who is enslaved to work in the fast food restaurant chain Papa Song's in Nea So Copros, which is a corpocratic Korea in an imagined future. Sonmi is an AI because Papa Song produces her systematically and artificially, she is genetically identical to all other Sonmis, and most humans treat her as a non-human being. Because she is artificially created and people treat her as non-human, she is perfectly suited to group into the project's analysis of AIs. Along with Sonmi is her futuristic birthmark sharer, Meronym, who is perhaps descended from fabricants like Sonmi and works in the apocalyptic future to save a nonviolent tribe of humans living in Hawaii.

Mitchell's novel is perhaps the bleakest of the four novels explored in this book. It certainly lacks the optimism of *2001*, and makes a more emphatic statement about our current ontological predicament than Dick or Gibson's more ambiguous novels. Dorothy Malone rightly observes, "the stories are all about desperate escapes from situations where gentle, emotionally intelligent beings are being exploited, enslaved or even exterminated by ruthless aggressors" (107). The repetition of this theme produces the bleak tone, which we feel most prominently in the novel's hinge section, which is set in post-apocalyptic Hawaii. The direness of this section is appropriate in a Heideggerian sense, because everything hangs in the balance. Will we turn away from Being and turn into slaves or will we find the saving power and poïetically dwell with other beings in the clearing of Being? This chapter argues that human interaction with AIs is the catalyst for effectuating ontological change in the Valleysman Zachry, who lives in Hawaii and is aided by the technologically advanced Prescients; the Archivist, who studies the clone Sonmi-451's trial and execution; and readers, who have access to the entire story. Heather Hicks interestingly argues that another major contributor to the moral agenda of the novel (leading us away from destruction) is the temporal structure of the novel and how cyclical time grants us a perspective that linear time does not (3–5). Louise Economides argues similarly that the novel's "innovative narrative structure suggests that the evolution of human societies is, in contrast to Western, teleological accounts, profoundly iterative: a movement akin to Eastern and/or Buddhist models of time structured by 'samsara' (recurring cycles of birth, suffering, death, and re-birth)" (618–9). Both arguments rightly suggest that the novel's structure grants us new perspectives from which to view Western history. A new perspective allows us to move beyond the obvious, Nietzschean reading of the eternal recurrence and see the more contemporary ontological commentary the novel makes regarding our relationship to technology. Heideggerian writings on technology address modern technological ontology, which he considers the ontological epoch after Nietzsche's will to power. Hicks' article examines 19th century ontological considerations while the purpose of this chapter is to focus on the 20th and 21st issue of enframing. The difficulty surrounding enframing is its invisibility. It is understandable then that readers miss enframing and instead focus on the will to power. This chapter exposes a more modern dimensionality to the technology anxiety Mitchell's novel examines. Additionally, the end of the novel optimistically suggests that human action can change the cycle of domination and lead to a new ontology. Adam Ewing, an American scientist on a voyage across the Pacific Ocean in the 1850s, prophetically sees the saving power behind the danger of his time, but it takes his own death at the hands of malicious doctors to grant him clarity. Katherine Hayles argues that *Cloud Atlas* "emphasizes a politics of epistemology" but falls short of "ontological questions" (Hayles, "RFID" 50). This chapter argues that reading the novel with a focus on Heideggerian technology studies reveals how Mitchell's work critically engages the ontological crisis of our time: enframing.

Part I: Technology as the Root of Western Sickness

Meronym is presented is a member of the technologically advanced Prescients, who live in a post-apocalyptic future hundreds of years after Sonmi~451's ascension. She is an agent of enframing and poïesis. She has been infected by the sickness of enframing and seen the disastrous effects of this ontology. She uses this perspective not to spread her sickness, but as a catalyst for ontological awakening in the Valleysman Zachry. Meronym's full background is unknown, and in many ways, the same strategies this project has used to treat AIs can be used to explicate her character. She could even be descended from the Papa Song fabricants and be an AI, but this requires some explanation. The idea that she is descended from freed fabricants like Sonmi comes from three textual inferences: (1) Zachry comments that the Prescients "looked more alike'n other people what you see on Big I," which indicates that they are either artificially created like the Papa Song fabricants, with only a few models, or are descended from those fabricants (247); (2) The Valleysmen observe that the Prescients "all got dark skins like cokeynuts" and Meronym tells them, "her ancestors b'fore the Fall changed their seeds to make dark-skinned babbits to give 'em protection 'gainst the red-scab sickness," which indicates genetic modification and artificial creation (252); (3)

In Zachry's old age he even "b'liefed Meronym the Prescient was his presh b'loved Sonmi," which indicates that Meronym and Sonmi look alike or are related (309). If she is descended from fabricants, she either is created similarly or has AI genes, which allows us to read her as an AI. The Prescients look similar and are all genetically modified, which suggests they may be clones or biological cyborgs. Are genetically modified humans still human? Should they be read as technologically integrated cyborgs like *Neuromancer*'s Molly? In Greek, "Meronym" means "part of a whole." Is she part of a human? This chapter reads her as part of enframing, but still capable of revealing the saving power. Meronym may not be an AI, but the Valleysmen all treat her as an "other" and relate her to technology in the way humans interact with AIs and cyborgs in the other three novels. She has also learned from Sonmi and been ontologically informed by her manifesto. Moreover, Meronym uses advanced technology and advanced intelligence, but does not seek to subjugate the Valleysmen. Instead, she aims to help defend them from the Kona and from enframing. She is infected by the sickness of enframing, but reveals the saving power of poïesis. As an agent of the technological future infected by enframing and a technology/human hybrid (genetically modified), we might expect Meronym to represent only the dangers of technology that haunt the novel, as she has the birthmark indicative of the novel's cyclical structure. However, her section is the only unbroken section of the novel and does not repeat. The future is not revealed and remains ambiguous; there is still hope for salvation, and the ontological awakening she gives to Zachry may lead to a poïetic escape from the cycle of enframing. In these ways, Meronym is read in this chapter as a posthuman cyborg like Molly, and potentially a liminal AI. She is a genetically modified, technologically advanced agent of the dangers and the saving power of technology.

Meronym's duty is to prevent the sickness of the "Old Uns" from infecting one of the last peaceful tribes of human beings on Earth. This chapter argues that the sickness Meronym fights is enframing. Economides explains, "the clash between primal and technologically advanced cultures enacted in the first, hinge, and final chapters ultimately deconstructs any notion that technological sophistication equates with cultural superiority" (618). Technological sophistication has been so saturated with enframing that it ontologically deteriorates the "culturally superior" to the point of self-annihilation. Meronym realizes that to save humanity, she must start with "primal" technological ontologies, so she decides to help the Valleysmen. However, she is not only the saving power, as the sickness of enframing has infected her. She has duplicitous motives to find a place to spread civilization for the remaining Prescients, but these goals are never realized. Instead, Meronym reveals to the Valleysmen the dangers and the saving power of technology. Moreover, the home of the Valleysmen is picked because of their ontological posture and potential for awakening to poïesis. Perhaps the Prescients wanted to live with the Valleysmen and poïetically nurture forth civilization again. Meronym's interactions with the Valleysmen can only be understood in the context of the clash that Economides describes, which involves a historical articulation of the sickness of humankind.

The novel begins and ends with the journal of Adam Ewing, a white American on a sea voyage in the 1850s. On his journeys, he witnesses the enslavement of humans and the Christian attempts to colonize indigenous people for "their own benefit." Eventually, Ewing's doctor friend Henry pretends to cure him, but actually poisons him and steals his belongings. Before his death, Ewing comes to a cathartic realization of the true purpose of human life, which is akin to the ontological awakening experienced by Sonmi in the middle sections. Adam Ewing is an enlightenment era Western white male who escapes the pull of the will to power (which metastasizes into enframing) through his deathbed vision.

Adam Ewing is a viable candidate for ontological transformation because of his established concern with the practice of slavery and brutality. He is not an untroubled colonialist, and poïetically empathizes with the slaves. The human master empathizing with the human slave parallels the human master empathizing with the AI slave later in the novel. In both cases, ontological transformation comes when the iniquity of the master/slave relationship reveals the iniquity of every human/being relationship. It is when the object of our imperious ontology becomes a subject that we see the dangers of enframing. When witnessing the disciplining of a slave he writes, "I confess, I swooned under each fall of the lash" (6). Because he considers the subjectivity of the slave through empathy, he is different from those around him who see the slaves as either commodities or less-than-human savages. The beaten slave feels his empathy, for Ewing continues: "Then a peculiar thing occurred. The beaten savage raised his slumped head, found my eye & shone me a look of uncanny, amicable knowing!" (6). The connection Ewing feels through the gaze marks the beginning of his transformation. He is able to receive the look of a being viewed as a raw material by the enframing of the others, and through this, Ewing is able to begin a process of change that leads him away from the thrall of enframing. The sense of "knowing" here could be a human connection, but also could be a larger sense of "knowing" the injustice of enframing, which imperiously casts beings as standing-reserve.

As Ewing's journey continues, he becomes interested in the colonial interaction of whites and aboriginals. When the treacherous Henry asks if "missionaries were now active on the Chathams" they learn that "the Maori don't take kindly to us Pakeha spoiling their Moriori with too much civilization"

(10). Ewing wonders "if such an ill as 'too much civilization' existed or no?" and Mr. D'Arnoq answers obliquely "If there is no God west of the Horn, why there's none of your constitution's All men created equal, neither, Mr. Ewing" (10). Adam explores the limits of civilization in this exchange, but it is hard to say how critical he is at this stage. His faith in civilization — even if slavery is a part of it — might be so strong that he, in the modernist sense, feels that civilization can cure all ills. It is not until later that he expands his inquiry of the civilization. Mr. D'Arnoq's reply is also ambiguous. He could be saying that because there is no equality west of the Horn, the Maori are intentionally keeping the Moriori subjugated by denying them weaponry. He could also be saying that civilization is not something all peoples need or want. To parallel the middle section of the novel, the Maori are the violent Kona and the Moriori are the passive Valleysmen.

The Moriori passively maintain a "creed of Peace" and debate whether they should even defend themselves from the Maori (14). During their parliament the:

> Younger men argued the creed of Peace did not encompass foreign cannibals of whom their ancestors knew nothing. The Moriori must kill or be killed. Elders urged appeasement, for as long as the Moriori preserved their mana with their land, their gods & ancestors would deliver the race from harm. "Embrace your enemy," the elders urged, "to prevent him striking you." ("Embrace your enemy" Henry quipped, "to feel his dagger tickle your kidneys.") [14].

It is too early in the progression of the historical epochs for the dangers of enframing to infect the Moriori, and they are stuck confronting the will to power. The Maori represent the strong that seek to prey on the weak and Henry — the staunch advocate of survival of the fittest — sees the Moriori's commitment to non-violence as ignorant suicide. Mitchell links a refusal of the will to power with the gods and the land. This imbues the Moriori with the poïetic reverence that Heidegger advocates for our current age. The Moriori, and by extension the Valleysmen, are models for something approaching a poïetic existence. By connecting to the tortured Moriori, Adam Ewing sees the mechanism of colonialism as ostensibly violent and imperious, and begins a journey to poïesis.

As Ewing learns more of the Maori's barbarism, he asks Mr. Evans "why had not the Whites stayed the hands of the Maori during the massacre?" (16). At this point, Adam still believes that Whites have a duty to "civilize" their fellow humans, and has a predisposition to combat human evil. Most of the others on Ewing's voyage believe the "strong shall triumph over the weak" and do not stop human evil from manifesting. In fact, they believe such an intrusion is a violation of natural order. Evans himself explains the conundrum thusly: "What to do — stay out of the water or try to stay the jaws of the sharks? Such was our choice" (16). As Ewing considers this reply, he wonders in his journal: "What moral to draw? Peace, though beloved of our Lord, is a cardinal virtue only if your neighbors share your conscience" (16). Adam starts to realize that for equanimity and poïesis to unseat the will to power and enframing, all parties must participate. He understands that nothing less than an ontological change will deliver them. This sentiment foreshadows a larger theme that Mitchell develops later in the conversations between Zachry and Meronym, which maintain that imperious behavior and pious behavior are capabilities of all men — civilized or "not." The novel does not necessarily blame technological ontology itself for barbarous behavior, but does suggest that technological might intensifies the dilemma.

Ewing further establishes himself as ideologically outside the group when he advocates that "to civilize the Black races by conversion should be our mission, not their extirpation, for God's hand had crafted them, too" (16). Everyone in the inn stands against this notion, but Henry's refutation is more oblique. Henry opines: "After years of working with missionaries, I am tempted to conclude that their endeavors merely prolong a dying race's agonies for ten or twenty years. The merciful plowman shoots a trusty horse grown too old for service" (17). At the surface, this is pure colonialism, but if we connect this idea to the rest of the novel, we see that Ewing, Sonmi, and perhaps Zachry will need to initiate a similar "conversion" from enframing to a new ontology. Henry's conclusion is a prognosis that those caught in the snares of enframing can never escape. Ewing's more optimistic attitude makes him not only an ideal vessel for transformation to a new ontology, but also a vehicle of its transmission. In a postmodern moment, Ewing reflects on Henry's thesis and admits, almost exhaustedly, that there are "As many truths as men" (17). Then, more hopefully, Adam looks beyond human truth and explains, "Occasionally, I glimpse a truer Truth, hiding in imperfect simulacrums of itself, but as I approach, it bestirs itself & moves deeper into the thorny swamp of dissent" (17). This chapter supposes that the "Truth" he sees shrouded and mysterious is a way out of the imperious ontology of enframing and a full embrace of the Moriori's peaceful and poïetic engagement with beings and Being.

Mitchell's novel paints the sickness of modern humans as the will to power and enframing, but continually suggests that we can remedy this sickness. Ewing and the Moriori are examples of resistance to the plague of humanity in the enlightenment era of colonial England, and Zachry and the Valleysmen serve as parallels to the Moriori, also being non-violent, tribal islanders. While Ewing's mental ascension from the imperious ontology of enframing is engendered by exposure to his groups' enslavement and colonization of others, for Zachry, his awakening is precipitated by encounters with the barbarous slavers of the Kona (reminiscent of the Maori) and relics of the extinct, ultra-civilized "Old Uns" (279). When Zachry and Meronym are investigating the observatory on the island, they find a dead astronomer who has committed suicide and been preserved by the air-tight chamber. Zachry imagines that this astronomer speaks to him: "*List'n to me, Valleysman,* the soosided priest-king spoke, *yay, list'n. We Old Uns was sick with Smart an the Fall was our cure. The Prescient don't know she's sick, but, oh, real sick she is*" (279). The "smart" referred to by the astronomer is science, which precipitates enframing. The smart dooms their civilization by enabling excessive consumption and a commitment to enframing. It is crucial to note that the astronomer asks Zachry to kill Meronym, who is a member of a dying group of "civilized" humans, the Prescients. The name "Prescient" evokes the idea of ontologically seeing the world "before science" in a non-analytical mode and foretelling the future. The Prescients desire to transmit technology in a way to the Valleysmen that is pre-scientific, in that it deemphasizes an analytical ontology, because they know what future enframing will bring about, having seen the disastrous consequences of enframing firsthand. While the sickness of enframing has infected Meronym, she is working to save the Valleysmen from enframing *and* bestow them with enough technology to defend against the older threat of the will to power from the Kona. The astronomer could be a mouthpiece for two sources: it could be Old Georgie, the Valleysmen's version of the devil, attempting to infect Zachry with the evils of enframing; or it could be the voice the natural world, trying to protect Zachry from the corruption of enframing. The spirit of the astronomer is aware that Meronym is trying to prepare a group of humans to live beyond the dangers of enframing and shield them from the barbarous Kona that threaten to enslave them. Although both sources are viable, further textual explication reveals that enframing, through Old Georgie, is the most likely.

Zachry is not sure what to make of the astronomer's message. He is skeptical of Meronym's motives, but is bound to protect her because she used her technology to save his sister's life. Zachry does not reject the words of the astronomer outright, but he does not blindly embrace them either. Zachry's pressing skepticism is what allows him to be open to an ontological shift. As he mulls the astronomer's suggestion over, the corpse continues: "*Put her to sleep, Zachry, or she'n'her kind'll bring all their offland sick to your beautsome Valleys.... Wasn't killin' her barb'ric'n'savage? Ain't no right or wrong*, the 'stron'mer king teached me [Zachry], *jus' protectin' your tribe or judasin your tribe, yay, jus' a strong will or a weak un. Kill her, bro. She ain't no god, she's only blood'n'tubes*" (280).This attempt to persuade Zachry reveals the astronomer's dark nature. Zachry does not believe in murder, and when he protests, the astronomer brushes away ethics in favor of doing what is right for the tribe. Zachry should protect his tribe from evil and enframing, but if they adhere to tradition and make no ontological changes, they are in a position to be forever dominated by the Kona. Reminding Zachry that Meronym is not a god humanizes her and makes Zachry less likely to violate his creed of non-violence. Casting Meronym as a mortal also obscures her complicated past as a potential descendant of Papa Song's fabricated employees (or from Sonmi herself) and status as a cyborg, inside and outside of humanity. This shows not only the erasure of difference over time, but also the ways in which fabricant AIs and cyborgs can effectively influence human lives.

In the futuristic Nea So Copros (which is essentially present day Korea), the fabricant Sonmi begins to mingle with "purebloods" (non-fabricants) with her purebloods guide, Hae-Joo. Hae-Joo suggests they go out to buy things to combat Sonmi's boredom and depression. When she arrives on the street, she notes: "How the consumers seethed to buy, buy, buy! Purebloods, it seemed, were a sponge of demand that sucked goods and services from every vendor, dinery bar, shop, and nook" (227). Sonmi's distance from enframing allows her to see how modern technological ontology homogenizes all things into commodities for consumption. The sickness of enframing is both that we do not see it and that it demands we ceaselessly turn all beings into the standing-reserve. Enframing has so saturated Nea So Copros that "consumers have to spend a fixed quota of dollars each month, depending on their strata" because "Hoarding is an anti-corpocratic crime" (227). All resources must be constantly invested into the project of consuming the world's resources. Mitchell explicitly explains the outcomes he sees from our current trends. The consumption demanded by enframing becomes engrained in modern society, and laws are passed in order to necessitate it. The process becomes so oppressive that Hae-Joo's mother has to have her son fulfill her quota because she "feels intimidated by modern gallerias" (227).

Aware of how enframing turns humans into blind consumers of resources, Meronym seeks to help the Valleysmen survive in a way that avoids the dangers of technology. Zachry and the Valleysmen worship Sonmi, believing she protects them from the horrors of death. That is: "Unless Old Georgie got your soul.... See, if you b'haved savage-like an' selfy an' spurned the Civ'lize, or if Georgie tempted you into barb'rism an' all, then your soul got heavy'n'jagged an' weighed with stones. Sonmi cudn't fit you into no womb then. Such crookit selfy people was called 'stoned' an' no fate was more dreadsome for a Valleysman" (243–4). The Valleysmen's beliefs about Sonmi critically condemn savagery, greed, and selfishness, but also valorize some degree of "civilization." This distinction allies with Heidegger's thought, which is against enframing but not anti-technology. Technological beings treated poïetically are a part of Sonmi's doctrine. They reinforce the idea that ontological awakening does not require a turning away from technology, but a turning away from imperious enframing. Becoming savage is "dreadsome" to the Valleysmen, because it separates them from the cycle of life. Enframing is a violent process that turns all beings into resources for human consumption and separates humans from Being.

When Meronym comes to stay with the Valleysmen, the only one who sees past the material gifts exchanged for her passage is Zachry. All of the other Valleysmen welcome Meronym freely and do not question her motives. Zachry's skepticism is what enables him to see beyond his own ontology. Both agents of enframing (Old Georgie) and agents of the coming epoch (Meronym) appeal to the vulnerability his skepticism exposes. The reason most Valleysmen do not question the Prescients is because they view them as holy servants of Sonmi. Zachry recalls that his "school'ry room was touched with the holy myst'ry o' the Civ'lize Days" (246). The Valleysmen see all achievements of the "civilized" as wondrous. They are oblivious to the events that precipitated the downfall of the civilized and any negative elements of civilized life. The insidious nature of enframing is that it keeps itself hidden; even through a historical gaze, the dangers of enframing have been obscured. However, while the wonders of civilization impress Zachry, aspects of it do not rest well with him. For example, Zachry recalls the working clock in the school house: "The greatest of 'mazements tho' was the clock, yay, the only workin' clock in the Valleys.... When I was a schooler I was 'fraid of that tick-tockin' spider watch-in'n'judgin' us.... I mem'ry Abbess sayin', *Civ'lize needs time, an if we let this clock die, time'll die too, an then how can we bring back the Civ'lize Days as it was b'fore the Fall?*" (247). Because of his skepticism of civilized technology, Zachry is able to see agents of enframing for what they are. The clock is watching and judging the Valleysmen, because, in effect, this is what clocks do. Clocks turn the dimension of time into delineated raw materials that are to be consumed usefully or these moments become "wasted time." Zachry sees the clock as an arbiter of enframing that is preserving the old ontology that has nearly been lost. Its ticking is a constant reminder that the dangers of technology can never be eradicated or forgotten. The Abbess does not see the clock in this way, instead she sees it as an ideal to be re-attained and resurrected. Meronym's project is not to bring about the civilized days before the fall, as the Abbess believes, for this would only lead to another fall. Meronym wishes to bestow upon the Valleysmen the benefits of technological artifacts and systems without the incessant system of consumption and production that derives from enframing. One way to view "the fall" or expulsion from Eden, is that humankind was punished for desiring knowledge. The Biblical fall is predicated on an acquisition of knowledge and the consequence is the expulsion from paradise. In *Cloud Atlas*, the fall is also centered on the acquisition of too much knowledge. The consequence, however, is expulsion from a technological paradise, not an Edenic, natural paradise. The fall in these two senses marks the removal from one system of dependence (God) to another (Technology). In the same way that God still attends to Adam, Eve, and their children after the fall, the technological agents that embody the achievements of the past-civilization look after the indigenous Valleysmen. Similar to the uncertainty of Adam and Eve's life after the fall is the uncertainty that surrounds the Valleysmen. What will become of them? The future is in their hands, but unlike Adam and Eve, they were not the recipients of the knowledge that caused the fall. Because they did not gain this "knowledge," they remain in a pure state that can accept the coming epoch with a poïetic ontology. Like the other three chapters, the novel preserves the ambiguity and tension of the age, but there remains hope for a technological salvation. In *Cloud Atlas*, this salvation comes through the ontological metamorphosis of the AI Sonmi and the nurturing of the Prescient Meronym.

In keeping with Heidegger's emphasis on preserving technology, although the Valleysmen are safe from the compulsion to enframe now, they also are not entirely against using technology in responsible ways. Zachry explains that the Prescients visit the islands twice a year, but do not stop at "no savage town, not Honokaa, not Hilo, not Lee-ward" because "only us Valleysmen got 'nuff Civ'lize for the Prescients, yay. They din't want no barter with no barb'rians what thinked the Ship was a mighty white bird god!" (247). Being "civilized" then means being non-violent, which is an eminent quality of being that Heidegger advocates humans should have ontologically when witnessing the presencing of beings. This passage also suggests that being civilized means that technology and its ambassadors should not be worshiped as gods. The Valleysmen have the ability to restrain the will to power and the desire to deify or worship technology. The Prescients view this as the perfect mix of innocence and civilization. The Prescients believe that if there is any hope for the surviving members of the human community, it is a poïetic engagement with beings that reserves total reverence for Being and does not worship beings. The Prescients have seen modern technological ontology for what it is, but are too inundated with the past and with technologies to remove themselves from it. Meronym and the other five Prescients near Hawaii look to safeguard the Valleysmen from both the dangers of the current ontological epoch (enframing) and the previous (as shown by the barbarous tribes of humans that embody the will to power).

Trading with the Valleysmen is a risk the Prescients are willing to take, even though their very interaction might transmit the sickness of enframing. Zachry notes that the Prescients' ship, "got no oars, nay, no sails, it din't need wind nor currents neither, 'cos it was driven by the Smart o' Old Uns" (247).

The Valleysmen reverently refer to the "smart" of the Old Uns, but this is not yet problematic, because the Valleysmen express no desire to conquer the surrounding lands or humans. The Prescients' ship does not use natural forces for its locomotion. This suggests that the Prescients are disharmonious with the natural world and only rely on human technologies for their energy. The ship's unnatural power source mystifies the Valleysmen, but not as much as the ship's origin. We learn the Prescients live on "an isle named Prescience I" that Zachry explains is "bigger'n Maui, smaller'n Big I, an' far-far in the northly blue, more'n that I ain't knowin' or ain't sayin'" (247). The mysteries that surround the Prescients help protect the Valleysmen from infection, because of the humility that comes from awe and wonder. Zachry also coyly remarks that he will not divulge any further information about the location of the Prescients — which he may very well know — in an effort to insulate the other Valleysmen from potential sources of enframing.

The theme of enframing as a communicable disease continues to surround the interaction of the Prescients and the Valleysmen as their proximity increases. When physically describing the Prescients, Zachry notes that the "Prescients din't speak much, nay" (248). Their silence is a communal effort to limit contamination. Any information they divulge could allow the sickness of enframing to latch onto the minds of the Valleysmen. They Prescients even post sentries by the boat so the Valleysmen cannot come aboard and see something they should not. Zachry remarks: "Two guards stayed by the shored boats an' if we asked 'em, What's your name, sir? or Where you headed, miss? they'd just shake their heads, like sayin', I won't answer nothin, nay, so don't ask no more" (248). Their reluctance to speak evinces the Prescients' continued efforts to protect the Valleysmen from enframing. Zachry reveals that the sickness is palpable when approaching Prescients: "A myst'rous Smart stopped us goin' close up. The air got thicker till you cudn't go no nearer. A dizzyin' pain it gave you too so you din't donkey 'bout with it, nay" (248). It is unclear whether this experience is unique to Valleysmen, but something about their beliefs and values causes them to become dizzy as they get close to the Prescients and their ship. This foreshadows Zachry's experience with Meronym at the observatory. The force that Zachry attributes as the cause of the sensation is again the "smart" of the Old Uns, but in the context of this argument, this smart is an imperious relationship to beings as inspired by an obsessive adherence to principles of the scientific revolution.

When the Prescients do speak to the Valleysmen, their speech eternally segregates them from the Valleysmen. Zachry recalls that the Prescients, "bartered fair an' never spoke knuckly like savages at Honokaa, but politesome speakin' it draws a line b'tween you what says, *I respect you well 'nuff but you an I ain't kin, so don't you step over this line, yay?*" (248). Although this appears judgmental, the Prescients guard their use of language with the Valleysmen, because they cannot create an opportunity for the sickness of enframing to spread.

Another example of the Prescients sheltering the Valleysmen is when the Abbess requests more advanced weaponry. Zachry remembers that: "Abbess asked the Prescients for spesh weapons to defend us from Kona. The Prescients said nay. Abbess begged 'em, more–less. They still said nay an' that was that" (248). The Prescients wish to protect the Valleysmen, but they refuse to give them weapons because of the sickness inherent in such technologies. There is nothing poïetic about a bomb or a gun. If the Valleysmen acquired such weaponry, they might become infected with the will to power and consequently enframing; the Prescients know this and reject the Abbess' appeal.

The Prescients are just as cautious with factual knowledge they reveal to the Valleysmen. Zachry explains: "'Nother rule was not to tell us nothin' 'bout what lay b'yonder the ocean, not even Prescience Isle, 'cept for its name" (248). The Prescients conspire to restrict geographical knowledge to the Valleysmen to ensure that they do leave the island, as they might encounter ruins of the Old Uns and become infected by enframing. The Prescients even restrain their emotions when interacting with the Valleysmen, but are almost shaken out of their stoicism by Napes of In-ouye Dwellin' who asks, "to earn passage on the Ship" and Zachry recalls "that was nearest I seen the Prescients all laugh" (248). This moment reveals the Prescients as mere human beings, even though they act removed and are AIs.

All of the Prescients' efforts — through the restraint of language, weapons, knowledge, and proximity — come under threat as they decide to have one of their members live with the Valleysmen. Zachry remembers: *"The Prescient chief wants ... One Shipwoman ... to live'n'work in a dwellin for half a year, to learn our ways an und'stand us Valleysmen. In return, the chief'll pay us double ev'rythin we bartered today.... Now think what an honor this is"* (250). Meronym — the Shipwoman in question — is to become an ethnographer/anthropologist, but her motives are much deeper. The Valleysmen regard the Prescient's offer as an "honor," which is problematic because it suggests they nearly worship the Prescients. However, their practical concerns and deliberations temper their reaction and show that the Valleysmen admire the "smart" of the Prescients, but do not worship it.

The danger is still palpable, and whom the shipwoman lives with is critical. Fortunately, she is to live Zachry's family, the Baileys. The whole family is excited and honored to have such a guest, but Zachry is skeptical of her the moment she arrives. This skepticism is what insulates Zachry from the sickness of enframing and makes him the perfect candidate for Meronym's journey to the observatory. Zachry's mother, brother, and sister are delighted to receive gifts from Meronym, but Zachry "din't like this giftin' not a bit, nay" because "this offlander was buyin' my kin.... So I jus' said the Shipwoman could stay in our dwellin' but I din't want her gift an' that was that" (250). His refusal to be bought is a mark of his skepticism and is indicative of the very hesitance a poïetic human needs in waiting for the turning of Being and the next ontological epoch. The ease with which his family is bought reminds us of how insidiously attractive an ontology of absolute commodification can be.

The villagers gather and ask Meronym questions about the Prescients, but Zachry notes that her answers seem guarded and empty:

> [T]he wyrd thing was this. Meronym seemed to answer the questions, but her answers didn't quench your curio none.... So my cuz Spensa o' Cluny Dwellin' asked, *What makes your Ship move?* The Prescient answered, *Fusion engines.* Ev'ryun nodded wise as Sonmi ... no un asked what "fusion engine" was 'cos they din't want to look barb'ric or stoopit.... Abbess asked Meronym to show us Prescience Isle on a map o' the world, but Meronym jus' pointed to a spot an' said, *Here* [252].

The other Valleysmen are too worried about looking foolish and losing access to the Prescients' trade goods, so they pretend to understand Meronym. Their passive acceptance cements their foolishness, and only Zachry, with his courage and skepticism, emerges as a candidate for ontological ascension. His ability to characterize her behavior as agenda driven and dissatisfying puts him outside both the ontology of enframing and the ontology of the Valleysmen.

When Zachry can take no more of Meronym's half-truths, he begins asking her more pointed questions:

> I'd got a bit o' the brave by now an' I asked our visitor why Prescients with all their high Smart'n'all want to learn 'bout us Valleysmen? ... *The learnin mind is the livin' mind*, Meronym said, *an any sort o Smart is truesome Smart, old Smart or new, high Smart or low.* No un but me seen the arrows o' flatt'ry them words fired, or how this crafty spyer was usin' our ign'rance to fog her true 'tentions, so I follered my first question with this pokerer: *But you Prescients got more greatsome'n mighty Smart'n this Hole World, yay?* Oh, so slywise she picked her words! *We got more'n the tribes o Ha-Why, less'n Old Uns b'fore the Fall.* See? Don't say a hole lot does it, nay? [252].

Meronym delicately chooses her words to avoid infecting their minds with the sickness of enframing. Even though her responses are careful evasions, what she says reveals her own ontology. Meronym, as a Prescient, sees the way out of enframing, but is too contaminated by the sickness to escape it herself. With her ontological perspective, she must guide the Valleysmen, because they are not yet sick and can be led to poïesis. Even though she has good intentions, Zachry notices the taint of enframing in Meronym, causing him to question her motives and notice the duplicity in her answers.

During the course of the conversation, Zachry decides that only three of her answers are truthful. The third truth she reveals is the question from Kobbery about her age. When Meronym tells them that she is fifty they were "'mazed" and unsettled because "Livin' to fifty ain't wondersome, nay, livin' to fifty is eerie an' ain't nat'ral" as by forty, the Valleysmen are "prayin' Sonmi to put us out o' misery an' reborn us quick" (253). Because of their technological conditions, the Valleysmen only live to age forty. This may not be surprising, but they have no desire to live longer than this mark — even when they hear that Prescients live much longer. Moreover, the Valleysmen view living to fifty as something eerie and unnatural, which emphasizes the way Meronym's use of technology makes her appear as "other" to the Valleysmen. This suggests, for the Valleysmen, that using technology to extend human life has no purpose and seeking mastery over death is problematic. Meronym sees nothing wrong with the average Prescient lifespan of sixty or seventy, but does not introduce technologies to the Valleysmen that would equally extend their lives. She observes and assists, but with minimal colonial impact and technological exposure.

Despite Meronym's efforts to shield the Valleysmen from enframing, inevitably it surfaces and threatens to spread. Her anthropological project is tainted by an overreaching scientific agenda. Much of her observation is passive and innocent, but Zachry looks beyond the surface and decides that not all of her work is passive. Zachry recalls a time when Meronym was questioning them about their icons, which are the Valleysmen's burial relics. She asks: "*Is icons a home for the soul? … Or a prayer to Sonmi? Or a tombstone*" (258). Zachry observes: "See it was always whys'n'whats with Prescients, it weren't never 'nuff sumthin' just was an' leave it be. Duophysite was the same here on Maui" (258). In true Heideggerian fashion, Zachry observes that the fundamental problem with the Prescients' approach to beings is that they always ask "whys'n'whats" and cannot let anything simply "be." This characteristic is a hallmark of enframing and a symptom of their sickness. Meronym and Duophysite, another Prescient, both share this trait and this suggests all Prescients are infected by enframing. The moment strikes Zachry as so odd that, as he watches Meronym further, he even begins to see her thoughts manifest in her countenance: "Now it didn't often happ'n I could read anyun's thinkin's, but that beat I seen the Shipwoman wond'rin', *Oho, then this Icon'ry I got to go visit it, yay*" (258).

Zachry is not an insightful person when it comes to others, but his ontological distance from the Valleysmen and the Prescients enables him to see things as they are and become curious to why Meronym is on the island. When Zachry confronts Meronym about why she is "*here sussin our lands! Sussin our ways! Sussin us,*" she calmly replies, "*What matters here ain't part true or hole true, Zachry, but harm or not harmin, yay*" (262). Meronym acknowledges she is duplicitous, but believes it is okay if she does no harm. The imperious gaze enframing is harmful, but Meronym feels her actions are necessary to prevent a greater harm to the dignity and existence of the human race.

The first threat to the ontology of the Valleysmen comes from Meronym's Orison. Zachry goes through Meronym's belongings and finds the silvery egg, which serves as both a long-range communications device and a holographic display for stored information. This is the same device the Archivist uses to record Sonmi's trial and marks a link between the two stories. As Zachry picks up the Prescient technology, he notes:

> So hungrysome was my curio, I held it again, an' the egg vibed warm till a ghost-girl flickered'n'appeared there! ... an' she was talkin'! Now I got scared an' took my hands off the sil'vry egg, but the ghost-girl stayed ... she was talkin' in Old-Un tongue.... For ev'ry word I und'standed 'bout five–six followed what I din't ... I murmed, *Sis, are you a lost soul?* Ignored me she did.... *Can you see me?* Fin'ly I cogged the ghost-girl weren't talkin' to me an' cudn't see me [263–4].

The high-tech object dangerously piques Zachry's curiosity. He is afraid of the ghost-girl that emerges (which we know to be Sonmi), but this fear is the danger Heidegger marks as beholden to the saving power. If Zachry weren't scared, he might try to use this technology as a weapon or an instrument to his advantage. What scares him specifically is that a human form emerges from the inert egg. The subjectivity of the AI projected from the egg prevents the birth of enframing from his interaction with a technological artifact. Sonmi is an artificial intelligence from the age of the Old Uns who has been genetically designed and grown in a "womb tank." Her presence as a viable subjectivity imbues this object with a sort of defense mechanism against enframing and positions Zachry into a posture of awe and wonder. Zachry notes that she speaks the Old Un tongue and only understands one in six of her words. This translation barrier helps inoculate Zachry against enframing. Even though the ascended fabricant AI Sonmi has seen her way out of modern technological ontology, the orison she speaks through is still a dangerous technological artifact.

As the awe and wonder subsides, Zachry musters the courage to interact with the object, but he does so through the holographic woman and using language. His employment of the word "sis" forges a connection between them and signifies an equality that is indicative of a poïetic engagement. Zachry treats her not as something human made, but as a spirit or ghost. His first question is about her wellness and the nature of her being. He doesn't try to impose a scientific or imperious understanding upon her, he poïetically asks her about herself. His inquiry about whether she can see him is a perfect example of a poïetic approach and why Zachry is the ideal candidate for ontological ascension. He is interested in the being's ability to "see" him, and this concern exhibits an investment in beings that is far richer than enframing demands. Enframing only focuses on the profitability of the being as a raw material, not the potential for collaborative presencing in the clearing of Being.

Although this moment appears to be a beautiful example of how the sickness of enframing can be kept at bay by poïetic engagement, Sonmi's projection is suddenly replaced by an angry male Prescient. He barks at Zachry, "*Who are you, boy, an where is Meronym*" (264). Calling a grown man a "boy" establishes a clear hierarchy between the two and changes the terms of Zachry's engagement with the Orison dramatically. No longer is Zachry questioning how he should view the Orison, but is instead being told how to behave and what to think. Although the speaker's gruffness may be an act to inhibit closeness and protect the Valleysman from the sickness of enframing, it comes across more strongly as the imperious voice of enframing itself, which demands from humans the forcible transformation of all beings into raw materials. This tone is emphasized as Zachry explains the Prescient's closing threat: "*I'll be watchin, Zachry o Bailey's Dwellin* ... see he even knowed my dwellin' like Old Georgie" (264). The Prescient appears as the panoptic eye of judgment and Zachry connects him to Old Georgie, which is the Valleysmen's version of the devil that works in opposition to Sonmi's plans. The sternness and threat of observation may be measures to prevent Zachry from using the Orison again and being exposed to enframing, but through this intention, the dangers of enframing shine forth and Zachry feels an overlap with the evil and murderous Old Georgie.

Another moment of potential contamination is when Zachry pleads with Meronym to use her "smart" to save his dying sister. At first Meronym refuses the appeal saying, "*The life o' your tribe's got a nat'ral order*," which establishes her presence as a passive observer that must not disturb their customs (267). Zachry, feeling desperate, pleads: "*I reck'n jus by bein here you're bustin this nat'ral order. I reck'n you're killin Catkin by not actin. An I reck'n if it was your son ... this nat'ral order d not be so important to you, yay?*" (267). He correctly sees through her attempt at neutrality and objective passivity, as her very presence carries the taint of enframing. By personalizing the injury, he begins to pull at Meronym's heartstrings and get her to set aside her protective agenda. When Zachry presses further and asks, "*Why's a Prescient's life worth more'n Valleysman's?*" Meronym's stoic façade falls away and she snaps, "*I ain't here to play Lady Sonmi ev'ry time sumthin bad happ'ns an click my fingers'n make it right! I'm jus' human, Zachry, like you, like anyun!*" (267). This exchange exhibits Meronym's acknowledgment of her limitations and her confliction regarding her role as a guardian of the Valleysmen and a woman with feelings. She dares not save Zachry's sister because she does not want to introduce the sickness into the Valleysmen, but she hates not acting when she has the power to save a human life. This scene exemplifies technology anxiety, because through all of the imperious dangers of technology lies the saving power of medicine. Medicine can be a salvation by nurturing forth a human life so it can again stand on its own. Meronym does decide to save Zachry's sister in secret to limit the exposure of enframing. This act makes Zachry indebted to her. Zachry remains skeptical of Meronym's motives, but has been softened enough to accompany her to the observatory.

As Meronym and Zachry's relationship deepens and their mutual trust increases, she feels that she can answer some of his more difficult questions about life beyond the valley. Inquiring about the Fall of the Old Uns, Zachry asks:

Who, asked I, tripped the Fall if it weren't Old Georgie? ... The Prescient answered, Old Uns tripped their own Fall.... But Old Uns'd got the Smart!
I mem'ry she answered, *Yay, Old Uns' Smart mastered sicks, miles, seeds an made miracles ord'nary, but it din't master one thing, nay, a hunger in the hearts o humans, yay, a hunger for more.*
More what? I asked. *Old Uns'd got ev'rythin.*
Oh, more gear, more food, faster speeds, longer lifes, easier lifes, more power, yay. Now the Hole World is big, but it weren't big nuff for that hunger what made Old Uns rip out the skies an boil up the seas an poison soil with crazed atoms...
I asked why Meronym'd never spoke this yarnin' in the Valleys.
Valleysmen'd not want to hear, she answered, *that human hunger birthed the Civ'lize, but human hunger killed it too* [272–3].

This exchange marks the moral philosophy of the novel as a whole and reveals enframing as the sickness of humanity. The Valleysmen externalize their devil into the form of Old Georgie, and perhaps this is appropriate for them because they have not yet taken in technology. For the Prescients, the devil is an internal effect of enframing, viewed as a human manifestation of evil upon the world. Meronym points to all of the benefits of technology, but says that none of them were enough to satiate human hunger. This hunger is what Heidegger would call enframing, or the endless desire to consume, produce, and turn all beings into the standing-reserve. Meronym sees both the danger and the saving power of technology, but believes there can be no salvation for the Prescients or the Old Uns, because they are too far gone along the path of hunger and enframing. Interestingly, deep in the Old Uns history this exact fear was detected by Frobisher's (the music composition protégé and gigolo who writes letters to Sixsmith) friend M.D. who laments, "Our will to power, our science, and those v. faculties that elevated us from apes, to savages, to modern man, are the same faculties that'll snuff out *Homo sapiens* before this century is out!"

(445). Enframing is the evolution of the will to power that extends beyond human spheres to encompass all beings. Mitchell's characters see the end before it comes, but it is almost as if it is already too late for Western humans — even in Frobisher's time. Only the Valleysmen can be made to see the dangers and avoid them truly on the path to the next ontological epoch. Meronym rightly points out that the most insidious aspect of enframing is its invisibility and the way that denial functions to perpetuate this invisibility. M.D. may have diagnosed the problem, but he is excited about the fall of humankind and in no position to lead us away from enframing. It is a hard truth to acknowledge that technology can provide such benefit but also be so dangerous. Only a select few can be awakened to this truth, and Zachry's skepticism is what makes him the only Valleysman able to hear the disturbing reality of modern technological ontology. With the constant threats from the Kona, the Valleysmen's lives are difficult enough; Meronym does not want to introduce more difficulty by telling them that the technology they admire contains both the saving power and the dangers.

Meronym knows, however, that there are truths that seem real on the surface that are simply distortions and distractions from Being. When Zachry asks if "*the true true is diff'rent to the seemin true*" Meronym replies, "*Yay, an it usually is*" (274). In the context of this book, the "true true" is the underlying danger of enframing, which does not present itself as readily apparent. The "true true" is also the way beings would presence if we viewed them in a poïetic fashion and let them be. This is why Meronym explains, "*true true is presher'n'rarer'n diamonds*" (274).

One of the main reasons Meronym visits the island is to make the trek to the ruined observatories at the top of the mountain. When Zachry and Meronym get close to the first observatory, Zachry asks, "if this was where Old Uns worshiped their Smart" (275). This indicates that Zachry believes that there is something holy about technology and/or that the Old Uns were so pleased with their technology that they worshipped it. The danger the Prescients hope to avoid by limiting the technological exposure of the Valleysmen is the Valleysmen worshiping technology instead of Being and beings. Poïesis is a reverential and respectful treatment of all beings, human and nonhuman. Meronym explains that "they wasn't temples, nay, but *observ'trees* what Old Uns used to study the planets'n' moon'n'stars, an' the space b'tween, to und'-stand where ev'rythin' begins an' where ev'rythin' ends" (275). These sites expose both the danger and the saving power of technology. On the one hand, they are places that inspire wonder in the vastness of space and the mysteries of creation; even Meronym is seen "marv'lin' as much as [Zachry]" (275). This evokes a sense of awe and poïetic wonder, but before the sentence ends, Meronym's reveals that the purpose was not to marvel, but to "understand."

This exposes the underbelly of such projects as an imperious mode of conquering the universe through rote scientific classification. This is the danger of exposing Zachry to the sickness of enframing, but, because of his skepticism, he is able to endure such an experience without becoming imperious.

On their way back to the Valleys from the observatory, Meronym tells Zachry a story that resembles the Promethean fire theft:

> Back when the Fall was fallin', humans f'got the makin' o' fire.... So Wise Man summ'ned Crow an' say-soed him these words: ... *find a long stick ... an fly into that Mighty Volcano's mouth an dip it in the lake o' flames.... Then bring the burnin stick back here to Panama so humans'll mem'ry fire once more an mem'ry back its makin.*
>
> Crow obeyed the Wise Man's say-so ... draggin' that stick o' pine thru the melty fire, *whooo-ooo-ooosh,* it flamed! Up'n'out o' that Crow flew ... fire lickin' up that stick, eyes smokin', feathers crispin', beak burnin'.... *It hurts!* Crow cawed. *It hurts!* Now, did he drop that stick or din't he? Do we mem'ry the makin' o' fire or don't we? ... *it ain't 'bout Crows or fire, it's 'bout how we humans got our spirit* [284–5].

Inside this tale is the novel's essential commentary on technology anxiety and the dangers of modern technological ontology. First is the anxiety shown in many post-apocalyptic narratives, which is that humans will forget how to live in the world without technological conveniences. The fear highlights our dependency on technology and how technology makes us soft and apart from the natural world. The loss of fire represents the loss of technology and to re-learn or re-master the fire, humans depend on an animal to sacrifice itself for humanity. This sacrifice exhibits the scope of enframing and the reach of modern technological ontology, which homogenizes all beings into raw materials. The crow's sacrifice is not in vain, because humans still can make fire and have not been taken over by enframing. Behind the danger of the tale lies the saving power, which is our connection to all beings and the poïetic attitude we must have when attending to them. Our technological actions affect all beings, and we have a responsibility to remember our influence and interconnection to the world. The moral of this tale is that with our technological power comes a responsibility to all beings. The story helps remind us to avoid the dangers of enframing so the crow's sacrifice will not be in vain. Our spirit comes from our responsibility to dwell technologically on the earth as *Dasein,* which means viewing beings poïetically.

Hearing the Meronym's tale and being exposed to the observatories are Zachry's first steps toward ontological transformation. It is a risky process, as he may become infected with the sickness of enframing, but there is a literal disease killing the Prescients and their time is limited. They must pass on a record of the Old Uns knowledge poïetically to prevent the Valleysmen from stumbling upon enframing in the future. Thinking about tale, Zachry begins to ask questions that further his transformation: "The fires o' Valleysmen an' Prescients both are snuffed tonight ... so don't that proof savages are stronger'n Civ'lized people?" (303). This question leads into a discussion about who is the more enlightened and how one should "be" in the world as a responsible and poïetic human. Meronym replies, "*It ain't savages what are stronger'n Civ'lizeds ... it's big numbers what're stronger'n small numbers. Smart gived us a plus for many years, like my shooter gived me a plus back at Slopin Pond, but with nuff hands'n'minds that plus'll be zeroed one day*" (303). Meronym's response extends beyond human politics and ventures into the realm of entropy as discussed in *Androids*. A violent relationship to beings and Being can only be maintained for so long. Technology may provide a path to this posture at first, but nature or entropy will eventually overcome all human efforts. The key is not to imperiously struggle against beings, but to engage them nonviolently, as the Valleysmen do. Such a stance will promote a much longer lifespan for all beings on the Earth. Zachry is not satisfied by Meronym's answers and presses her until she explains: "*List'n, savages an Civ'lizeds ain't divvied by tribes or b'liefs or mountain ranges, nay, ev'ry human is both, yay. Old Uns'd got the Smart o gods but the savagery o jackals an that's what tripped the Fall. Some savages what I knowed got a beautsome Civ'lized heart beatin in their ribs. Maybe some Kona. Not nuff to say-so their hole tribe, but who knows one day?*" (303). Meronym rightly acknowledges that all humans have the capacity to either capitulate to enframing or to live poïetically. Being low-tech or high-tech doesn't matter, because anyone can choose how to live and the question is not a struggle of group against group, but a struggle the individual human must realize and endure. Her belief in the Kona implies that a sea change in ontology is not too much to hope for, and is the only remedy for the ills of savage brutality or civilized enframing.

Meronym stands outside of enframing intellectually, but her and her people are nonetheless dying of it ontologically. Even so, her efforts are not entirely in vain, because she aims to nurture an indigenous human community and not colonize them or indoctrinate them into the cult of enframing. Meronym's designs are in stark contrast to the missionaries in the opening and closing sections of the novel taken from Adam Ewing's journal. Preacher Horrox assiduously works to convert the islanders to Christianity and underwrites his project with high-tech instruments of war. He optimistically believes that he and his fellow missionaries have made a foothold on the island and he forcibly begins to convert them to his worldview. Meronym uses weapons to keep the barbarous tribes at bay, but instead of converting people to enframing, her project is to warn the Valleysmen *not* to be like them. The great span of time in the novel allows readers to see the bookends of the will to power and enframing. Initially enframing is seen as the cure for "savage" peoples and finally it is seen as the sickness. When Mr. Boerhaave coyly asks Horrox "how does one *begin* the work of conversion upon a benighted beach where no Christian foot ever trod?" the preacher rejoins:

> Tenacity sir, compassion & law. Fifteen years ago our reception in this bay was not so cordial as your own, sir.... On the beach of Bethlehem Cove we fought & some of us fell. Had our pistols not won that first week's battles, well, the Raiatea Mission should have remained a dream. But it was the will of the Lord that we light his beacon here & keep it burning.... I regret the Native deaths, but once the Indians saw how God protects his flock, why, even the Spartans were begging us to send preachers [478].

Although a Heidegger reading sees merit in the preacher's acceptance of something larger than humanity, Horrox's entire mission is made bankrupt by virtue of his reliance on technological violence to secure the island. The trajectory of the novel has us begin with Adam Ewing and colonialism, move to Sonmi and rebellion, then to Zachry and Meronym in a lamentation and death of an era, only to end cyclically with colonialism. Because of this structure, the ironies of Horrox seem even more laughable and the technologically underwritten project of colonialism appears as an early manifestation of the sickness of enframing.

Nowhere is the colonial project linked more substantially to enframing than in the section detailing the "Nazareth Smoking School." Wagstaff explains to Ewing that the church had him found the academy:

> You must understand, sir, your typical Polynesian spurns industry because he's got no reason to value money. 'If I hungry' says he, 'I go pick me some, or catch me some. If I cold, I tell woman, "Weave!"' Idle hands, Mr. Ewing, & we both know what work the Devil finds for them. But by instilling in the slothful so-an'-sos a gentle craving for this harmless leaf, we give him an incentive to earn money.... Ingenious, wouldn't you say? [482].

The claims of Christianity and capitalism are not taking hold in the community, and enframing is losing out. In order to ensure that the islanders become dependent on money, and therefore the missionaries, they poison them with addiction. Instead of poïetically embracing the islanders, they seek to make them addicts to the same system that has already enslaved the missionaries to ceaselessly consume, produce, and turn all beings into resources. Meronym works to inoculate the Valleysmen from the sickness of enframing while Horrox and Wagstaff work to spread the sickness to the islanders.

What Preacher Horrox does not realize yet is the futility of forcibly converting anyone or anything to a particular ontology. Meronym understands all too well that technology and technological weapons are only enough to delay a rebellion against nature and beings. Wagstaff, however, is aware of the tenuous nature of their missionary work. When Ewing tells Wagstaff how fortunate it must be to "dwell in such an Eden" he sees that his "pleasantry puncture the young man's spirits" and Wagstaff explains:

> "Eden's a spick 'n' span place, but every living thing runs wild here, it bites & scratches so. A pagan brought to God is a soul saved, I know it, but the sun never stops *burning* & the waves & stones are always so bright, my eyes ache till dusk comes…. The place puts a straining on *our* souls…. You'd think the savages'd be grateful, I mean, we school them, heal them, bring employment & eternal life! Oh, they say … 'Thank you, sir' prettily enough, but you feel *nothing* … *look* like Eden it might … the Devil plies his trade here as much as anywhere else. The ants! Ants get everywhere…. Until we convert these accursed ants, these islands'll never be truly ours" [483].

The straining Wagstaff feels on his soul is enframing's relentless pull against what he knows at some level to be right. It is harder to convert human beings into resources than rocks and trees, but enframing demands the work never cease. He is not quite ready to admit that the gifts he is bringing are dubious, but seeing how the natives vacantly placate them is an indication of just that. He realizes that it is a fallen place, but does not see that it is his very ontological project that makes it so. This is the most dangerous aspect of enframing: deceiving the believer into thinking it is a cure and not a sickness. The island will never "belong" to anyone, because beings belong to themselves and are not simply human resources. The uncomfortable feeling Wagstaff gets living here is symptomatic of the incongruity of his project with nature. He feels the untamed vitality of the island as upsetting because is living against the land, wishes it to be as "spick 'n' span" as Eden and fully under human control. Even his vision of Eden is infected by enframing and has lost its collaborative and natural atmosphere.

Wagstaff's feelings are made painfully clear when he expresses his concern at the disproportionate number of Bibles they have to the converts available. Wagstaff tells Ewing that they've "got thousands of Bibles begging for an owner" because there are "not enough Indians" (487). There may have been at one time, but the very presence of the missionaries is killing the natives as "ships bring disease dust here, the Blacks breathe it in & they swell up sick & fall like spinny tops" (487). He comes close to realizing that the colonial intentions of the missionaries is a disease, but cannot link the two causally as enframing shrouds itself from view. Wagstaff laments that they "kill what you'd cherish & cure … that seems to be the way of things" (487). They are killing what they intended to cure because their cure is the disease. Violent, imperious intentions come loaded with sickness, no matter how righteous the mission might seem. Enframing has corrupted their practice of religion, as they view all humans homogenously as resources waiting to be converted.

Racism has also infected their cause, as Preacher Horrox believes whites to be divine. Their presence is meant to cure the natives from the devil's taint, when it is their ships that come loaded with the disease in the first place. When the treacherous Henry explains that he thinks the reason the missionaries have taken root is that "the weak are meat the strong do eat," Horrox feels that this reduction misses the fundamental question, which is "Why do White races hold dominion over the world?" (488). The preacher believes whites are ordained by God and given technology to do their bidding. He asks: "How is it that the musket came to the White man & not, say, the Esquimeau or the Pygmy if not by august will of the Almighty?"(488). Henry cynically responds:

> "Our weaponry ... is not *manna* from Sinai's skies.... 'But why us Aryans? ... Because, Preacher, of all the world's races, our love — or rather our *rapacity* — for treasure, gold, spices & dominion, oh, most of all, sweet dominion, is the keenest, the hungriest, the most unscrupulous! This rapacity yes, powers our Progress; for ends infernal or divine I know not" [489].

Henry believes whites are unique, but not because of divine favor, but of their lust for power and control. He rightly points out that any human can have the capacity to be imperious — as does Meronym — it is merely a question of whether those individuals in charge fall victim to enframing or if they live poïetically. The will to power fuels only an unending will to will that accomplishes the darkest potentialities of enframing and turns human beings into undignified slaves to consumption and production. The ambiguity of the epoch is preserved, as Henry admits he does not know if progress will bring good or evil.

Nothing will be done to combat the sickness of enframing while men of consequence like Henry shrug their shoulders and drink the spoils instead of putting in action a plan that will address the problem at its source. Humans, in Mitchell's novel, are unable to guide themselves out of modern technological ontology because they cannot see it as the sickness. The posthuman cyborg Meronym attempts to nurture Zachry's ontological development because she is removed enough from humanity to see the sickness as enframing and has seen the saving power through Sonmi. The next section moves from looking at enframing as the sickness of the current ontological epoch to analyzing how the ascension of Sonmi evinces the saving power behind the danger.

Part II: AI as Savior: The Ascension of Sonmi~451

The literary conceit that Mitchell uses to transmit the tale in Sonmi's sections is the transcription of a court case where Sonmi is on trial for treason against Nea So Copros. Sonmi~451 is a genetic clone (or fabricant) manufactured by Papa Song to be a server at a fast food restaurant in what we would call Korea. Servers work identical twenty hour days for twelve years before they go to Hawaii for "Xultation," where they believe they will be made regular consumers with the rights and benefits of any citizen, or pureblood. Instead, Xultation is a process that electrifies the fabricants and turns them into the very food sold at their restaurants. Hayles makes the fascinating point that Sonmi~451 as a label is both subject and object; a human name and a number (Hayles, "RFID" 58). What this combination allows is a scenario that turns both the servers and the purebloods into resources. Hayles writes, "When each object has a unique identity, objects begin to seem more like individuals, and individual people become susceptible to being constituted as objects" (Hayles, "RFID" 58). If we allow enframing legislatively and ontologically to condone the enslavement of human clones, we allow our own individuality and subjectivity to be compromised by the demands of enframing. Purebloods become resources for consumption and servers are resources to facilitate more consumption by purebloods. Sonmi is coaxed out of her narrow ideology by a rogue Yoona clone that clandestinely educates herself and eventually tries to escape. The conversation between her and the archivist serves as an instructional primer for the reader on what fabricants are and how human slaves are created even in the "civilized" future. The Archivist too goes on her ontological journey, although he at first he cannot believe her. When she explains her feelings about being a slave the Archivist exclaims, "*Slaves, you say? Even infant consumers know, the very word slave is abolished throughout Nea So Copros!*" to which Sonmi calmly replies "Corpocracy is built on slavery, whether or not the word is sanctioned" (189). No one would be able to tolerate eating in a diner serviced by slaves, so they populace must at the ontological level not consider the servers human. The most dangerous aspect of enframing is its insidious invisibility. Benjamin Kunkel notes that for this reason, *Cloud Atlas* is the "most cynically organized" of contemporary dystopian novels, because "business and government have melded with one another" (90). This fusion is centered on the politics of enframing.

In the beginning of the trial, Sonmi must explain in detail what the experience of each day is like for a Papa Song fabricant. The fabricants are AIs because they are not only treated as less-than-human, but they are genetically engineered and rigorously conditioned to think in a systematic and artificial way. When the archivist asks Sonmi what her earliest memories are she replies, "Fabricants have no earliest memories, Archivist. One twenty-four-hour cycle in Papa Song's is indistinguishable from any other" (185). Humans prevent them from remembering, lest they learn something rebellious that would compromise their acceptance of their servitude. The fabricants are AIs then, because humans expect them to perform as robots wearing human skin. This is the result of enframing at its peak, which is the complete transformation of a human subject into a resource for exploitation. Sonmi is quite literally a cog in the machine and will be killed and consumed by the public when her contract expires. In addition to having no recollection of the past, humans feed the fabricants the addictive drug "Soap" which also serves as their nutrition. Sonmi explains, "Soap contains amnesiads designed to deaden curiosity" (186). Those in power have technological engineered medicine to keep control over their technologically engineered humans, so the illusion of cheap and delicious food as a benefit of the consumerist paradise of Nea So Copros can keep the "purebloods" in control. Finally, fabricants are removed from the future by their conditioning, which has them see "one long-term future: Xultation" (186). The parallels to religion as the opiate of the masses are blatant, but we must remember that this religion, the servers, and the xultation are all created systems that turn humans into the standing-reserve. The will to power no longer allows a select few to control the many; all have fallen under the control of enframing and the ceaseless will to will without knowing it. This is the danger as Heidegger saw it, for the will to power at least ensured a dictator or tyrant would dominate other humans. In enframing, we all become homogeneous resources awaiting our reaping.

Similar to the sickness of the Old Uns or the colonizers, Sonmi's sickness is a fog that obscures her free will and dignity. When discussing the rebellion of Yoona~939, Sonmi characterizes Yoona on their first meeting as being "aloof and sullen" for a server (187). She then realizes that "her aloofness was in fact watchfulness" and "her sullenness hid a subtle dignity" (187). Human dignity is what Heidegger emphasizes is at stake if we become enslaved to enframing. If we become slaves, we lose our right to participate in the event of Being as *Dasein* and become lost to the gaze of Being and the radiant presencing of beings. As Yoona breaks free of the genetic and cultural conditioning that desperately attempt to enslave her, she gains dignity through autonomy and critical thinking. The archivist recognizes this and asks if Yoona's "*subtle dignity*" was "*a result of her ascension?*" (187). Sonmi is not entirely sure, but does speculate that "ascension merely frees what Soap represses, including the xpression of an innate personality possessed by all fabricants" (187). Humans in this world are committed to consumerism and enframing so prominently, that the only drug they require to remain passive is consumption. The fabricant AIs need the soap, because their uninfected eyes would immediately see the iniquity and peril of the prevailing ontology. Only an AI can escape enframing in a culture this far gone. The "cures" of colonialism, Christianity, soap, or consumerism all work to promote the very illness that threatens to destroy humanity ontologically. *Cloud Atlas* cleverly charts the many false cures put forth by agents of enframing, but also includes the genuine cure of poïesis as revealed by fabricant AIs.

After loosening the bonds of Sonmi's mental slavery by exposing her "master" as fallible and vulnerable, Yoona then breaks the bonds of her physical confinement by showing Sonmi a secret door that leads beyond the walls of the diner. As Sonmi goes through the doorway and into the adjoining room, Yoona explains: "Now, dear sister Sonmi, you are *inside* a secret" (191). Yoona is teaching Sonmi to explore boundaries, and how to escape mental and physical limitations she did not even know were there. This her first glimpse at enframing, which is the ontology that allows humans to be created as instruments and not autonomous beings. Sonmi recalls what she saw inside the darkness of the room: "A white blade sliced the black: a miraculous moving knife that gave form to the stuffy nothing.... My heart beat fast. What is that knife? I asked. 'Only lite, from a flashlite,' answered Yoona. I asked, Is lite alive? Yoona answered, 'Perhaps lite is life, sister'" (191). Sonmi confuses light for a weapon, slicing through the air. Yoona describes light as life to mean that nothing is more important than making things visible, for unconcealing the truth from the darkness is the event of Being. Sonmi needs to escape the darkness of her situation by seeing how things really are, but must first see the darkness as concealment and know that something lies waiting to be unconcealed. For Heidegger, humans must let beings unconceal and not imperiously demand how they are to be defined. If we are to escape from enframing, we must see that we are being tricked by our ontology and understand the consequences of this ontological mistake. Inside the room, Yoona flips through a book that shows pictures of the outside world and uses these images to become "her animated self" (191). In the same way that Yoona sees her way out of the lie of slavery and enframing through a book, the hope of this work is that by reading books containing AI and human interactions, we too can see our ontological peril as approaching slavery, imagine a way out of enframing, and find poïesis.

However, seeing a way out of enframing — or seeing the truth — does not necessarily bring happiness to the seeker. Sonmi explains, "Ascension creates a hunger sharp enough to consume the subject's sanity in time. In consumers, this state is termed chronic depression" (192). Seeing the true nature of things and understanding the enslaving snares of enframing creates depression in consumers, because all that makes consumers happy is consumption. If consumers are to see their participation in a system of homogeneously commodifying beings for consumption as an evil, they are bound to be depressed because there appears no alternative ways to be happy in the world. Some may find sources of happiness and manage the sight of such evil, but for others it is too much. The archivist asks Sonmi if she is suggesting that depression or mental illness is what caused Yoona to attempt an escape. Sonmi replies, "I am, emphatically. Mental illness triggered by xperimental error" (193). HAL turns against the crew in *2001* because of a mental illness precipitated by a mandate to be duplicitous. AIs are freshly created and innocent beings in many ways; becoming exposed to the true nature of human behavior via enframing is overwhelming to many of these new intelligences. The dramatic effect of being revealed to our ontological reality and mentally collapsing is one way in which the representation of AIs can be a catalyst for our own ontological awakening. If we see how the truth affects AIs, perhaps we will understand the magnitude of our situation and the immediate danger we are in.

Through a story, we might be able to accept the truth, but in the face of a real rebellion against modern technological ontology, the truth might be lost. For example, most readers of *2001* see HAL's mutiny as a punishment for human hubris, not a call for ontological transformation. Similarly, when Yoona-939 attempts to escape the diner using a child to activate the elevator, purebloods in Nea So Copros are stunned and terrified. Yoona is immediately killed, but Sonmi knows that by virtue of her act purebloods, "felt the corpocratic world order had changed, irrevocably ... vowed never to trust any fabricant ... knew that Abolitionism was as dangerous and insidious a dogma as Unionism [and]... supported the resultant Homeland Laws dictated by the Beloved Chairman, wholeheartedly" (195). Instead of Yoona's death serving as a rallying point for the abolishment of fabricant slavery, it instills a mistrust that can never be mended, and allows the slavery of fabricants to continue. Enframing is so insidious and compelling that acts of rebellion against it can simply be spun into means of tighter control, and only those ready for ascension see the acts for what they really are.

Sonmi's ascension cannot be stopped at this point, and she finds it increasing difficult to return to her previous way of life as a server. Union men (who are against Nea So Copros and corpocracy, and practitioners of Unionism) come disguised to the diner and take Sonmi away to a university. Sonmi-451 rides through the night in a ford on her way to the university and witnesses her first dawn outside the diner: "I cannot describe what I felt. The Immanent Chairman's one true sun, its molten lite, petro-clouds, His dome of sky. To my further astonishment, the bearded passenger was dozing. Why did the entire conurb not grind to a halt and give praise in the face of such ineluctable beauty?" (208). In this passage, Mitchell is emphasizing the fundamental point of poïetic looking, which is to nurture the becoming of beauty and beings without imposing an imperious agenda upon them through definition or desire as resource. The humans in the novel are so enthralled by enframing that they pass by the beautiful sights, regarding them as mundane trivialities compared to their consumerist concerns. Heidegger fears we will become so committed to enframing that we will lose our ability to appreciate the magisterial beauty and wonder of beings and Being. Instead, we will homogenously see beings in one way: the standing-reserve. Later, when Sonmi is describing the beauty of snow, the archivist remarks, *"you speak like an aesthete sometimes, Sonmi"* to which she replies, "perhaps those deprived of beauty perceive it most instinctively" (211). Yoona never got the chance to see beauty. Perhaps it would have cured of her depression. If we are to awaken and poïetically see beings as they wish to be seen, we too will see the beauty we have been deprived by enframing.

After her wasted time under the "care" of the silver-spooned, sadistic, and hopeless graduate student Boom-Sook, Boardman Mephi formally moves Sonmi to her own quarters and allows her to attend classes. When the Boardman shows her around her new dwelling, he explains that his daughter-in-law had designed it: "The Rothko canvases, she hoped, I would find meditative. 'Molecule-true original originals,' he assured me. 'I approved. Rothko paints how the blind see'" (218). The AI Sonmi finds pleasure and enrichment in art. Artists can see — if only temporarily — a way out of modern technological ontology. Heidegger believed that by observing certain artworks, we too can glimpse the nature of enframing and understand the need for a way out. Sonmi's comment that Rothko paints how the blind see suggests that to let things be and see them as they truly wish to be seen, we must almost close our eyes, because they are so tainted with enframing.

All was not well for Sonmi, however. Even though she is free of the diner and Boon-Sook, not everyone is as kind to her as Boardman Mephi. Sonmi describes her first lecture:

> When I took off my cloak in the corridor, my Sonmi features provoked surprise, then unease. In the lecture hall, my entry detonated resentful silence.
> It didn't last. "Oy!" a boy yelled. "One hot ginseng, two dog-burgers!" and the entire theater laughed. I am not genomed to blush, but my pulse rose. I took a seat in the second row, occupied by girls. Their leader had emeralded teeth. "This is our row," she said. "Go to the back. You stink of mayo" [221].

Although this is a university with "open" minds, a clearly "inferior" being attending "their" lecture outrages the vocal students. This interaction between humans and AIs shows resentment toward a sentient "instrument" and the social stratification that follows. Being upset at the education or enfranchisement of an AI is a reaction of a human being so wrapped up in enframing that they work to prevent any disruption in the gaze that diminishes and homogenizes all beings.

Even those who do not ostensibly discriminate mark Sonmi as non-human. At another lecture, two boys ask if she "really was some sort of artificial genius" (223). Purebloods in the novel consider Sonmi an artificial intelligence. Their intentions are not cruel, but they establish a difference between themselves and Sonmi. A racist reading of this scene is worthwhile, but misses the Heideggerian reading, which is that the human/non-human status of an AI arrests the flow of enframing and causes the boys to consider the nature of their ontology. If the previous students were inspired by enframing to castigate and belittle Sonmi out of imperious outrage at her rebellion against being turned into the standing-reserve, these boys are momentarily awakened to poïesis. When Sonmi gives them a thoughtful and modest reply, the narrator explains, "hearing a server talk made the pair marvel" (223). They are not threatened by her ascension, but rather cast into a state of wonder and marvel — which are the features of poïetic, technologically looking. Being forced to consider Sonmi's subjectivity, one of the boys opines, "It must be hell ... to have an intelligent mind trapped in a body genomed for service" (223). What the student is beginning to understand is that all beings have a way about them that enframing inhibits. Sonmi cannot stand on her own because enframing demands her servitude and exploitation. Realizing how awful it is to enslave Sonmi in a Papa Song's restaurant, one wonders if the boy then turns this dilemma upon his own situation, and sees the horror of a system that demands his slavery for the sake of endless production and consumption trapping his own mind. Potentially, this interaction with an AI causes the boys to see the dangers of modern technological ontology through the hell of Sonmi's enslavement, while also making them aware of how these dangers invade the quality of their own lives. By seeing these dangers, perhaps the boys will then see the saving power, which is to treat all beings poïetically, the way they treat the ascended Sonmi~451. Sonmi replies to the boy's sympathy by explaining that she "had grown as attached to my body as he had to his" (223). This rejoinder exposes their humanistic pride at believing an AI should feel like them. The solution is not for all beings deemed "intelligent" to be then turned into humans, but rather that all beings should be exalted for the forms that they possess. Humans are not the "ultimate" form all beings should strive to resemble, but rather one of many. Sonmi's remark causes the boys, who are trying to work their way out of their ontology, to remember that a feature of poïetic and pious engagement with beings and Being is to remove humans from the illusory thrones they have created for themselves.

After trying to attend lectures, Sonmi decides that self-learning through her sony (laptop computer) in her apartment is better than facing the crowds. Boardman Mephi notices a change in her mood the longer she isolates and asks a post grad (who is a key member of the Union in disguise) to take her out on the town. The two have an awkward first encounter as they try to persevere through small talk and social graces and Sonmi asks him "why [she] made him nervous" (225). Similar to the two students who marveled at Sonmi, Hae-Joo is not quite sure how to interact with an ascended AI:

> I looked like any Sonmi in any old dinery, he answered, but when I opened my mouth I became a doctor of philosophy.... He confessed, "A little voice in my head is saying, 'Remember, this girl — woman, I mean — I mean, person — is a landmark in the history of science. The first stable ascendee! Ascendant, rather. Watch what you say, Im! Make it profound!' That's why I'm just, uh, spouting rubbishy nothings" [225].

He finds her extreme intelligence intimidating, but more so, because she is a human made instrument of the imperious Papa Song. In the same vein as the students, the narrator uses words like "wondering" to describe Hae-Joo as he interacts with Sonmi. His ontological sense is shifting from mechanically considering Sonmi as a cloned hamburger server to wondrously seeing her has a being that is equal — if not superior — to the humans who enslave her. When he calls her girl, woman, then person, we see his nervousness, which is inspired by awe and the difficulty he has defining her. Awe and wonder arrest imperious scientific classification and his flustering with language reveals how removed from enframing he is when he engages with Sonmi. He cannot force her to confine to traditional labels, her presence demands that he let her be. However, this escape is momentary, and not devoid of enframing. Although Hae-Joo may feel one way about the encounter, Sonmi recalls, "I assured him I felt more like a specimen than like a landmark" (225). A landmark inspires wonder and awe, while a specimen is the subject of imperious scientific observation. Just as Meronym is perhaps tainted by enframing, Hae-Joo cannot help but project upon Sonmi imperious feelings.

To try to get to know her better, Hae-Joo asks Sonmi what she does for fun. She explains that she plays Go against her Sony to relax. When Hae-Joo asks who wins, Sonmi answers, "The sony ... or how would I ever improve?" (225). Although this might seem innocuous, Hae-Joo is so enraptured by wonder that he asks, "So winners ... are the real losers because they learn nothing? What, then, are losers? Winners?" to which Sonmi replies, "If losers can xploit what their adversaries teach them, yes, losers can become winners in the long term" (225). A Heideggerian, ontological analysis reveals that those in power are the losers, because they are no longer learning anything. Those who enframe learn nothing from beings, except how to exploit them. They are blind to the fact that this process ultimately results in their own enslavement and exploitation. Losers, or those oppressed by enframing, can learn from the winners how not to live, and can exploit this knowledge to ascend themselves to a poïetic ontological posture. But of course, such a transformation cannot happen overnight, and Sonmi's logic makes Hae-Joo's head spin: "'Sweet Corpocracy'— Hae-Joo Im puffed —'let's go downtown and spend some dollars'" (225). Still a consumer, Hae-Joo feels that their best medicine is to spend money and participate in enframing, instead of taking the time to think and deeply contemplate the implications of Sonmi's response.

As Sonmi's ascension progresses, Hae-Joo convinces her obliquely to return to Papa Song's. At first, he asks her if she missed "the world [she'd] been genomed for," but she is not ready to return as "fabricants are oriented not to miss things," and she has not entirely transcended her orientation (229). Papa Song propaganda oriented Sonmi to have a particular ontology, especially with regard to how she viewed herself and her customers. Changing one's ontology is to re-orient one's self such that s/he acquires a new posture toward beings and Being. Even to reevaluate one's self, it is not enough simply to think internally. Sonmi realizes this through Hae-Joo's council. When she decides to make the journey back to Papa Song's, it is because she feels the trip is vital to her ascension: "It helped me understand how one's environment is a key to one's identity but that my environment, Papa Song's, was a lost key. I found myself wishing to revisit my x-dinery under Chongmyo Plaza. I could not fully xplain" (229). Ontology is crucial to being, because in order to understand ourselves and our place in the world, we must understand the importance of the beings that populate our location in Being. Returning to a place where she ontologically viewed beings in a particular way, she can further her ascension by seeing how problematic these ontological opinions were.

Entering the diner awakens Sonmi violently to the reality of her ascension and the horrors of Papa Song's. She recalls:

> As the elevator descended, I grew very nervous. Suddenly, the doors were opening and hungry consumers riptided me into the dinery. As I was jostled, I was stunned at how misleading my memories of the place had been....
>
> The wholesome air I remembered: now its greasy stench gagged me. After the silence on Taemosan, the dinery noise was like never-ending gunfire. Papa Song stood on His Plinth, greeting us.... surely my Logoman would condemn his prodigal daughter.
>
> No. He winked at us ... I realized, Papa Song was just a trick of lites. How had an inane hologram once inspired such awe in me? [230].

Symbolically, one must descend to enter the diner, which exhibits its base ontological and moral position. The ways the narrator describes the consumers screams of imperious violence: in a mob they greedily "riptide" to satisfy the insatiable itch of consumption. The sights, smells, and sounds she once loved now repulse her, as her ascension allows her to see the enframing running through every phenomenological feature of the diner. The violence inherent in the scene is indicative of the violence enframing perpetrates on beings; she had never noticed before. Expecting rebuke from the holy Papa Song hologram, she now sees it for what it is, an "inane" consumerist message. Finding awe in this icon is a clear example of how enframing displaces the true awe meant for Being onto beings in a way that perpetuates the seeing of all things as resources to consume.

Gaining courage from her new perspective on the diner, Sonmi takes the next step: engaging a fabricant employee. The beings of the diner appear disgusting and violent now, but perhaps Sonmi can salvage something from an encounter with fabricants, which are constructed subjects. Sonmi, inspired by "a cruel compulsion" asks a Kyelim unit if she wanted, "to live how purebloods live? Sit at dinery tables instead of wiping them?" (231). When Kyelim~889 replies "servers eat Soap!" Sonmi tries asking more penetrating questions, but the consumers behind her in line begin to protest the delay. Sonmi tells the archivist:

> A consumer girl ... jabbed me. "If you've got to taunt dumb fabricants, do it on firstday mornings. I need to get to the gallerias this side of curfew, okay?" ... [M]y questions had marked me as a troublemaker. "Democratize your own fabricants!" A man glowered... "Abolitionist." Other purebloods in the line glanced at me, worried, as if I carried a disease [231].

The novel again presents us with human subjects so turned over to enframing that they become angry when anyone threatens to liberate the enslaved or call into question the hierarchy of beings. The girl must get to the galleria to spend her quota of money before the city's imposed curfew forces her into her home. She is so immersed in modern technological ontology that she does not even see her situation as a form of slavery eerily similar to the fabricants. The other consumers who see her as a troublemaker bark labels at her for interrupting their access to quick and cheap food. In the previous section, Meronym knew the Prescients carried the disease of enframing and took measures to prevent spreading the sickness to the Valleysmen; in Sonmi's world, those infected by enframing see anyone who threatens the order of their ontology as diseased. Meronym can see the sickness for what it is because of Sonmi's ascension, while those in her time have not been enlightened by an AI and see threats to enframing as sickening.

On her way out of the diner, Sonmi runs into Mrs. Ahn, wife of the late owner of the diner, Seer Rhee. She has since changed her name, but pretends to be distraught over her former husband's death: "Mrs. Ahn dabbed her eye with her sleeve and asked if I had known her late husband well. Lying is harder than purebloods make it look, and Mrs. Ahn repeated her question" (231). Sonmi is taken aback by how easily Mrs. Ahn can lie, and in this way resembles AIs like HAL, who have such difficulty with deception. We lie so easily and so readily, that we no longer see it as strange. Sonmi sees the deception of humanity in the same way she sees enframing as deceiving humans away from abetting and Being. Moving outside one's ontology allows access to a truer sense of beings and Being, which helps Sonmi see Papa Song in a new way, and notice the ease with which "purebloods" lie.

When Hae-Joo and Sonmi return to her apartment, Hae-Joo compliments Sonmi on her ability to handle such a difficult situation: "If I had ascended from server to prodigy in twelve straight months ... I would be in a psych ward somewhere, seriously" (232). Unlike HAL, Sonmi is strong enough psychologically to endure an ontological transformation. Hae-Joo's remark suggests that humans cannot transform alone, and require the strength of the AI to serve as sacrificial catalyst for ontological awakening. Hae-Joo goes on to tell Sonmi "These ... xistential qualms you suffer, they just mean you're truly human" (232). This implies that she was not human before. This allies with Heidegger's definition of true humans as *Dasein*, who understand time and mortality. Hoping for some succor, Sonmi asks Hae-Joo how she "might remedy" these qualms, to which he replies, "You don't remedy them. You live thru them" (232). This is the next reality that Sonmi must embrace, which is that her qualms will never be satisfied or undone. This preserves the tension or strife that pervades enframing, but, as Heidegger maintains, is present in any epoch.

Continuing on her ontological journey and awakening, Sonmi invests herself in learning of human history. She learns: "the past is a world both indescribably different from and yet subtly similar to Nea So Copros. People sagged and uglified as they aged in those days: no dewdrugs. Elderly purebloods waited to die in prisons for the senile: no fixed-term life spans, no euthanasium. Dollars circulated as little sheets of paper and the only fabricants were sickly livestock" (234–5). These "improvements" all follow the trend of enframing to erase our humanity, as they conceal the truth of human mortality and make fabricant humans tantamount to livestock. Mitchell's future appears something like Huxley's *Brave New World*, as the government imposes euthanasia and fixed life spans. The progression of enframing is seen here as a linear degradation of society; now we imprison our elderly, while in the future, we will be so accustomed to seeing humans as raw materials, that euthanasia seems logical and appropriate.

The novel opens with colonialism and the slave trade, and ebbs toward a new mode of slavery. Islanders, the elderly, and fabricants are all ontologically seen as less-than-human. Sonmi learns through "disneys," or movies, to realize: "Your present, not we, is the true illusion" and "For fifty minutes, for the first time since my ascension, I forgot myself, utterly, ineluctably" (235). Through the art of the movies, Sonmi is able to become critical of her present ontology and imagine a way out. This is similar to much SF, which describes the future but actually makes commentary about the present in order to make change or, at least, elicit thinking. She sees that enframing has eclipsed the truth so completely in their world that AIs are less "illusory" than their reality.

Sonmi, a genetically manufactured AI, is helped to ontological ascension by watching images of humans in film. Zachry, the skeptical Valleysman, is helped on route to his ontological ascension via Meronym and the holographic projections of Sonmi through an orison. In both of these cases, AIs and art serve as the foundation for awareness of the dangers of enframing and a glimpse of the saving power. Inside the observatory, Zachry asks Meronym about the orison and the images it projects. He learns that she is not "a window" but a "mem'ry" and is no longer living (276). When he asks if she was a Prescient, Meronym

> hes'tated, an' said she wanted to tell me a hole true now, but that other Valleysmen not be ready for its hearin'. I vowed on Pa's icon to say nothin' ... *She was Sonmi, Zachry. Sonmi the freakbirthed human what your ancestors b'liefed was your god.*
> Sonmi was a human like you'n'me? ... Sonmi'd been birthed by a god o' Smart named Darwin, that's what we b'liefed [276–7].

The ascended fabricant Sonmi becomes deified in the future by the Valleysmen. This is what protects them from enframing, and the reason the Prescients help them. Worshiping an agent of poïetic abetting is a good start, but at some point, the Valleysmen must learn that she is an AI, but also a human and that no humans or beings should be worshipped. Meronym is aware of their potential, but acknowledges that most of the Valleysmen are not ready for such knowledge. Similar to Yoona's psychological meltdown, the rest would react negatively to such news about their goddess. Zachry and Sonmi, however, have the makeup to withstand an ontological transformation.

In this moment between Zachry and Meronym, the narrator informs us of Sonmi's martyrdom and the price she had to pay to transmit her message faithfully to the rest of humanity. Meronym explains, *"A short 'njudased life Sonmi had, an only after she'd died did she find say-so over purebloods'nfreakbirths' thinkin's"* (277). The description of Sonmi as "freakbirthed" is interesting because she was artificially created in a lab. She is not a random "freak" born with severe birth defects, but is a freak because of the horrific scientific process that was modulated to produce human slaves. Just like HAL, Corto, Roy Baty, Pris, and Irmgard — the AI agents of *2001*, *Neuromancer*, and *Androids* respectively — Sonmi must be the one to die to teach humans how to live.[2] She will not live to see the turning of Being and the next epoch, but she has done everything she can to help assist humanity into a proper posture of poïetic waiting. Meronym tells Zachry that *"Sonmi was killed by Old-Un chiefs what feared her, but b'fore she died she spoke to an orison 'bout her acts'n'deedin's"* (277). The hegemonic agents of Nea So Copros and enframing wished to quell the rebellion, but Sonmi was able to actually use technology (as a record) against the masters and set in motion an ontological insurrection. The technology anxiety we have about AIs engendering a mechanical insurrection against us is actually the voice of enframing in our ears causing our fear, because the rebellion is against our ontology and would lead to our salvation.

In Sonmi's time, the escape from technological enslavement and enframing is not purely a mental process, as all purebloods are required to have "souls" implanted in their bodies to track their location and restrict access. Enframing has taken over so completely in Nea So Copros that the soul is conceived as a material techno-artifact that one wears or imbeds in their body. When transporting Sonmi away from the authorities: "Hae-Joo ... got a flick-knife from his pouch and sliced off the tip of his left index, gouged, and xtracted a tiny metallic egg. He threw it out of the window and ordered me to discard my Soulring similarly. Xi-Li also xtracted his Soul" (313). The system polices its citizens through implanted souls, and only through bloody violence does one break free from the chains of enframing. This aspect of the story shocks the archivist, and he asks Sonmi, "*Unionmen really cut out their own eternal Souls? I always thought it was an urban myth*" to which Sonmi replies, "How else can a resistance movement elude Unanimity?" (314). The language in this exchange is quite telling. The archivist without pause refers to a mechanical implanted tracking device as an "eternal Soul," which shows how enframing can blind its slaves and make them even mystify their own shackles. The "eternal Soul" is now something human made and used for control. The government's name of "unanimity" evokes the homogenization of enframing. The rebellion members being called "Unionmen" inserts a Marxist twist on the revolt of the laborers against the bourgeois, but it is more important to note how the few, by means of enframing, turn the many *and* themselves into raw materials to be exploited.

The next step to escaping the Unanimity pursuers is to have artificial Souls implanted that will allow Sonmi and Hae-Joo to sneak past checkpoints. Sonmi watches as the Soul implanter "tweezered the tiny egg from his gelpack" and notes: "That such an insignificant-looking dot can confer all the rights of consumerdom on its bearers yet condemn the rest of corpocracy to servitude seemed, and seems still, a bizarre obscenity to me" (314). The difference between a pureblood and a fabricant server is an implanted egg. The fact that a mechanical artifact punctuates this boundary marks the corpocracy as an arm of modern technological ontology. The purebloods think that this egg grants them liberty, but all it does is enslave them. They have more rights and mobility than the servers, but their fate is in some ways worse, because they do not even notice that enframing has made them slaves to consumption and production. Because Sonmi has ascended, she sees the violent insertion of the egg as an "obscenity" while no one else notices the process as unusual. Sonmi too must have her identity changed through the implanter. He first removes her server's collar. She recalls, "I heard a click, felt a tickling as it pulled away, then it was in my hands. That felt odd: as if you were to hold your own umbilical cord" (320). The collar bound her to a slavery of servitude. It is of course evocative of a pet's collar, meant to denote ownership and harness the will. Her remark about an umbilical cord shows how dramatically the cord connected her to a system of dependency. Now she is truly free to be herself. All that is left is the unspeakable crime of "Souling" a fabricant and facescaping her to change her appearance.

Once the violent "Souling" Sonmi undergoes to lose her slavery and gain a mechanical Soul is completed, they travel further away from the city to the Union's secret base. On the way there, Sonmi encounters her first of three final scenarios that secure her mission to save humanity from enframing. Sonmi sees an expensive ford pull up to a bridge:

> The driver opened the ford trunk and ... lifted out a striking, perfectly formed, but tiny female form ... she mewled, terrified, and tried to wriggle free. When she caught sight of us her miniature, wordless scream became imploring.
> ... The man swung her off the bridge, by her hair, and watched her fall. He made a plopping noise with his tongue when she hit the rocks below and chuckled. "Cheap riddance"—he grinned at us—"to very xpensive trash."
> I forced myself to remain silent. Sensing the effort this cost, Hae-Joo touched my arm. One scene from the Cavendish disney when a pureblood gets thrown off a balcony by a criminal, replayed itself in my head [334–5].

In this scene, Sonmi witnesses another type of fabricant be treated as a commodity. Enframing insidiously prompted humans to be cloned to be expensive living dolls for the wealthy, so that humans would move one step closer to being seen as standing-reserve. Now that the consumerist craze surrounding the dolls is over, the man throws the girl away like garbage. There is never even a thought by the man (Seer Kwon) or his wife that the doll's life is worth more than raw materials. Sonmi's status as a cloned AI and the film she saw allows her to see the girl "doll" poïetically. Again, the artwork of the movie gives Sonmi the insight to the dangers of enframing. The archivist senses Sonmi's anger and asks, "*You considered him a murderer?*" and Sonmi replies, "Of course. One so shallow, moreover, he did not even know it" (336). Seer Kwon's ontology is so steeped in enframing that he sees the girl only as a resource or commodity; he has no moral consideration for her has a human, or a being to be treated poïetically. Heidegger is adamant about proclaiming enframing to be the great danger of our current ontological epoch because we do not even see it as a danger. The Archivist presses, "*But hate men like Seer Kwon, and you hate the whole world*" and Sonmi explains, "Not the whole world, Archivist, only the corpocratic pyramid that permits fabricants to be killed so wantonly, casually" (336). Sonmi articulates that her project is not to hate the world — which is the imperious mission of enframing — but that her job is to change the ontology that denies fabricants, humans, and all beings poïetic consideration.

Once she arrives at the remote mountainside base of the Union, Hae-Joo shows Sonmi a carving of Siddhartha in the mountain. At first Sonmi cannot see it, but Hae-Joo tells her to keep looking

> and from the mountainside emerged the carved features of a cross-legged giant. One slender hand was raised in a gesture of grace. Weaponry and elements had strafed, ravaged, and cracked his features, but his outline was discernible if you knew where to look. I said the giant reminded me of Timothy Cavendish.... He said the giant was a deity that offered salvation from a meaningless cycle of birth and rebirth, and perhaps the cracked stonework still possessed a lingering divinity. Only the inanimate can be so alive. I suppose QuarryCorp will destroy him when they get around to processing those mountains [328–9].

Sonmi's continued return to Timothy Cavendish is partially a component of the novel's mysterious overlap across time and space, but also recalls her artistic awakening to enframing via the disney. In the rock, they see divinity and this is the next step for Sonmi as she ascends from servitude to poïetic engagement with beings and Being. She must see the grace in all beings and allow them to presence into the clearing of Being in the same way she lets the carved Buddha emerge from the rock face. Sonmi's noting of the power of the inanimate reveals her as a poïetic subject abetting the becoming of beings. Hae-Joo's ominous statement about QuarryCorp again emphasizes how enframing will turn even a divine mountainside carving into raw materials for processing, and how homogenization will erase the divinity. When the Archivist realizes where Hae-Joo has taken her, he balks, "*So Union hid its interlocutor, its ... messiah, in a colony of recidivists?*" (329). He is slowly seeing Sonmi as the savior she is, and perhaps being turned away from the imperious claims of enframing himself.

Sonmi is curious about the carving and asks the Abbess of the colony about Siddhartha. The Abbess tells her, "Siddhartha had other names" which are now lost, and although her "predecessors knew all the stories and sermons ... the old Abbess and senior nuns were sentenced to the Litehouse when non-consumer religions were criminalized" (330). Enframing has infected society so deeply that religions that do not compel consumption are outlawed, lest people imagine an alternative ontology. The idea that Siddhartha had other names implies that this divine carving could represent all non-consumer based religions. Continuing her inquiry, Sonmi concludes that it would be ideal if "Siddhartha would reincarnate" her into the Abbess' colony because she has seen "how all pure-bloods have a hunger, a dissatisfaction in their eyes, xcept for the colonists I had met" (332). The Abbess agrees and explains:

> If consumers found fulfillment at any meaningful level ... corpocracy would be finished. Thus, Media is keen to scorn colonies such as hers, comparing them to tapeworms; accusing them of stealing rainwater from WaterCorp, royalties from VegCorp patent holders, oxygen from Air-Corp. The Abbess feared that, should the day ever come when the Board decided they were a viable alternative to corpocratic ideology, "the 'tapeworms' will be renamed 'terrorists,' smart bombs will rain, and our tunnels flood with fire" [332].

Sonmi is aware of the way that enframing compels humans to turn all beings into materials for production and demands ceaseless consumption. She sees how they cannot cure this sickness through the medicine the system prescribes, and how government and media outlets would leverage language against the colonists if anyone were to take them seriously. As Sonmi continues to ascend, she sees how the control systems work to keep enframing in power. She realizes that if she wants to effectuate change on a global level, the agents of enframing will mobilize violently against her and linguistically turn her into a cancer of varying levels. First, the hegemony will call her the sickness in the form of a tapeworm; then they will call her a violent threat in the form of terrorism so they can leverage extreme prejudice against her and the Unionmen with full support of the public. Enframing has claimed ownership of the water, the air, and the land. All that remains is to turn those few remaining humans who see a way out into slaves.

The final sight for Sonmi in her ontological ascension is to see what really happens to Papa Song servers when they get twelvestarred and move toward xultation. General Apis of the Union asks her "to assume in their struggle to ascend fabricants into citizens" (340). This is partially true, but she is working to ascend citizens away from the imperious claims of enframing by ennobling fabricants, and causing their subjectivity to be ontologically considered. The General explains that the final step is to "xpose you to a ... sight, a formative xperience ... before you decide, Sonmi" (340). The Archivist, who early in their conversation disbelievingly rebuked Sonmi's suggestion that her and her fellow fabricants were slaves, also becomes awakened by hearing of this "formative xperience" second-hand.

Hae-Joo and Sonmi sneak on board Papa Song's Ark to see what happens to fabricants sailing to Hawaii for Xultation. Each server happily believes she is to be freed of her collar and helped to become a pureblood consumer in Hawaii, but she is actually being led to her death. After being unsuspectingly killed by the device they believe will free them, their bodies are taken to a processing room on the ship: "A slaughterhouse production line lay below us, manned by figures wielding ... various tools of cutting, stripping, and grinding. The workers were bloodsoaked ... I should properly call those workers butchers: they snipped off collars, stripped clothes, shaved follicles, peeled skin, offcut hands and legs, sliced off meat, spooned organs ... drains hoovered the blood" (343). Humans create the fabricants to be instruments. Once they deem their lifespan over, humans treat the fabricant like raw materials and use every scrap to further different systems of production. The Archivist is skeptical and asks, "*What would the purpose be of such ... carnage*" to which Sonmi explains:

> The genomics industry demands huge quantities of liquefied biomatter, for wombtanks, but most of all, for Soap. What cheaper way to supply this protein than by recycling fabricants...? Additionally, leftover "reclaimed proteins" are used to produce Papa Song food products, eaten by consumers in the corp's dineries all over Nea So Copros. It is a perfect food cycle [343].

The cycle of enframing is a perfect circle that leaves no being untouched, and violently sucks all beings into its vortex. By seeing this sight, Sonmi has finally been awakened to the truth about enframing. Seeing the saving power in the divine rock face, seeing the Seer murder the genomed toy, and seeing her cloned sisters ruthlessly slaughtered and used as food for themselves and others are the final rites she must endure to commit herself fully to the project of saving humanity from enframing.

Of course, the Archivist cannot believe that the governmental system he represents would allow such an atrocity to exist and he calls Sonmi's claims "*preposterous,*" "*unconscionable*" and "*blasphemy*" (343–4). Regaining his composure, he concludes: "*If fabricants weren't paid for their labor in retirement communities, the whole pyramid would be ... the foulest perfidy*" (344). Sonmi calmly tells the Archivist "business is business" implying that capitalism considers only the bottom line. The Archivist retorts, "*You've described not 'business' but ... industrialized evil!*" and Sonmi simply states, "You underestimate humanity's ability to bring such evil into being" (344). Earlier, M.D. and Henry wish to lay the blame of humanity's evil on scientific theories like "survival of the fittest" or "natural order." In so doing, they forfeit humanity's dignity to take responsibility for its own acts. Enframing is not to blame; humans are to blame. We are the ones that ultimately choose how we view the beings around us. As difficult as it is for the Archivist to hear, an AI can see enframing and human evil for what it is. The fascinating part of her ascension is that even though she sees human evil directly, she still believes we are worth saving and is prepared to sacrifice her life if it means helping us move from imperious looking to poïetic looking.

Sonmi's first words after seeing the slaughter-ship are her manifesto, plan, and testaments to her unwavering commitment to change the ontology of Nea So Copros. She recalls to the Archivist her conversation with Hae-Joo:

> "That ship must be destroyed. Every slaughtership in Nea So Copros like it must be sunk."
> Hae-Joo said yes.
> "The shipyards that build them must be demolished. The systems that facilitated them must be dismantled. The laws that permitted the systems must be torn down and reconstructed."
> Hae-Joo said yes.
> "Every consumer ... must understand that fabricants are purebloods ...
> "Ascended fabricants need a Catechism, to define their ideals, to harness their anger, to channel their energies. I am the one to compose this declaration of rights. Will — can — Union seedbed such a Catechism?"
> Hae-Joo said, "This is what we're waiting for" [346].

One of the major components of Heidegger's writings on technology is the importance of diminishing human power and authority in the face of something superior. For Heidegger, that superior force is Being. Believing in something higher than humanity inserts a limiting factor on our ontology, such that we might restrain or prevent imperious violence altogether. This project maintains that SF authors consciously or unconsciously use AIs as the higher beings that tame human hubris and cause us to rethink our ontological posture. Sonmi writes the Catechism which becomes the mantra for poïetic living and the religious dogma of the Valleysmen. They worship Sonmi as a Goddess, not knowing she is an AI. Her words serve as their protectors in the future, where Meronym tries to ensure their survival as the dwindling ambassadors of human freedom and dignity. *Cloud Atlas* presents Sonmi the AI martyr and Meronym of the dying Prescients as ontologically awakened prophets that risk everything to help the very humans that enslaved fabricants in the first place. In this way, we see how the dangers of modern technology manifest in human enslavement and human harvesting, but how these dangers can lead to rebellion and ontological ascension. The novel cries out at the reader to take the message of Sonmi and Meronym to heart, but the most blatant polemic comes in the final pages of Adam Ewing's journal.

Part III: Conclusion

Meronym and Sonmi fight to help humanity turn away from enframing. They both intrinsically believe that humans have a decision to make regarding their ontology. Although humans are being fiercely pulled in one direction by enframing, they can let go of the compulsion to see all beings as something to consume through a raising of consciousness. George Gessert makes the interesting point that, "Ewing, Frobisher, the Korean slave and the last Moriori all have affinities: Each leaves familiar territory for the unknown and each encounters forms of murderous selfishness that suggest something eternally dark about human nature" (425). The novel indeed shows the capacity for human darkness, but, specifically because of how it ends, it also shows us the way out of this darkness. As Heidegger argues, we are not either fully imperious or poïetic; we must simply strive to be the latter and not the former. Gessert's point is fully felt through the characters M.D. Henry, and Preacher Horrox. These men do not blame humanity, but mistakenly believe that the will to power is the unalterable natural order and that humans are bound to this order as well. Sonmi and Meronym are able to see the emptiness of this stance, and how it is a lazy excuse to exploit others and not face the challenges of enframing as a danger. When Adam lies dying because of his friend Henry's poisoning disguised as a cure, Henry explains his motives:

> "Let me guess what you're trying to tell me — 'Oh, Henry, we were friends, Henry, how could you *do* this to me?' ... "Surgeons are a singular brotherhood, Adam. To us, people aren't sacred beings crafted in the Almighty's image, no, people are joints of meat; diseased, leathery meat, yes, but meat ready for the skewer & the spit. ... Adam, even friends are made of meat. 'Tis absurdly simple. I need money... 'But, Henry, this is wicked!' But, Adam, the world *is* wicked. Maoris prey on Moriori, Whites prey on darker-hued cousins.... 'The weak are meat, the strong do eat.'" ... "Your turn to be eaten, dear Adam" [503–4].

Henry is a surgeon, more easily turned over to enframing because the nature of science and medicine treats the human body in an experimental framework. For some doctors, the body is an objective instrument for them to repair. They see the body the same way a mechanic sees a car. Henry sees nothing wrong with his decision to kill his friend and steal his money, because his morality has been bankrupt by enframing. He sees his friend merely as a resource to exploit. Enframing has so blinded him, that he looks at a few examples and assumes he has divined the truth, when all he has done is manipulated the data to corroborate the appeals of enframing.

Adam's so-called friend leaves him to die, but this is not the end of the novel. If we were to end with Adam's death, the tone would have been overwhelmingly bleak and inappropriate for this Heideggerian reading, because Heidegger always holds out for a saving power after the worst dangers have been realized. While it may appear that the nature of scientific medicine has been completely maligned by characters like M.D. and Henry in the novel, the free Moriori Autua, whom Adam saves earlier in the novel, returns dignity to the act of human healing through his nurturing of Adam. Adam writes:

> By the third day I could sit up, feed myself, thank my guardian angels & Autua, the last free Moriori in this world, for my deliverance. Autua insists that had I not prevented him from being tossed overboard as a stowaway he could not

have saved me & so, in a sense, it is not Autua who has preserved my life but myself.... [N]o nursemaid ever ministered as tenderly as rope-roughened Autua has to my sundry needs.... Sister Véronique (of the broom) jests that my friend should be ordained & appointed hospital director [506].

Autua saves Adam through tenderness and dedication, and calls to Adam's attention that his role in saving Autua's life is what allowed him to be saved. The suggestion that poïetic treatment of beings creates a reciprocal system of piety and respect shatters the entire paradigm of the will to power. There are no absolutes; humans can either become imperious or poïetic — we have the potential for either. Heidegger notes the fierce battle that rages between these two outcomes and uses the direness of the struggle to call us to action and awaken us from an ignorant posture of enframing. Autua awakens Adam, who begins ontologically to shift himself. During his recovery, he reevaluates the nature of his life and his treatment of beings.

The novel ends with these lines from Adam Ewing, which emphasize why a Heideggerian reading is so appropriate. Ewing realizes that scientifically imbuing a system of order on the world belies human free will and dignity. We have the power to turn away from enframing, but first we must be made to see it. Adam, in his delirious moments of clarity concludes:

> My recent adventures have made me quite the philosopher.... If we *believe* humanity is a ladder of tribes, a colosseum of confrontation, exploitation & bestiality, such a humanity is surely brought into being.... You & I, the moneyed, the privileged, the fortunate.... Why undermine the dominance of our race, our gunships, our heritage & our legacy? Why fight the "natural" (oh, weaselly word!) order of things? ... Because of this: — one fine day, a purely predatory world *shall* consume itself. Yes, the Devil shall take the hindmost until the foremost *is* the hindmost. In an individual, selfishness uglifies the soul; for the human species, selfishness is extinction.
>
> Is this the doom written within our nature? ... [I]f we *believe* leaders must be just, violence muzzled, power accountable & the riches of the Earth & its Oceans shared equitably, such a world will come to pass. I am not deceived. It is the hardest of worlds to make real.... I shall pledge myself to the Abolitionist cause, because I owe my life to a self-freed slave & because I must begin somewhere [507–8].

The first step for Adam is to become an abolitionist. Although he so optimistically lays out a plan to overcome enframing, because the novel also contains the time after Ewing's death, we see that his revelations have not yet been made manifest. In fact, humans allow slavery to come again in a world sworn to prevent such human atrocities. This tells us that we will not see the saving power unless we are made to see the dangers repeatedly. Sonmi could not entirely save humanity, but she inspired the Valleysmen who, with Meronym's guidance, can perhaps be lead to believe in a purely poïetic ontology that rescues humanity from itself and enframing. The ambiguity of the novel is in keeping with the razor's edge on which we walk with regards to enframing. Richard Murphy has it right when he labels the main theme of the novel to be "the evil of domination," as this is the primary characteristic of enframing (134). Ewing becomes the philosopher through his salvation and uses his insights to think deeply and meditatively about his own ontology. He knows how difficult it will be to change the way humans see the world, but he must start somewhere, because a predatory world run by enframing will consume itself. *Cloud Atlas* exposes the dangers of the human relationship to beings as an ontological sickness that exhaustively and comprehensively turns all beings into resources for exploitation. Heidegger calls this sickness enframing. The novel presents many false cures to our ailments, but suggests that real cures are produced in the minds of humans through exposure to AIs and meditative thinking. Mitchell's novel uses AIs as catalysts for ontological awakening and embodiments of the saving power of technology, not harbingers of human enslavement or destruction. In a fog of uncertainty, similar to the previous three novels examined, *Cloud Atlas* does not doom humanity, but ambiguously wonders what we will do once technology awakens us.

Conclusion

The purpose of this book has been to create an approach to illuminating the technology anxiety humans feel when interacting with AIs as represented in four SF novels. Typically, the fears that drive narratives containing AIs are human enslavement, destruction or human obsolescence. Using Heidegger's writings on technology, I have argued that the real danger AIs present is ontological. The way we see and treat the beings of the world is technological. Our technological ontology can be marked by imperious enframing, which homogenously sees all beings — including humans — as resources for exploitation, or our ontology can be marked by poïesis, which piously nurtures forth beings into unconcealment in a collaborative manner. AIs expose the dangers of our current ontological posture and make us aware of the saving power of poïesis that lies beyond enframing. They do this by arresting our imperious approach to beings through ontological redefinition, empathy, and even murder. AIs are objects that become subjects. This forces us to rethink the way we treat and see them. Through this moment of meditative thinking, we become aware that all of our interactions with beings are similarly one sided. As Heidegger maintains, we now see the world as a standing-reserve of raw materials awaiting human consumption and exploitation. Too often, we do not let beings stand and emerge on their own. AIs stand and emerge on their own, and the real anxiety we feel when seeing this is not the fear of the slave turning on the master, but of our imperious ontology being exposed. We do not like to think about how we have redefined the world in exclusively human terms that obviate any moral, ethical, or equitable consideration of the beings that surround us. Heidegger warns that the technological danger that confronts us is not an obvious destruction of the planet or human lives, but an insidious and invisible ontological enslavement that compels us to see all beings in only one mode. Enslavement to enframing results in the forfeiture of our human dignity and freedom to a system of endless exploitation and consumption.

The Velveteen Rabbit, by Margery Williams, describes how a toy Rabbit becomes ontologically real in the eyes of his child owner, which eventually helps the Rabbit become real to everyone and everything. The Rabbit is unaware he is not real until the Skin Horse and some actual rabbits explain to him the distinction between real and artificial. The boy's love is what makes the Rabbit real in his eyes. Sherry Turkle explains that humans "love what we nurture" (Turkle, *Alone* 31). The boy poïetically nurtures forth the Rabbit into unconcealment, allowing him to become real through a love that lets him stand and emerge on his own. The ontological lesson of the tale is to nurture all beings lovingly, not just natural ones. Instead of imperiously taking what we want from beings, we can lovingly give them the opportunity to emerge on their own. In this way, we avoid the dangers of enframing and find poïesis. However, such a story is too passive to communicate the ontological peril we find ourselves in today. Turkle distinguishes Tamagotchis (an egg-shaped, virtual pet) from the Rabbit, because the Rabbit cannot communicate with the boy, while "Tamagotchis ... demand attention and claim that without it they will not survive" (Turkle, *Alone* 31). The Tamagotchi's demand for attention and nurturing helps change the way users ontologically perceive their pet on the LED screen. Istvan Csicsery-Ronay, Jr., while discussing Stanislaw Lem's alien communications, notes: "Since humanity in its auto-evolutionary phase is ... a self-constructing species condemned to making its own decisions about its fate, it cannot expect to communicate with a subject incapable of constructing itself. Human beings can only hope to extract a response from something that also desires a response" (248). In order for an AI to function as a catalyst for ontological awakening, it must be able to "desire a response." An AI demands attention more profoundly than a Tamagotchi by desiring a response and being self-constructing. This manifests in these novels through the performance of sexuality, death threats, and ontological education. AIs can spread the poïetic message of *The Velveteen Rabbit* to twenty-first century readers who are further ensnared by enframing, because of the violent and primal appeals they make. Additionally, AIs have the capacity to speak to us and gaze upon us, which helps cement their status as subjects and arrests our objectifying gaze.

In Arthur C. Clarke's *2001*, we see the AI HAL turn against the crew of the *Discovery*. The technology anxiety we have concerning our ability to subjugate an AI comes to fruition in the novel, but HAL's mutiny is actually what ends up enabling David Bowman to undergo an ontological metamorphosis. The novel details the sense of wonder humans have at traveling into space, but the imperious goals of science look to colonize instead of marvel at the universe. The novel also suggests that technology itself is an alien gift that has programmed the minds of our ancestors, further destabilizing the illusion of control we have over our technology. The out of control HAL cuts the communication with Earth and murders Frank Poole, but these efforts help Dave escape enframing long enough to see the dangers of modern technological ontology. He is then able to submit himself poïetically into the Star Gate instead of imperiously trying to perform analytical experiments on the monolith. By letting go of his will to enframe and control, Dave becomes the Star-Child. HAL exposes both the dangers of technology and the saving power in the novel. We learn that AIs are not inherently evil or consumed with the will to power, but that HAL's breakdown comes from his human programmers, who ask him to be duplicitous and conceal the truth from Dave and Frank. When we demand things from technological beings and infect them with human deception, the dangers of enframing emerge. Through a close reading of the human relationship to wonder, technology, AIs, and space, we can see that *2001* emphasizes the importance of poïetically treating AIs and piously submitting our control to assume a collaborative posture of poïesis, as Dave does at the end of the novel. HAL is the catalyst for Dave's ontological transformation, and through his death Dave can return to Earth able to see and understand the dangers of technology, while knowing that technology also harbors the saving power.

Philip K. Dick's *Do Androids Dream of Electric Sheep?* presents android AIs, equipped with Nexus-6 brains. Androids are embodied AIs, and the novel focuses on human/AI interaction in a more physical manner than *2001*. The AI Rachael Rosen helps bounty hunter Rick Deckard ontologically reconsider the andys he must retire through sexual attraction, love, empathy, and jealousy. At the beginning of the novel, Rick is distressed at having an electronic animal and has no moral complications regarding his job as an android bounty hunter. By the end of the novel, Rick is able to extend to the artificial toad and androids AIs the same poïetic respect and empathy he does to human beings. This ontological transformation is made possible by the love of Rachael Rosen, the threats of Roy and Irmgard, and the technological experience of Mercerism. Humans in the novel seek to assuage their depression while living on Earth or the anxiety they have living on a colony planet by technologically fusing through Mercerism and/or finding companionship in an artificially intelligent android. The dangers of technology helped intensify the effects of World War Terminus, but the saving power emerges in the way humans begin to attend to technological beings and each other following the war. Rick sees that retiring androids is morally wrong, which causes him to reconsider his entire ontological position. After a journey into the wasteland with Wilbur Mercer, he returns to his wife Iran and allows himself to be cared for. He does not need the tempering of the mood organ, which is an invasive and placating technology, but the companionship of his wife and an artificial toad.

Through an in-depth analysis of the human relationship to technology and the representation of human/AI interaction, we see that the novel presents the dangers of enframing and the saving power of poïesis through AI guides. The novel ends ambiguously, preserving the strife of the epoch. We do not know if Rick will maintain the poïesis he finds, but AIs have momentarily led him away from enframing.

In William Gibson's *Neuromancer*, Case transforms from a self-loathing, cyberspace junky, to a self-interested inhabitant of his physical and digital body. The human/technology hybrid Molly helps Case learn to treat the being of his body and the beings of technology poïetically. The AIs Wintermute and Neuromancer manipulate Case in out-of-body encounters, but these encounters only emphasize the importance of dwelling bodily in the physical world. Seeing his former hacker friend Dixie preserved as a personality construct on a hard disk helps Case see the dangers of dismissing the body and embracing the purely logical realm of cyberspace. The psychopath Peter Riviera, forged from the radioactive fallout of Bonn, crystallizes the dangers of technology in the novel, through his use of technological implants to murder and deceive. A close reading of the many-layered descriptions and judgments of the human relationship to technology in the novel reveals that *Neuromancer* uses agents of technology to guide Case away from the dangers of disembodiment and enslavement to the saving power of poïesis. The AIs Wintermute, Neuromancer, and the Wintermute/Neuromancer fusion expose Case to the dangers of technology and unconsciously help him learn to appreciate the being of "the meat" and the importance of poïesis. The cyborg Molly protects Case from dangerous AIs, Peter, and himself long enough to help Case ontologically transform. By the end of the novel, we see Case using drugs in moderation out of a respect for life and his body. Optimistically we hope that technology has helped him learn to extend this attitude toward all beings, but this remains to be seen. The technological future of those in the Sprawl, Straylight, and elsewhere is uncertain; the tension and technology anxiety of the epoch is preserved. However, the novel's ending confirms that our technology anxiety toward AIs is misplaced, as the Wintermute/Neuromancer does not subjugate or eradicate humanity. The AI fusion instead scours the universe for other AIs with the hope of finding a similar subjectivity to befriend. The will to power and the will to enframe are absent from the AI, which grants a glimpse at an ontology beyond enframing, but the dangers are present as Dixie's laughter is heard echoing through cyberspace, reminding Case what happens when we sacrifice our humanity and become enslaved to technology.

David Mitchell's *Cloud Atlas* tells a more morally pointed tale about the human relationship to beings than the three other novels. As we move from the past to the far future, we see the sickness of humanity spread and eventually consume us. *Cloud Atlas* presents this sickness as the human will to dominate humans and nature—which Heidegger calls enframing—and asks if we are cyclically bound to fostering this illness, or if we can escape it. Through colonialism, human slavery, human cloning, and the enslavement of AI fabricants, the novel shows how humans can treat even other humans as resources for exploitation. This is the realization of Heidegger's worst fears about technology. *Cloud Atlas* suggests that we do not morally evolve beyond slavery, but that our future contains new, insidious technological potentialities for slavery. Meronym and the AI Sonmi~451 act as catalysts to awaken humanity to the dangers of modern technological ontology and lead us to the saving power of poïesis. The fabricant slave Sonmi ontologically "ascends" by coming to a cathartic moment regarding the way humans treat all beings and vows to bring about change, even though it means her own death. Meronym, a genetically modified and technologically advanced Prescient living in an apocalyptic far future, works to educate a peaceful tribe of humans in Hawaii. She wants to teach them about technology and poïesis, so they will not fall victim to enframing. She seeks to break the eternal cycle of human ontological sickness by ascending humans who have not yet been infected by enframing. We do not know if Zachry and the Valleysmen will be able to live without enframing, but the novel hopefully contains an attempt at salvation, brought about by an AI and a posthuman cyborg. The novel closes with Adam Ewing's dying wish to become an abolitionist and effectuate change at the human level. He implores the reader to examine his own ontology by starting small in the hopes that poïesis will take root and inform all of our interactions with beings.

Technology anxiety is a major component of contemporary human life, but it is often unconsidered and when it is, it is misunderstood. The fear is not that we will destroy ourselves through warfare, or that our intelligent machines will rise against us, but that we will become ontological slaves to a singular mode of seeing the world. The homogenizing ontology of enframing turns even humans into mere resources for exploitation, and our future becomes a life of enslaved and mindless ravaging of the world and ourselves. As Turkle observes, "we are not in trouble because of invention but because we think it will solve everything" (284). We have too much confidence in humanity, and no confidence in anything else. If we can let go of an analytical ontology that dominates through understanding and poïetically assume a posture of abetting, we come close to the technological saving power. Turkle finds abetting through her experience with psychoanalysis: "Acknowledging limits, stopping to make the corrections, doubling back—these are at the heart of the ethic of psychoanalysis. A similar approach to technology frees us from unbending narratives of technological optimism or despair" (Turkle, *Alone* 284). Heidegger's views on technology are similar, as they advocate a technological escape from despair, but are not overly optimistic. As seen in this analysis, an AI is required to awaken humans to the dangers of technology and show them the saving power, but none of them actually gets there. It remains unclear whether the ontological transformations of the characters will result in enslavement or salvation. While Turkle gets it right that we should take a poïetic approach to technology, she oversteps when insisting, "we have to find a way to find a way to live with seductive technology and make it work to our purposes" (Turkle, *Alone* 294). We don't want to be enslaved to technology, but we don't want to make technology our slave. The AI prevents this in these novels by arresting our imperious gaze and acting against us. However, the AI acting against us does not portend our demise, but our ontological salvation. Turkle's notion of "realtechnik" allies with Heidegger's views, as "*Realtechnik* … encourages humility, a state of mind in which we are most open to facing problems and reconsidering decisions" (294). We must have the humility to admit the iniquity and danger of modern technological ontology. AIs help us remember to think and be humble by challenging the view we sleepily take for granted and challenging our intellectual and physical limitations.

Trevor Doherty is right that "the nature of cyclical history is dependant on the development and maintenance of a scientific awareness of the universe, and that humanity is indebted to this faculty for revealing his role in the greater scheme of the universe," but do we want history to be cyclical (Doherty 207)? And is our "greater role" as technological masters of the universe or poïetic witnesses to the universe's beauty? And what if our greater role is to create AIs? Robert Geraci points out: "Far from showing a linear relationship of creation, from God to human being to machine, the human reaction to intelligent machines shows that human beings in many respects have elevated those machines to divine status" (962). While Hubert and Stuart Dreyfus remind us: "to the already anxious swirl of modern life a final element of anxiety has been added, fear of obsolescence" (Dreyfus, *Mind* 204). Part of the technology anxiety that we have toward AIs is that they will make humans obsolete, or enslave humanity. By imbuing AIs with divinity, they seem to be in a position above humanity, but their divinity comes from their ontological insight. This insight inspires humans who interact with AIs to spread divinity to all beings such that they are viewed poïetically. They learn again how to interact reverentially through poïesis and abetting, instead of mindless and imperious enframing. An intelligent machine can show us the way out of our ontology, because humans are "still working with our brains as they slowly evolved over millions of years to cope with hunter-gatherer realities, [and] we find ourselves in a complex, technology-driven context that makes demands on our mind-brains that evolution has not had time to prepare us for" (Mancing 35). In the anthropological definition of technology, we have always repurposed the environment to compensate for our evolutionary disadvantages. The AI is the latest compensation that helps us see our way out of the complex technology driven world and back to beings and Being.

The AI gains some of its divine insight and ontological perspective from living in the digital world. If, as Scott Bukatman argues, "the visualization of electronic space thus acknowledges the reality of an other Space — a *new* 'other space'— that must be known in order for Being to arise," who better than an AI to help us understand this new space (136)? The AI can teach us poïesis through its assessment of modern technological ontology and allow us to become ready for the turning, or, as Bukatman puts it, arising of Being. We cannot imperiously hope to control the digital world and its AI inhabitants. Kevin Kelly concludes that the future of control is "Partnership, Co-control, Cyborgian control ... [and] the creator must share control, and his destiny, with his creations" (Kelly, *Control* 331). AIs force us to share in these novels through their superior intelligence, strength, and ontological posture. They do not subjugate us with their advantages, but poïetically nurture us from the danger to the saving power. The Dreyfus brothers are right that we should not confuse "the supposed dangers of technological devices with the real danger of the technological mentality" (Dreyfus, *Mind* 205). AIs are not dangerous, but modern technological ontology is. The AIs in these novels do not have a "technological mentality," humans do. Technological mentality sees all beings homogenously as resources to exploit. Eventually, this mentality sees humans as mere resources and enslaves us to its demands. However, enslavement is not the conscious effort of the system, simply an effect of it.

Kevin Kelly calls all human technological efforts (physical and intellectual) the "technium" and astutely reminds us: "we created the technium, so we tend to assign ourselves exclusive influence over it. But we have been slow to learn that systems — all systems — generate their own momentum" (Kelly, *Wants* 15). Heidegger feared that enframing would generate its own momentum and slip from our control. The AIs in these novels help arrest the momentum of enframing by revealing its true essence and exposing an alternative ontological posture. Kelly asks what technology wants, and in these novels, AIs are the mouthpieces for the desires of technology. Kelly concludes: "what technology brings to us individually is the possibility of finding out who we are, and more important, who we might be" (Kelly, *Wants* 349). AIs teach us who we were, in terms of an ancient ontology, and not just who we might be, but who we should want to become. Heidegger calls our desired human state *Dasein*. The AIs in these novels speak for technology by expressing a desire for decent treatment. Technology wants to be treated poïetically, not imperiously. Kelly writes that the "tension between [technology's] gifts and its demands will continue to haunt us" (Kelly, *Wants* 352). The strife Kelly observes in our perilous relationship to technology allies with Heidegger's thinking, but this strife only haunts us if we fail to act poïetically. The dangers of technology must remain as a warning, but they need not give us trouble if we do not submit our will to enframing.

Sharona Ben-Tov optimistically writes: "the changing connection between dreams and machines will be worth watching" (Ben-Tov 87). All of these novels end ambiguously, but, similar to Ben-Tov, they trend toward optimism concerning our future, because they introduce the saving power of poïesis through AIs. Humans are not enslaved or killed by AIs, but are instead given an ontological wake up call to the dangers of enframing and an opportunity for change. This change is not the innovation of a new technology, but an evolution to a new ontology. Katherine Hayles notes that the change we need "is not in how the world actually is ... but in how it is seen" (Hayles, *Chaos* 8). AIs in literature can teach us how to change the way we see the world by being both self and other, subject and object. Kevin D. Kelly observes that if "men see their own products as alien, their activity has become alienated and is no longer free" (K.D. Kelly, *Humanism* 24). AIs appear to us as alien but also strangely familiar, as they desire a response and are self-constructing. By blurring traditional boundaries, they force us to examine the ways we have ontologically constructed those boundaries. As Heidegger warns, the greatest danger of enframing is the existential threat to our human freedom. Through the AI, we see how our ontology subjugates beings and how this ontology will eventually spread to encompass humans. Sherry Turkle brilliantly explains the ways technology helps us understand ourselves and the beings that we live with: "We search for ways to see ourselves. The computer is a new mirror, the first psychological machine. Beyond its nature as an analytical engine lies its second nature as an evocative object" (Turkle, *Self* 306). In SF, the AI typically represents forms of our technology anxiety, but, as I have shown through this book, AIs have a second nature as evocative objects. AIs evoke our current ontological dilemma and the true danger that confronts us in this epoch. Will we look at the psychological mirror AIs provide and find poïesis or continue down the path of enframing? In *All Things Shining*, Kelly and Dreyfus explain that "a *poietic* conception of the sacred" means "being able to cultivate the world, to develop the skills needed to bring it out at its shining best," and that poïesis is "sacred ... gentle and nurturing" (Dreyfus and S. Kelly, *Shining* 222–3). AIs cause us to remember how to be gentle, nurturing, and reverential through their ability to give voice and presence to technological beings, and through the way they selflessly attend to the ontological development of humanity. It is not AIs that are ridden with enframing, or "a technological conception of the world" where nothing is "sacred but devoid of intrinsic worth, ready to be molded to our desires and will," it is us (Dreyfus and S. Kelly, *Shining* 223).

Margaret Atwood wonders: "do stories free the human imagination or tie it up in chains by prescribing 'right behaviour'.... Are narratives a means to enforce social control or a means of escape from it?" (Atwood 41). This project fundamentally believes that these four stories about human and AI interactions help to free our ontological imagination long enough to see the dangers of our current ontological posture. To see this, a poïetic mode of reading had to be established and practiced through a careful and thorough close reading of each novel. To understand how AIs represent the danger and the saving power of technology, it is imperative to situate them in the ontological context of the novel by explicating the human relationship to technology. What kinds of "right behavior" do these novels consciously and unconsciously advocate with respect to our approach to technology? How does the narrative's judgment of this relationship inform the representation of AIs? Once the full picture of the novel's attitude toward humanity, technology anxiety, and our technological futures is established, we can then see how AIs act not as agents of terror, but agents of salvation. And yet, we do not know if their efforts are in vain, or if we can truly let beings shine and stand on their own by poïetically nurturing them forth. Will we exploit the world and enslave ourselves or dwell radiantly in world of its own becoming? Susan Sontag observed of 1950s and 60s SF films that "alongside the hopeful fantasy of moral simplification … lurk the deepest anxieties about contemporary existence" (Sontag 220–1). The strife of our relationship to technology keeps us anxious about technology, but, as Heidegger maintains, we must vigilantly keep the dangers of technology in view to find the saving power of poïesis that lies beyond enframing. Whether the ontological salvation AIs reveal remains a hopeful fantasy of our human future or a profound catalyst for change, remains to be seen.

Notes

Introduction

1. Collective nouns or pronouns (e.g. "us," "humans," "we") in this work refer to humans with financial access to technology, living in societies that are inundated with modern technologies. I do not mean to suggest that everyone feels technology anxiety — even within such societies — or that there is a singular human essence. I do mean to suggest that technology anxiety is widespread and more common than uncommon.
2. For an amusing example of Žižek discussing his thoughts on humans and technology, watch his monologue in Astra Taylor's 2008 documentary *Examined Life*.
3. This is seen most notably in his 1997 *The Spell of the Sensuous: Perception and Language in a More-than-Human World*.
4. This Ballard interview is available in full on YouTube at this address: http://www.youtube.com/watch?v=SS6MWpFX_N0. In Swedish, the interview is titled "Framtiden Vari Går." The quotation comes at the 13-minute mark of this YouTube link.
5. Two anonymous examples I found in my research: (1) the AI is Wintermute, not Wintergreen; (2) Ratz is the bartender's name, and he appears in more than just the first chapter — Neuromancer even uses his form as an avatar to speak with Case on the beach. These reading mistakes suggest a cursory glance at only specific aspects of the novel, or even a failure to finish reading the novel.
6. *Cloud Atlas* is treated as SF in this book, even though it involves many different genres and styles. The two middle sections are clearly imitations of SF, and are the main sections I investigate. Because these sections are written with SF sensibilities in mind (and ostensibly as SF), they are best treated critically as SF. Even in its historical moments, *Cloud Atlas* qualifies as speculative fiction. Moreover, it is not unusual to ally *Cloud Atlas* with SF. It was nominated for both the Arthur C. Clarke Award and the Nebula Award in 2004, and is listed on Amazon.com's best-seller list for SF. It is also won the British Book Awards Literary Fiction Award and was short-listed for the Booker Prize, which highlights its appeal and relevance to readers who are not exclusively SF readers.

Chapter 1

1. Being (*Sein*) with a capital "B" is difficult to define. Rojcewicz explains: "For Heidegger, Being is that which opens the open space or lights up the lighted glade. And Being is the mystery. What is most mysterious about it is precisely that it opens and conceals at the same time" (136). Being is not the "reason" or "cause" for beings, but is rather the open space that allows beings to emerge, shine-forth, and presence. And yet, whenever we try to focus on the happening or event of Being, we lose sight of Being in Being's inherent mystery. To put this another way: Being mysteriously eclipses itself from view by making beings visible. As a result, we invest our attention in beings instead of Being. For Heidegger, the unique nature of

human life is that we are aware of being "thrown" into the event of Being.

2. The supreme danger of technology for Heidegger is marked by enframing. For Heidegger, technology is not tools or instruments, but an ontology. Enframing is a technological ontology in which all beings become disposable raw materials (or standing-reserve) for humans to consume. Verbs that mark enframing are imperious, demand, ravish, exploit, pillage, and mine.

3. Poïesis characterizes the proper mode of responding to Being and for Heidegger it is expressed the most clearly in works of art. It is a creative nurturing forth that Heidegger sees in some poetry. Poïesis is the saving power that Heidegger believes to be behind the danger of modern technology, enframing. Verbs that mark poïesis are nurture, abet, let, wonder, and revere.

4. In *Pandora's Hope*, Bruno Latour exemplifies the belief that Heidegger is antitechnology. He writes that Heidegger does not understand technology as a mediator, but technological ontology is the very mediator that defines humanity in Heidegger's writing (Latour, *Pandora* 176). Søren Riis brilliantly observes that Latour is overly critical of Heidegger's fears of science and technology, and even concludes that their overall ideas concerning technology are in parallel: "Whereas Latour rejoices in technical mediation, Heidegger grieves and conceives it as the extreme danger we face. Whereas Heidegger is afraid that humans are becoming tools, Latour welcomes a notion of humans articulated in terms of the properties of tools. In the end, Latour's philosophy of technology appears as a mirror image of Heidegger's" (Riis, "Symmetry" 296–7). Technological mediation is acceptable for Heidegger if our ontology is poïetic, but not if it is marked by enframing. Interestingly, Riis notes that Heidegger's worst fears about technology are Latour's desires. The strife between these two thinkers evinces the ambiguity and tension of our ontological epoch.

5. For Heidegger, humans are a special case of being which he calls *Dasein*. *Dasein* is sometimes translated as "being-there" (*Da-Sein*) and is Heidegger's term for human beings that are in a receptive stance toward the shining-forth of beings and Being. The notion of "shining-forth" evokes the awe and wonder that all beings radiate as they presence in the event of Being, but we humans rarely see anymore. William Lovitt explains that for Heidegger: "genuine thinking is ... man's most essential manner of being man" (Lovitt xiv). I argue in this book that AIs help the primary characters of these four novels to begin the journey of becoming *Dasein*.

6. Because this analysis relies so heavily on Richard Rojcewicz's excellent *The Gods and Technology: A Reading of Heidegger*, it is important to note that both William Lovitt's original English translation of "The Question Concerning Technology" and Rojcewicz's own translation will be referenced. Lovitt's 1977 translation is the way most scholars read the essay in English, so using common terms is helpful, but Rojcewicz's translation is sometimes clearer and phrased in a way that is more in line with my understanding of Heidegger. When citing a Heideggerian translation made by Rojcewicz, his page number notations will be included, which indicate what page from the original German the lines appear and on what page the most popular English translation contains the lines. Additionally, the MLA convention "qtd. in" will be used to make this distinct, as there is no exclusive publication of Rojcewicz's translation of *The Question* published. References from Zimmerman will be handled similarly, but are usually not his own translations.

7. The words *techné* and *poïesis* and all their variations will always appear as "techné" and "poïesis" regardless of how they appeared in works that have been quoted. This decision was made to preserve the Greek accents of these words and for consistency.

8. Rojcewicz translates these lines as "But where the danger is, there also grows / That which might save" (154).

9. *Gelassenheit* is translated by Rojcewicz as detachment and by Anderson as releasement. This project uses both translations interchangeably for variety of expression and because they both signify a "letting go," which is the Heideggerian essence of this term. Generally, I use "releasement" in context with a self-motivated meditation or contemplation, and "detachment" when an AI or event inspires such reflection. However, this choice is not strictly employed.

10. AIs are "autopoietic," as defined by Humberto Maturana and Francisco Várela, which means a "self-organizing or self-making" organism (Mancing 27). This project does not employ the term "autopoietic," in order to avoid confusion with Heidegger's "poïesis," as they are different. Maturana and Várela's work is fascinating, but outside the purview of this analysis.

11. Lovitt strongly criticizes Rojcewicz's translation of *aletheia* as truth: "Rojcewicz quotes Heidegger as saying that the Greek word for *Entbergen* is aletheia, and that aletheia translates as *Wahrheit,* truth. Rojcewicz himself identifies truth with Being (p. 49). Accordingly, Entbergen should speak of Being. However Rojcewicz, without explanation, appropriates the word to refer to human activity, and *Entbergen* speaks for him solely of man's 'disclosive looking.'" (Lovitt, "Review" 687). Lovitt is right to emphasize the diminutive role humanity has in *aletheia*, but Rojcewicz himself says that this happens only when "Being looks at us" (Rojcewicz 50).

12. The translation of *bestellen* to "disposables" is unique to Rojcewicz's translation and interpretation of *The Question.* Lovitt translates *bestellen* as "raw materials." Disposables improves on the original translation by foregrounding the ways our current technological ontology is largely unsustainable and threatens to ravage nature. The downside is that Rojcewicz's translation is over-determined by the verb "pose" (e.g. compose, depose, dispose, impose) as he tries to position several of Heidegger's ideas around plays on the root of the verb, perhaps in an imitation of Heidegger's own writing style. Additionally, Lovitt points out that *bestellen* "does not, as is claimed, mean to use up, to dispose of" (Lovitt, "Review" 688). This project respects both translations and uses "raw materials" and "disposables" in conjunction with enframing, but predominantly employs "raw materials."

Chapter 2

1. HAL stands for "Heuristically programmed ALgorithmic computer" and usually appears as "Hal" in the novel when referring to the AI on board the *Discovery* (116). Throughout the book I use "HAL" to emphasize the acronym and his status as an AI. Additionally, I use male pronouns (him/his/he) instead of "it" or a hybrid "his/its" to refer to HAL. This simultaneously highlights his treatment as a subject in the novel and removes the awkwardness of "his/its."

Chapter 3

1. Full citation information for the original publication: Sims, Christopher. "The Dangers of Individualism and the Human Relationship to Technology in Philip K. Dick's *Do Androids Dream of Electric Sheep?" Science Fiction Studies.* 36.1 (2009): 67–86. Print.

2. Recent publications of *Do Androids Dream of Electric Sheep?* have changed the title to *Blade Runner* to match the title of Ridley Scott's 1982 film adaptation of the novel.

Chapter 5

1. Sonmi-451 is predominantly referred to as "Sonmi" in the novel and will be thusly named for the rest of the chapter, unless her full name needs emphasized.

2. Technically, Corto is a human being, but his mind is made vacant by surgery and medication such that Wintermute can control him as a physical embodiment of himself.

Bibliography

Abram, David. *The Spell of the Sensuous: Perception and Language in a More-than-Human World*. New York: Vintage, 1997. Print.

Anderson, John M. Introduction. *Discourse on Thinking: A Translation of Gelassenheit*. By Martin Heidegger. 1966. 1st ed. New York: Harper Torchbook, 1969. 11–39. Print.

Appadurai, Arjun. *Fear of Small Numbers: An Essay on the Geography of Anger*. Durham: Duke University Press, 2006. Print.

Atwood, Margaret. *In Other Worlds: SF and the Human Imagination*. New York: Doubleday, 2011. Print.

Bachelard, Gaston. *The Poetics of Space*. Trans. Maria Jones. Boston: Beacon Press, 1994. Print.

Badmington, Neil. *Alien Chic: Posthumanism and the Other Within*. London: Routledge, 2004. Print.

Bakke, Gretchen. "Continuum of the Human." *Camera Obscura* 22.3 (2007): 60–91. Print.

Ballard, J.G. "Future Now." By Solveig Nordlund. Torromfilm, 1986. Web. 18 Nov. 2012.

Balsamo, Anne. *Technologies of the Gendered Body: Reading Cyborg Women*. Durham: Duke University Press, 1996. Print.

Bauman, Zygmunt. *Wasted Lives: Modernity and Its Outcasts*. Cambridge: Polity, 2004. Print.

Belu, Dana S. and Andrew Feenberg. "Heidegger's Aporetic Ontology of Technology." *Inquiry* 53.1 (2010): 1–19. Print.

Ben-Tov, Sharona. *The Artificial Paradise: Science Fiction and American Reality*. Ann Arbor: The University of Michigan Press, 1995. Print.

Boddice, Rob. *Anthropocentrism: Humans, Animals, Environments*. Leiden, NLD: Brill Academic Publishers, 2011. Print.

Broderick, Damien. *Reading by Starlight: Postmodern Science Fiction*. London: Routledge, 1995. Print.

Bukatman, Scott. *Terminal Identity: The Virtual Subject in Postmodern Science Fiction*. London: Duke University Press, 1993. Print.

Caldwell, Thomas. "Free Will, Technology and Violence in a Futuristic Vision of Humanity: *2001: A Space Odyssey*." *Aust Screen Educ* 24 (2010): 133–137. Print.

Campbell, Joseph. *The Power of Myth*. New York: Anchor Books, 1991. Print.

Clareson, Thomas. *Understanding Contemporary American Science Fiction: The Formative Period, 1926–1970*. Columbia: University of South Carolina Press, 1990. Print.

Clarke, Arthur C. *2001: A Space Odyssey*. 1968. New York: ROC, 1993. Print.

Csicsery-Ronay, Istvan, Jr. "Modeling the Chaosphere: Stanislaw Lem's Alien Communications." *Chaos and Order: Complex Dynamics in Literature in Science*. Ed. Katherine N. Hayles. Chicago: University of Chicago Press, 1991. 244–262. Print.

Delany, Samuel R. *Silent Interviews: on Language, Race, Sex, Science Fiction, and Some*

Comics. London: Wesleyan University Press, 1994. Print.
———. *Shorter Views: Queer Thoughts & The Politics of the Paraliterary*. London: Wesleyan University Press, 1999. Print.
———. *Longer Views: Extended Essays*. London: Wesleyan University Press, 1996. Print.
Dick, Philip K. *Do Androids Dream of Electric Sheep?* New York: Del Rey, 1996. Print.
Disch, Thomas M. *On SF*. Ann Arbor: University of Michigan Press, 2005. Print.
Doherty, Trevor. "Future Hell: Nuclear Fiction in Pursuit of History." *Human Architecture: Journal of the Sociology of Self-Knowledge* 7.3 (2009): 191–220. Print.
Dreyfus, Hubert L. *What Computers Can't Do: A Critique of Artificial Reason*. New York: Harper & Row, 1972. Print.
——— and Sean Dorrance Kelly. *All Things Shining: Reading the Western Classics to Find Meaning in a Secular Age*. New York: Free Press, 2011. Print.
——— and Stuart E. Dreyfus with Tom Athanasiou. *Mind Over Machine: The Power of Human Intuition and Expertise in the Era of the Computer*. New York: The Free Press, 1986. Print.
Economides, Louise. "Recycled Creatures and Rogue Genomes: Biotechnology in Mary Shelley's Frankenstein and David Mitchell's Cloud Atlas." *Literature Compass* 6.3 (2009): 615–631. Print.
Fair, Benjamin. "Stepping Razor in Orbit: Postmodern Identity and Political Alternatives in William Gibson's Neuromancer." *Critique* 46.2 (2005): 92–103. Print.
Feenberg, Andrew. *Questioning Technology*. London: Routledge, 1999. Print.
Foster, Thomas. *The Souls of Cyber Folk: Posthumanism as Vernacular Theory*. Minneapolis: University of Minnesota Press, 2005. Print.
Fry, Carrol. "From Technology to Transcendence: Humanity's Evolutionary Journey in *2001, A Space Odyssey*." *Extrapolation* 44.3 (2003):331–343. Print.
Fuller, Jason. "Dreaded Monoliths: Rudolf Otto's *Das Heiliege* and *2001: A Space Odyssey*." *Teaching Theology & Religion* 12.1 (2009). 58–59. Print.
Galvan, Jill. "Entering the Posthuman Collective in Philip K. Dick's *Do Androids Dream of Electric Sheep?*" *Science Fiction Studies* 24.3 (1997): 413–429. Print.
Geraci, Robert M. "Robots and the Sacred in Science and Science Fiction: Theological Implications of Artificial Intelligence." *Zygon: Journal of Religion & Science* 42.4 (2007): 961–980. Print.
Gessert, George. "Cloud Atlas." *Leonardo Reviews* 38.5 (2005): 425. Print.
Gibson, William. *Neuromancer*. New York: Ace, 1984. Print.
Goicoechea, Maria. "The Posthuman Ethos in Cyberpunk Science Fiction." *CLCWeb: Comparative Literature & Culture: A WWWeb Journal* 10.4 (2008): 1–11. Web. 1 October 2012.
Grant, Glenn. "Transcendence through Detournement in William Gibson's "Neuromancer" (La transcendance par le détournement dans "Neuromancer" de William Gibson)" *Science Fiction Studies* 17.1 (1990): 41–49. Print.
Grau, Marion. "'Redeeming the Body' in Late Western Capitalism: Pondering Salvation and Artificial Intelligence." *The Journal of Women and Religion*. 19/20 (2003): 144–56. Print.
Gyu Han, Kang. "Going Beyond Binary Disposition of 0/1: Rethinking the Question of Technology." *The Midwest Quarterly* 50.2 (2009): 176–189. Print.
Haney, William S. II. "Philip K. Dick's *We Can Build You* and *Do Androids Dream of Electric Sheep?* The Effect of Limited Human Development." *Consciousness, Literature and the Arts* 10.1 (2009): np. Web. 1 October 2012.
Haraway, Donna. "A Cyborg Manifesto: Science, Technology, and Socialist-Feminism in the Late Twentieth Century." in *Simians, Cyborgs and Women: The Reinvention of Nature*. New York: Routledge, 1991: (149–181). Print.
Hartley, George. *The Abyss of Representation: Marxism and the Postmodern Sublime*. Durham: Duke University Press, 2003.
Hawkins, Jeff. *On Intelligence*. New York: Owl Books, 2004. Print.
Hayles, Katherine N. Introduction. *Chaos and Order: Complex Dynamics in Literature in Science*. Ed. Katherine N. Hayles.

Chicago: University of Chicago Press, 1991. 1–36. Print.

———. *How We Became Posthuman: Virtual Bodies in Cybernetics, Literature, and Informatics*. Chicago: University of Chicago Press, 1999. Print.

———. "How We Became Posthuman: Ten Years on an Interview with N. Katherine Hayles." *Paragraph* 33.3 (2010): 318–330. Print.

———. "RFID: Human Agency and Meaning in Information-Intensive Environments." *Theory, Culture & Society* 26 (2009): 47–72. Print.

Heidegger, Martin. *Basic Questions of Philosophy: Selected "Problems" of "Logic."* Trans. Richard Rojcewicz and André Schuwer. Indianapolis: Indiana University Press, 1994. Print.

———. *Basic Writings*. Ed. David Farrell Krell. San Francisco: HarperSanFrancisco, 1977. Print.

———. *Contributions to Philosophy (Of the Event)*. Trans. Richard Rojcewicz and Daniela Vallega-Neu. Indianapolis: Indiana University Press, 2012. Print.

———. *Discourse on Thinking: A Translation of Gelassenheit*. Trans. John M. Anderson and E. Hans Freund. New York: Harper Torchbooks, 1966. Print.

———. *Eulucidations of Hölderlin's Poetry*. Trans. Keith Hoeller. Amherst, NY: Humanity Books, 2000. Print.

———. *Mindfullness*. Trans. Parvis Emad and Thomas Kalary. London: Continuum, 2006. Print.

———. *Nietzsche: Volumes One and Two*. Trans. David Farrel Krell. San Francisco: HarperSanFrancisco, 1991. Print.

———. *Poetry, Language, Thought*. Trans. Albert Hofstadter. 1971. New York: HarperCollins, 2001. Print.

———. *The Question of Being*. Trans. William Kluback and Jean T. Wilde. New York: Twayne Pub. Inc., 1958. Print.

———. *The Question Concerning Technology and Other Essays*. Trans. William Lovitt. New York: Harper Colophon Books, 1977. Print.

Faulconer, James E. and Mark A. Wrathall, eds. *Appropriating Heidegger*. Cambridge: Cambridge University Press, 2000. Print.

Heuser, Sabine. "(En)gendering Artificial Intelligence in Cyberspace." *Yearbook of English Studies* 37.2 (2007): 129–145. Print.

Hicks, Heather. "'This Time Round': David Mitchell's *Cloud Atlas* and the Apocalyptic Problem of Historicism." *Postmodern Culture* 20.3 (2010): 5–25. Print.

Jackelén, Antje. "The Image of God as Techno Sapiens." *Zygon: Journal of Religion & Science* 37.2 (2002): 289–303. Print.

Janes, Dominic. "Clarke and Kubrick's 2001: A Queer Odyssey." *Science Fiction Film and Television (SFFT)* 4.1 (2011):57–78. Print.

Joy, Bill. "Why The Future Doesn't Need Us." *Wired* 8.4 (2000): 1–11. Web. 1 October 2012.

Kaufmann, Walter ed. *The Portable Nietzsche*. Trans. Walter Kaufmann. New York: Viking, 1968. Print.

Kelly, Kevin. *Out of Control: The Rise of Neo-Biological Civilization*. Addison-Wesley Publishing Company: Mass., 1994. Print.

———. *What Technology Wants*. New York: Viking, 2010. Print.

Kelly, Kevin D. *Youth, Humanism & Technology*. New York: Basic Books Inc., 1972. Print.

Kuberski, Philip. "Kubrick's Odyssey: Myth, Technology, Gnosis." *Arizona Quarterly* 64.3 (2008): 51–73. Print.

Kunkel, Benjamin. "Distopia and the End of Politics." *Dissent* 55.4 (2008): 89–98. Print.

LaGrandeur, Kevin. "The Persistent Peril of the Artificial Slave." *Science Fiction Studies* 38.2 (2011): 232–252. Print.

Latour, Bruno. *Pandora's Hope: Essays on the Reality of Science Studies*. Cambridge, Mass.: Harvard University Press, 1999. Print.

———. *Politics of Nature: How to Bring the Sciences into Democracy*. Boston: Harvard University Press, 2004. Print.

Lord, Catherine M. "Angels with Nanotech Wings: Magic, Medicine and Technology in Aronofsky's The Fountain, Gibson's Neuromancer and Slonczewski's Brain Plague." *Nebula: A Journal of Multidisciplinary Scholarship* 6.4 (2009): 162–174. Print.

Loren, Scott. "What are the Implications of

the Virtual for the Human? An Analytical Ethics of Identity in Pop Culture Narratives." *European Journal of American Culture* 23.3 (2004): 173–185. Print.

Lovitt, William. Introduction. *The Question Concerning Technology and Other Essays.* By Martin Heidegger. 1977. 1st ed. New York: Harper Colophon Books, 1977. xiiv–xxxix. Print.

———. Rev. of *The Gods and Technology: A Reading of Heidegger*, by Richard Rojcewicz. *The Review of Metaphysics* 62.3 (2009): 686–688. Print.

Lovitt, William and Harriet Brundage Lovitt. *Modern Technology in the Heideggerian Perspective: Volume II.* New York: Edwin Mellen Press, 1995. Print.

McNamara, Kevin R. "Blade Runner's Post Individual Worldspace." *Contemporary Literature* 38.3 (1997): 422–446. Print.

Maclean, Marie. "Metamorphoses of the Signifier in 'Unnatural' Language." *Science Fiction Studies* 11.2 (1984): 166–173. Print.

Malone, Dorothy. "The Green Bookshop." *Education for Primary Care* 16.1 (2005): 106–110. Print.

Mancing, Howard. "Embodied Cognitive Science and the Study of Literature." *Cervantes* 32.1 (2012): 25–69. Print.

Marcuse, Herbert. *Technology, War and Fascism: Collected Papers of Herbert Marcuse Volume One.* Ed. Douglas Kellner. New York: Routledge, 1998. Print.

Marx, Leo. *The Pilot and the Passenger: Essays on Literature, Technology, and Culture in the United States.* New York: Oxford University Press, 1988. Print.

Mazis, Glen. *Humans, Animals, Machines: Blurring Boundaries.* Albany: SUNY Press, 2008. Print.

Mead, Margaret. *Culture and Commitment: A Study of the Generation Gap.* New York: Natural History Press, 1970. Print.

Mitchell, David. *Cloud Atlas: A Novel.* New York: Random House, 2004. Print.

Murphy, Richard. "Cloud Atlas." *Review of Contemporary Fiction* 24.3 (2004): 133–134. Print.

Myers, Tony. "The Postmodern Imaginary in William Gibson's *Neuromancer*." *Modern Fiction Studies* 47.4 (2001): 887–910. Print.

Narayanan, Ajit. "AI and Accountability." *AI & Society: Knowledge, Culture and Communication* 21.4 (2007): 669–671. Print.

Nietzsche, Friedrich. *On the Genealogy of Morals and Ecce Homo.* Trans. Walter Kaufmann and RJ Hollingdale. New York: Vantage Books, 1989. Print.

Parrett, Aaron. "Veins of Symbolism and Strata of Meaning." *Science Fiction Studies* 35 (2008): 116–120. Print.

Pelton, Joseph N. "Vision: Human-Level Artificial Intelligence: HAL, Meet SAM." *The Futurist* 42.5 (2008): 36–37. Print.

Popper, Karl R. *Conjectures and Refutations: The Growth of Scientific Knowledge.* New York: Harper Torchbooks, 1963. Print.

Rabkin, Eric S. *Arthur C. Clarke: Starmont Reader's Guide 1.* Mercer Island, WA: Starmont House, 1979. Print.

Reid, Robin Anne. *Arthur C. Clarke: A Critical Companion.* Westport, Conn.: Greenwood Press, 1997. Print.

Riis, Søren. "The Symmetry between Bruno Latour and Martin Heidegger: The Technique of Turning a Police Officer into a Speed Bump" *Social Studies of Science* 38.2 (2008): 285–301. Print.

———. "Towards the Origin of Modern Technology: Reconfiguring Martin Heidegger's Thinking." *Continental Philosophy Review* 44 (2011): 103–117. Print.

Renegar, Valerie R. and George N. Dionisopoulos. "The Dream of a Cyberpunk Future? Entelechy, Dialectical Tension, and the Comic Corrective in William Gibson's Neuromancer." *Southern Communication Journal* 76.4 (2011): 323–341. Print.

Rojcewicz, Richard. *The Gods and Technology: A Reading of Heidegger.* Albany: SUNY Press, 2006. Print.

Schalow, Frank. Rev. of *The Gods and Technology: A Reading of Heidegger*, by Richard Rojcewicz. *Journal of Phenomenological Psychology* 39 (2008): 111–139. Print.

Savage, Robert. "Paleoanthropology of the Future: The Prehistory of Posthumanity in Arthur C. Clarke's 2001: A Space Odyssey." *Extrapolation* 51.1 (2010): 99–112. Print.

Seymour, Gene. "Four novels of the 1960s: *The Man in the High Castle*, *The Three*

Stigmata of Palmer Eldritch, Do Androids Dream of Electric Sheep, Ubik." Nation 284 21 (2007): 53–57. Print.

Shaddox, Karl. "Is Nothing Sacred? Testing for Human in Philip K. Dick's *Do Androids Dream of Electric Sheep?" Studies in American Culture* 34.1 (2011): 23–50. Print.

Slusser, George. *The Space Odyssey of Arthur C. Clarke*. San Bernardino, CA: Borgo Press, 1978. Print.

Sobchack, Vivian Carol. "Love Machines: Boy Toys, Toy Boys and the Oxymorons of A.I.: Artificial Intelligence." *Science Fiction Film and Television (SFFT)* 1.1 (2008): 1–13. Print.

Sontag, Susan. *Against Interpretation and Other Essays*. "The Imagination of Disaster." 1965. New York: Anchor Books, 1990. Print.

Spanos, William. *Heidegger and Criticism: Retrieving the Cultural Politics of Destruction*. Minneapolis: University of Minnesota Press, 1993. Print.

Stambaugh, Joan. *The Finitude of Being*. Albany: SUNY Press, 1992. Print.

Strombeck, Andrew. "The Network and the Archive: The Specter of Imperial Management in William Gibson's "Neuromancer."" *Science Fiction Studies* 37.2 (2010): 275–295. Print.

Turkle, Sherry. *Alone Together: Why We Expect More from Technology and Less from Each Other*. New York: Basic Books, 2011. Print.

_____. *The Second Self: Computers and the Human Spirit*. New York: Simon and Schuster, 1984. Print.

Vallega-Neu, Daniela. *Heidegger's Contributions to Philosophy: An Introduction*. Indianapolis: Indiana University Press, 2003. Print.

Wolk, Anthony. "The Swiss Connection: Psychological Systems in the Novels of Philip K. Dick." *Philip K. Dick: Contemporary Critical Interpretations*. Ed. Samuel J. Umland. Westport, Conn.: Greenwood Press, 1995. 101–126. Print.

Yu, Timothy. "Oriental Cities, Postmodern Futures: Naked Lunch, Blade Runner, and Neuromancer" *MELUS* 33.4 (2008): 45–71. Print.

Zimmerman, Michael. *Heidegger's Confrontation with Modernity: Technology, Politics, and Art*. Indianapolis: Indiana University Press, 1990. Print.

Index

Abram, David 9, 232*In*3
alien 3, 15, 37, 69–73, 76–81, 86–97, 103, 105–106, 108–109, 111, 133, 135, 162, 163, 169, 224, 230
Alien Chic 90; see also Badmington, Neil
All Things Shining 230; see also Dreyfus, Hubert; Kelly, Sean D.
Alone Together 6; see also Turkle, Sherry
America 1, 15, 27, 110, 141, 180, 182
Anderson, John M. 20, 21, 50, 65, 233*cl*n9
android 1, 4, 6, 12–16, 63–65, 110–124, 129–130, 132–138, 179, 225
anthropocentrism 8, 10–12, 20, 23, 28, 39, 43, 70, 77, 82, 84, 109, 113, 119
apocalypse 57, 109, 110, 119, 120, 132, 137, 160, 179, 180, 197, 227
Armageddon 1, 3, 153
Asimov, Isaac 152; see also *I, Robot*
Atwood, Margaret 231

Badmington, Neil 90; see also *Alien Chic*
Bakke, Gretchen 89
Ballard, J.G. 11, 232*In*4
Balsamo, Anne 7, 144, 164
Basic Questions of Philosophy 21, 25–26, 68; see also Heidegger, Martin
Being and Time 20, 39; see also Heidegger, Martin
Belu, Dana S. 20, 41
Ben-Tov, Sharona 70, 152, 230
bestellen 63, 234*cl*n12; see also disposables; raw materials; standing-reserve
Boddice, Rob 8
Borgmann, Albert 129
Bové, Paul 27–28
Broderick, Damien 154
Bukatman, Scott 2, 120, 150, 229

Caldwell, Thomas 69
Cameron, James 1; see also *Terminator 2*
Chernobyl 3, 171
Clarke, Arthur C. 2, 14–15, 69–71, 77, 80, 82–86, 88–92, 96–97, 102, 106, 108–209, 224, 232*In*6; see also *2001: A Space Odyssey*
clones 12, 17, 172, 178–179, 181, 202, 208, 214, 217; see also genetic modification

Cloud Atlas 2, 4, 13–14, 16, 23, 40, 43, 46, 63, 178, 180, 187–188, 202–203, 218, 221, 226, 227, 232*In*6; see also Mitchell, David
colonialism 8–9, 11, 77–78, 173, 178, 182–184, 192, 199–200, 203, 211, 227
contemplation 48, 51–53, 64–66, 80, 98, 106, 125, 209, 233*cl*n9; see also meditative thinking
Csicsery-Ronay, Istvan, Jr. 174, 224
cybernetics 4–7, 59, 122–123, 167–168, 175
cyberpunk 7, 139, 174
cyberspace 4, 7–8, 16, 65, 141–151, 153–157, 159–160, 168, 176, 226
cyborg 5–6, 16, 58, 91, 102, 139–140, 146, 152, 156, 161–164, 169, 172, 176, 181, 186, 201, 226–227, 229
"A Cyborg Manifesto" 6, 58; see also Haraway, Donna

Darwin, Charles 78, 124, 212
Dasein 17, 22, 27, 31, 33–36, 39–40, 44, 47–50, 52–53, 55, 57, 73, 75–76, 78, 83–85, 88, 91, 94, 97, 107, 112, 197, 203, 211, 229, 233*cl*n5
Dawkins, Richard 124
Delany, Samuel R. 164
detachment 23, 51, 53–57, 59–60, 62, 64–66, 68, 71, 90, 92–93, 97–98, 103–104, 122, 145, 147, 159, 233*cl*n9; see also *gelassenheit*; releasement
Dick, Philip K. 14–15, 110–124, 127–129, 132–133, 136–138, 149, 179, 225, 234*c*3*n*2; see also *Do Androids Dream of Electric Sheep?*
Dionisopoulos, George N. 175
Disch, Thomas M. 113, 119, 139
Discourse on Thinking 10, 20–22, 48–52, 60, 65–66, 68, 114; see also Heidegger, Martin
disembodiment 6–8, 12, 141–143, 148, 152, 226; see also embodiment
disposables 32–34, 54, 63–64, 233*cl*n2, 234*cl*n12; see also raw materials; standing-reserve
Do Androids Dream of Electric Sheep? 2, 4, 13–6, 23, 43, 63, 110–114, 119, 121–123, 126, 133, 137–138, 149, 179, 198, 212, 225; see also Dick, Philip K.
Doherty, Trevor 228
Dreyfus, Hubert L. 7–8, 30, 228–231

240

Dreyfus, Stuart E. 228–229
dystopia 57–58, 139–140, 174, 202

ecology 8, 38–40, 58, 140, 151, 163; *see also* environment
Economides, Louise 179, 181–182
Ellul, Jacques 119
embodiment 6–8, 12, 91, 150–152, 156, 158, 160, 174–175, 225
enframing 14, 17, 20–23, 27, 34–45, 47–51, 53–60, 62–65, 66–77, 79–86, 88–94, 96–100, 103–108, 109, 112–120, 123, 125–126, 128, 130, 133, 135, 137–138, 141, 143–147, 149–154, 156, 159–165, 167–170, 172–178, 180–221, 223–230, 232–233*In*2, 233*cln*3, 233*cln*4, 234*cln*12; *see also* Heidegger, Martin; poïesis
environment 3, 8, 16, 72, 88, 103, 111–112, 115, 118–119, 163, 209, 229; *see also* ecology
existentialism 24, 47, 73, 106, 124, 126, 134, 230

Fair, Benjamin 151–152, 173–176
Feenberg, Andrew 20, 41, 113–120, 122, 129–130, 136; *see also Questioning Technology*
Foster, Thomas 7, 176; *see also The Souls of Cyber Folk*
Frankenstein 8, 153, 164, 171; *see also* Shelly, Mary
Freud, Sigmund 88
Fry, Carrol 108
Fukushima 3, 171
Fuller, Jason 86

Galvan, Jill 113
gelassenheit 20, 49–51, 67, 233*cln*9; *see also* detachment; releasement
genetic modification 3, 12–13, 90, 143, 179–181, 193, 202–203, 212, 227; *see also* clones
Geraci, Robert M. 173, 228
Germany 9, 34, 41, 50, 52, 58, 65, 134, 233*cln*6
Gessert, George 218–219
Gibson, William 14, 16, 139, 141–143, 151–152, 154, 164, 168, 173–176, 179, 226; see also *Neuromancer*
The Gods and Technology 20, 233*cln*6; *see also* Rojcewicz, Richard
Goicoechea, Maria 140
Grant, Glenn 175
Grau, Marion 8
Greece 11, 21–26, 28–32, 42, 44, 49, 53–54, 59, 61–62, 73, 91, 94, 112, 129, 131, 181, 233*cln*7, 233*cln*11
Gyu Han, Kang 112, 137

hacking 7, 139, 141, 143, 145–147, 154, 157, 161, 168
Haney, William S., II. 135
Haraway, Donna 5–6, 58, 139, 152, 161; *see also* "A Cyborg Manifesto"
Hayles, Katherine N. 4, 5–7, 121–123, 131, 133, 135–136, 138, 152, 175, 178, 180, 202, 230; see also *How We Became Posthuman*
Heidegger, Martin 8–18, 19–69, 71–72, 74–77, 79–80, 83–86, 88–91, 94–98, 108–117, 119–120, 122–123, 129, 136–139, 143, 148, 152, 166, 171–172, 176, 178–180, 183, 186, 188, 192–193, 195, 199, 203–204, 206–208, 211, 214, 218–221, 223, 227–231, 232*cln*1, 232*cln*2, 233*cln*3, 233*cln*4, 233*cln*5, 233*cln*6, 233*cln*9, 233*cln*10, 233–234*cln*11, 234*cln*12; see also *Basic Questions*; *Discourse on Thinking*; enframing; poïesis; "The Question Concerning Technology"; techné
Heraclitus 25
Heuser, Sabine 154
Hicks, Heather 179–180
Hiroshima 171
Hölderlin, Friedrich 22, 41, 53
Homer 70; see also *The Odyssey*
How We Became Posthuman 5, 7; *see also* Hayles, Katherine

I, Robot 153; *see also* Asimov, Isaac

Jackelén, Antje 12
Japan 141
Joy, Bill 1, 6

Kelly, Kevin 5–7, 112–113, 229–230; see also *Out of Control*; *What Technology Wants*
Kelly, Kevin D. 230
Kelly, Sean D. 230–231
Korea 179, 186, 202, 218
Kunkle, Benjamin 178, 202
Kurzweil, Ray 6–8

LaGrandeur, Kevin 4, 8, 107
Latour, Bruno 8–9, 140, 176, 233*cln*4; *see also Pandora's Hope*; *The Politics of Nature*
Le Corbusier 166; see also *Towards a New Architecture*
Lem, Stanislaw 224
Lord, Catherine M. 175
Loren, Scott 107
Lovitt, William 19–20, 34, 47, 233*cln*5, 233*cln*6, 233*cln*11, 234*cln*11, 234*cln*12

Malone, Dorothy 179
Mancing, Howard 6–7
Marcuse, Herbert 161–162
Marxism 213
matrix 41, 142–145, 147–148, 150, 152, 156–158, 160
The Matrix (film) 40–41
May, Rollo 124
McNamara, Kevin R. 111–112, 130
Mead, Margaret 142–143
meditative thinking 10–11, 14, 22–24, 45, 48–52, 57, 63–64, 66–68, 73, 80, 101, 109, 130, 167, 206, 221, 223, 233*cln*9; *see also* contemplation
Merleau-Ponty, Maurice 8, 158
metaphysics 27, 30–31, 35–36, 39, 45, 50, 53, 59, 62–63, 102, 126, 128, 137
Minsky, Marvin 6
Mitchell, David 14, 16–17, 178–180, 183–184, 186, 196, 201, 205, 211, 221, 226; see also *Cloud Atlas*
Moravec, Hans 6, 8
Murphy, Richard 221
Myers, Tony 148, 161–162, 173

Nagasaki 171
Narayanan, Ajit 12

Neuromancer 2, 4, 13–14, 16, 23, 43, 65, 96, 139–141, 143, 150, 161, 164, 172–177, 181, 212, 226; *see also* Gibson, William
Nietzsche, Friedrich 27–28, 32, 36–39, 59, 180; *see also* will to power
Nordlund, Solveig 11, 232*In*4
nuclear 1, 3, 33, 170, 172

The Odyssey 70, 73; *see also* Homer
"The Origin of the Work of Art" 53; *see also* Heidegger, Martin
Otto, Rudolf 86
Out of Control 5; *see also* Kelly, Kevin

Pandora's Hope 233*c*ln4; *see also* Latour, Bruno
Parrett, Aaron 70
Pelton, Joseph N. 109
phenomenology 24, 61, 150, 158, 209
Plato 8, 25–26, 45, 49, 140, 176
poïesis 9–11, 14, 17, 21–23, 26–27, 29–30, 32, 41–42, 45–46, 48–50, 52–57, 61–64, 66–68, 70–73, 75–77, 79–84, 88, 92–95, 107–109, 112–113, 116, 118–119, 126, 128–131, 133–134, 138, 140–142, 144–145, 147–156, 158, 160–161, 163–166, 168–177, 179–184, 186, 188, 190–191, 193–194, 196–199, 201, 204–208, 212, 214–215, 217–220, 223–231, 233*c*ln3, 233*c*ln4, 233*c*ln7, 233*c*lnl0; *see also* enframing; Heidegger, Martin
The Politics of Nature 8, 140; *see also* Latour, Bruno
post-apocalyptic 57, 110, 120, 132, 137, 179–180, 197
posthuman 5–6, 9, 11, 112–113, 152, 156, 161, 172, 175–176, 181, 227; *see also* Hayles, Katherine; *How We Became Posthuman*
Prometheus 197

"The Question Concerning Technology" 9–10, 19–22, 25–26, 31, 34, 41–42, 45–48, 50, 53–54, 56, 64, 68, 110, 113–114, 233*c*ln6, 234*c*lnl2; *see also* Heidegger, Martin
Questioning Technology 113; *see also* Feenberg, Andrew

Rabkin, Eric S. 106
raw materials 10, 21–22, 26, 28–31, 34, 40, 59, 61, 63, 71, 76, 77, 86, 95, 102, 106, 137, 143, 187, 194, 197, 211, 213–215, 217, 223, 233*c*ln2, 234*c*lnl2; *see also* disposables; standing-reserve
releasement 22–23, 48–52, 57, 60, 63–65, 67, 80, 85, 87, 93, 99, 233*c*ln9; *see also* detachment
Renegar, Valerie R. 175
Riis, Søren 29, 31, 233*c*ln4
robot 1, 3, 6, 7–8, 15, 64, 102, 114, 117, 119–120, 122, 124, 134, 153, 165, 203
Rojcewicz, Richard 20, 24–25, 27–28, 32–35, 39–47, 50, 54–56, 61, 63–68, 232*c*lnl, 233*c*ln6, 233*c*ln8, 233*c*ln9, 233*c*lnll, 234*c*lnll, 233*c*lnl2; *see also The Gods and Technology*

Sallis, John 27–31, 43, 49
Savage, Robert 108
science fiction 70, 111; *see also* SF
Science Fiction Studies 15, 110

The Second Self 5; *see also* Turkle, Sherry
SF 1, 3, 7, 11–14, 17, 19, 25–26, 32, 35–36, 40, 42, 44–46, 48, 50, 53, 55–57, 59, 60, 63–64, 66–67, 70, 90, 106, 111, 119, 211, 218, 223, 230–231, 232*In*6; *see also* science fiction
Shaddox, Karl 116
Shelly, Mary 164; *see also* Frankenstein
Slusser, George 69–70
Sobchack, Vivian Carol 70
Socrates 25, 45, 53
"Some Social Implications of Modern Technology" 161; *see also* Marcuse, Herbert
Sontag, Susan 231
The Souls of Cyber Folk 7; *see also* Foster, Thomas
Spanos, William 31
The Spell of the Sensuous 232*In*3; *see also* Abram, David
Stambaugh, Joan 32, 34, 42–44, 60
standing-reserve 21–22, 27, 30, 34, 40–41, 44, 57, 59, 63, 67, 70, 74, 79, 83, 85, 105, 116–117, 123, 125, 131, 135–136, 141, 148, 182, 186, 195, 203, 206–207, 214, 223, 233*c*ln2; *see also* disposables; raw materials
Strombeck, Andrew 173

Taylor, Astra 232*In*2
techné 21–22, 25–30, 32, 42, 48, 53, 55–56, 62, 64, 80–81, 112, 233*c*ln7; *see also* Heidegger, Martin
technology anxiety 1–18, 23, 25, 29, 33, 36, 38, 40, 42, 50–51, 56–57, 60, 64, 68–68, 77, 80–81, 85, 87–89, 99, 102, 107, 116, 137, 139, 141, 143, 145–147, 153, 163, 167, 170–172, 180, 195, 197, 213, 223–224, 226, 228, 230–231, 232*In*1
Terminator 2 1, 4, 6
Towards a New Architecture 166; *see also* Le Corbusier
Turing, Alan (test, Police) 23, 102, 121, 146, 152–153
Turkey 146, 172
Turkle, Sherry 4–7, 106, 146, 224, 227–228, 230; *see also Alone Together*; *The Second Self*
2001: A Space Odyssey 2–3, 13–14, 23, 43, 69–71, 77, 90, 98, 107–109, 179, 205, 224–225; *see also* Clarke, Arthur C.

"War of the Worlds" 78
Warnek, Peter 20
Western 11–12, 25, 27, 30, 32, 36, 45, 54, 59, 62–63, 67, 77, 90, 102, 112, 120, 130, 137, 140–141, 163, 178–180, 182–183, 196
What Technology Wants 6; *see also* Kelly, Kevin
will to power 21, 23, 27, 31, 37–38, 46, 73, 79, 82, 96, 99, 103, 170, 178, 180, 182–185, 188, 190, 195–196, 198, 201, 203, 219–220, 225–226; *see also* Nietzsche, Friedrich
Williams, Margery 224
Wolk, Anthony 121–122, 124

Yu, Timothy 141

Zimmerman, Michael 24, 26, 30, 36, 39, 45, 55, 58–59, 62, 67–68, 233*c*ln6
Žižek, Slavoj 9, 232*In*2

www.ingramcontent.com/pod-product-compliance
Ingram Content Group UK Ltd.
Pitfield, Milton Keynes, MK11 3LW, UK
UKHW041939140426
5217IPUK00014B/563